The Defining Skill
in Selling

Discover how a new model will catapult you towards your potential in selling.

M. Tim Welch

DORRANCE
PUBLISHING CO
EST. 1920
PITTSBURGH, PENNSYLVANIA 15238

Contact Information for M. Tim Welch: (tel) 801.319.5467
(email) tim.welch@att.net

Dorrance Publishing Co
585 Alpha Drive
Pittsburgh, PA 15238
Visit our website at *www.dorrancebookstore.com*

ISBN: 978-1-4809-8973-3
eISBN: 978-1-4809-9460-7

What Business Leaders Are Saying About *The Defining Skill in Selling*

Woven through the pages of this book is a clear, sorely needed message. Mastery is a choice and it is the only choice that leads to enduring Passion. In an age where instant gratification is the norm, many lose site of the fact that Mastery requires a plan, hard work, and years of patience. The principles in this book apply not only to sales but to all pursuits of excellence. I'm grateful that Tim Welch took the time to model his journey of discovery and mastery and then share that gift with all of us.

—Mark Oakes, Chief Executive Officer, Intellimar, Inc.

Amazing! The insight of Tim Welch is refreshing. In an era of paralysis for most, Tim reminds us and educates with sound principles that lead to success. Simply one of the best books I have studied in my 32-year sales career – wished I would have had this decades ago.

—Greg Sanders, President CEC/ KDG Distributing

Tim Welch has nailed it! In *The Defining Skill in Selling*, he uniquely teaches that no matter how appealing an enterprise's products or services are, successful companies are distinguished and driven by effective and committed people. Tim's book is a must read for sales and marketing professionals —— and an ought to read for anyone who is interested in coupling principle-based personal development with organizational effectiveness.

—Allen B. Alexander, Chairman and CEO,
Savage Companies

The Defining Skill in Selling is one book that every Sales Professional should read. Not just for themselves but for the customers they serve. The book is written with something for every learning style. The practical examples and exercises keep the reader engaged and focused. This is one time investment that will pay off exponentially.

—Jeff Hamby – Senior Strategic Account Manager –
McGraw-Hill Construction

Sales leaders are constantly seeking best practice for maximizing the performance of their sales teams. *The Defining Skill in Selling* not only provides the solutions, but presents practical, fundamental principles that can and will change the performance of a committed sales professional.

—David Murdoch-Director of Sales
-Bradley Corporation

The Defining Skill is a great blueprint and foundation for sales effectiveness and success!

—Mark Taylor-Vice President Channel Sales, Novell, Inc.

If you lead a sales team or wish to maximize your professional selling success, then buy this book! *The Defining Skill in Selling* accurately diagnoses the symptoms and cures that many of us have faced in our sales careers, without the preaching. Invest in yourself and your sales team. A very good read.

—Paul Boucherle, Principal,
Matterhorn Consulting, LLC

The Defining Skill in Selling offers insight into problems that we all share. It is an honest and revealing analysis of success (and failure) in the sales process. Tim Welch has reminded me that an excellent sales process by itself does not generate success; passion and dedication need to be present in the success formula.

—David Wicks, Western Region Sales, GMG Americas

This volume is a handbook to be valued by all who wish to hone their skills as sales professionals.

—Laird Walker, Senior V.P., U.S. West (retired)

Tim Welch captures the essential ingredients to a successful sales career. This work should be a must read for any sales team striving for excellence. His ability to detail the key professional competencies and their corresponding skills provides a clear roadmap to maximize your personal abilities.

—Greg Tillar, CEO, NuGrowth Solutions,

This book will increase sales! Tim provides step by step processes to manage and hold sales representatives accountable while maximizing productivity. In this challenging economic environment this is a must read for any business with a sales force. My productivity and sales management skills have improved twenty fold. Thanks Tim!

—Kris Cottrell, President, Back Office Results, Inc.

Finally a book that addresses the systemic reason for a sales professional's sustainable success…Personal Leadership. Tim Welch's, *The Defining Skill in Selling*, uniquely articulates the connection of foundational competencies such as Character, Vision, and Passion, with quantifiable sales planning, execution, and accountability. An important book to read and embrace if you truly desire to understand the psyche of the sales profession.

—Matt Bower, V.P. Sales & Marketing, Click Safety

Every top-gun senior seller understands how to run their sales territory like a business. Tim connects those dots for us in this results oriented book. No magic–but very magical when it's brought together like this.

—Pam Springer, President & CEO Manta Media

Tim Welch has created a handbook for the development and refinement of the personal constitution as it relates to not only the sales process but to life in general. He understands the essence of relationships and the vital necessity of examining and forging one's code of conduct to engender trust in our relationships. Tim is impeccable with his word and has been generous enough to share his insight and wisdom in such a way that we can internalize these enduring principles propelling us toward our potential. Well done!

—David Beck, Director of Experiential Programming,
Cirque Lodge

This book presents the authentic rules for effective selling. Tim speaks from experience, and his wise counsel will aid you in achieving greater success through personal leadership know-how. This is a book that can be read and enjoyed by veteran and rookie members of the sales team. If you are interested in dramatically improving sales results, read this book – a blueprint for sales success.

—Cory R. Moore, V.P. & Partner,
Big-D Construction Corp.

Tim Welch's new book, *The Defining Skill in Selling* surfaces what REALLY matters in high trust selling–who you are when you walk into the call. Vision,

Character, and Passion are the foundations of sales success in Tim's book– as they are in every salesperson that embodies enduring success. You will resonate with the principles, relate with the stories, and recommit yourself to renewed contribution in your sales career and life.

—Barry Rellaford, Founder of The Great Work
Company and co-author of *A Slice of Trust: The*
Leadership Secret with the Hot and Fruity Filling

In *The Defining Skill in Selling*, Tim Welch guides the reader on a path that leads to the intersection of successful selling through personal leadership. The skills outlined in his Personal Leadership model are everyday tools to drive results in sales, to meet the objectives of any salesperson who is trying to connect clients to solutions. In my experience, both in direct enterprise sales and supporting sales organizations, it is clear that skills modeled by Tim Welch are the ones that create success year in and year out for the professionals who are committed to strategic selling. For any salesperson who wants to expand their selling ability and create meaningful/consistent success over the long term, then Personal Leadership is the key and a roadmap is described in *The Defining Skill in Selling*. Using humor and real world perspective earned over years of successful selling and managing sales teams, Tim Welch has written a book that benefits anyone in sales and will be referred to many times after reading the book. If you are willing to expand your selling skills by making yourself the key to your professional success, this book is for you.

—Scott Harris, Adobe Systems:
Director–Demand Marketing

Every sales professional should add *The Defining Skill in Selling* to their sales tool box. Using these principles will bring real sales results with practical application and simple execution. Mr. Welch has written a sales handbook of core values like character and vision. This book will challenge you to assess your personal potential as well as those you lead, and invite you to a new level of sales and personal leadership.

—Paul Featherstone, Sales Executive and Independent
Film Producer, Lorien Entertainment

This book is a must-read for every serious sales professional, and for those who should take their profession more seriously. Personal Leadership has always been the key to maximizing success in selling and in business. In *The*

Defining Skill in Selling, Tim Welch uses real-world examples and stories to illustrate how desire, effort, planning, and execution all work together to help sales people reach their true potential. Whether you are a "seat of your pants" type sales person, a completely "process-driven" sales person, or somewhere in between, Tim's model and time-tested templates will help you improve your skills and overcome the eight symptoms of sales paralysis.

—Lane Monson, COO, Aviacode

Tim Welch has nailed it! *The Defining Skill in Selling* should be the "Gold Standard" for the art of selling.

—Leon Yulkowski, President & CEO, Total Door

Tim Welch's book, *The Defining Skill in Selling*, provides intriguing insights for sales professionals and business leaders. This energizing book can definitely be useful as a guide for those who wish to move their knowledge and skills in selling to the next level. Nicely done, Tim!

—Dr. Susan R. Madsen, Professor of Management,
Orin R. Woodbury Professor of Leadership and Ethics,
Utah Valley University Woodbury School of Business

To Michele

Acknowledgments

THE COMPLETION OF THIS PROJECT was greatly assisted by the encouragement, advice, and support of many longtime friends, colleagues, and family members. My wife Michele teaches English at a local university, and her margin notes on every draft improved not only sentence structure but more importantly the clarity of the ideas being communicated. She believed in this project-or at least she believed in me-from the very beginning, and that belief inspired me beyond words. In addition, I would like to thank the following people who read the manuscript and offered valuable insight about the role of personal leadership in selling:

Gary Judd	Barry Rellaford	Ted Decker
Karen Brown	Betty Mollet	David Larsen
Ben Welch	Lisa Call	David Rodeback
Ben Banks	Corinne Bodeman	Matt Bower
Kris Cottrell	David Murdock	Stephen Merrill

I am indebted to my son Ben for his tedious editing work and the restructuring of the content to more appropriately reflect the overarching emphasis on personal leadership. Karen Thielacker contributed substantially to this project with her design of the Personal Leadership Model and nearly all of the other graphic images in the book. David Rodeback refined the overall tone with a consistency, which it lacked in the original drafts. I also want to thank Ron Smart and the many members of the Won-Door sales team whose lives and professional careers have provided the workshop for the ideas and concepts in this book to develop fully. And finally I am grateful for three lifelong mentors whose encouragement and support provided a significant portion of the motivation for this project even though none of them lived to see it completed: C. Russell Hansen, Lee R. Allridge and Wayne S. Winters.

Contents

Introduction

HAVE YOU EVER WONDERED why some people seem to have a natural ability to produce stunning revenue totals and other, seemingly talented people struggle to come within a solar-system of their annual sales goal? Is it possible that what seems to be natural ability is really a transferable skill that could transform your professional life? My answer to both questions is a definite yes.

I would like to change a number of things about my experience leading sales teams over the past thirty years. None of these is more serious than miscalculating the relative importance of *Personal Leadership* in the sales process. My orientation to selling during the early portion of my career was driven primarily by products – in other words, by the things we were selling, not the people who were selling them. Our sales training meetings were heavily loaded with discussions about innovative product changes, the identification of new emerging market segments, favorable regulatory changes, and upbeat economic forecasts. All these topics have a legitimate place in a sales meeting. Unfortunately, when products dominate the agenda, we may ignore the essential contribution of people.

From our company's founding in 1962 until the early part of the 1980s, we sold our products through a traditional channel of wholesale distributors. In the latter part of 1982 an associate from our corporate office approached me about opening a branch of the company in a large metropolitan area in the Southwest. He was a recent college graduate and had no distinguishing sales experience on his resume. My suspicions about his lack of preparation to sell were assuaged by my high level of confidence in the market demand for our products. He opened our first branch office in January 1983. Soon most of my product-based sales philosophy came under careful scrutiny.

As 1983 began, our US distribution base consisted of approximately 62 independent distributors located in every major market area, and one shiny new branch office. Twelve months later the composition of the sales team was the same but revenue production had dramatically changed. Our new branch office with an inexperienced product representative had generated a revenue total that was roughly equal to all of the other 62 distributors combined.

For the first time in my short career as a sales manager, I was starting to resemble someone who actually knew what he was doing. It didn't take too long for me to confirm the suspicions of the skeptics. Our superlative success proved to be more of an organizational anomaly than a viable strategy for long-term success. Our desperate attempts to duplicate the model in other areas of the country were, in most instances, miserable failures. I was a whiz kid who had exhausted his fifteen minutes of fame.

The eventual post mortem on this experience of re-engineering our distribution channel, conducted with more mature eyes a few years later, suggested that the answer was immediately in front of us. I had simply chosen to ignore what became more and more obvious. The outcome of the experiment was exceptional, but I was blinded by my own product obsession. It prevented me from realizing that the variable in the equation producing the dramatic result was not the product, but rather the person. More specifically, it was not just a person but this person.

Most of us who lead sales teams can become overly enamored with the products we represent. We spend much of our lives sizing up our competitors and developing strategies to clearly differentiate how our products uniquely solve pressing customer problems. Sometimes this obsession with understanding how products work keeps us from focusing on how people work. Knowing how products work is essential; understanding how people work can change the landscape of virtually any business venture.

Personal Leadership is a learned skill that produces maximum results – the highest possible revenue totals – in the world of professional selling. When you are working at a level consistent with your potential, revenue numbers almost always become a secondary issue. This book is dedicated to bringing your performance in alignment with your sales potential.

If you have been selling for any length of time you know that certain attitudes, behaviors or beliefs can disrupt the selling process. They can emerge out of nowhere and morph rapidly into a type of numbing paralysis that can seriously compromise your effectiveness to work with customers and grow your business. Before we look at the new sales model I would like to examine eight common symptoms of Sales Paralysis that sidetrack careers and alienate customers. With the common ground of these symptoms on your mind it will make it easier to understand how this new sales model will literally catapult you to your greatest potential as a sales professional.

CHAPTER 1

Losing Forward Motion
The Eight Symptoms of Sales Paralysis

LIKE MANY sales professionals, most territories fluctuate over the course of several years. While some regression is understandable, sometimes even expected, in territories that have produced prolific growth, leaders find ways to keep revenue from suffering systemic reversals. This revenue regression typically follows one of two patterns. The first is short-term and often parallels economic cycles; the second quite often can be more long-term in nature and generally follows cycles, patterns, habits, and commitment levels established by the sales professional.

Selling is difficult and demanding work. I know of no other profession where the exasperation of rejection resides in such close companionship with the exhilaration of success. Leaders maintain a perspective about rejection. They have selective memories that allow them almost immediately to forget the *no*'s while being completely re-energized by the faintest hint of *yes*.

Losing Forward Motion

A few years ago, as my daughter and her husband were moving to Pennsylvania to attend graduate school, I heard myself offer to drive the rental truck on a 1900-mile cross-country excursion, carrying the bulk of their household possessions. I am sure it was my voice, but it was one of those experiences where my head had not fully informed my heart about the nature of the journey ahead.

Fully loaded, the 25-foot yellow Penske rental truck weighed about 12,000 pounds. Moving one of the family cars was also part of my job description. The front wheels rested on a small trailer behind the rental truck; the rear wheels were on the road. This rather benign complication would soon contribute to one of the most serious blunders of my life.

About sixteen hours and 900 miles into the trip, I arrived at the end of the first leg of the journey in Lincoln, Nebraska. The only stops during the day were for gas, and, as soon as I left behind the traffic of the city, I strangely started to enjoy the exhilaration of riding high and moving my load. The balance of the second day was equally uneventful, with the exception of maneuvering through miles of road construction near Chicago, Illinois.

The desk clerk at the Marriott Courtyard off I-80 in Toledo was very accommodating in finding me a room, despite the fact that I had not made a reservation. I had not previously stayed at this particular hotel, but it was not noticeably different from many, many other Marriott properties where I have stayed over the years. The hotel itself is rectangular. Imagine the rectangle with the two short sides facing east and west and the long sides facing north and south. The main entrance was located in the middle of the south side.

Being a bit road-weary from two long days of travel, I climbed back into the truck and began looking for a place to park. Assuming I could drive around the hotel to park, I pulled forward and turned left at the end of the hotel. The parking lot was filled with cars, and I watched through the side mirrors as the trailer made the turn a safe distance from the cars. At the completion of the left turn, with the trailer lined up straight behind the truck, I looked ahead at an obvious dead end. There was no way out.

What the helpful people at the rental office don't always carefully explain is that when you tow a car on a trailer with the rear wheels dragging, it can become your worst nightmare if you travel in reverse for even a short distance. When you back up the trailer with the rear wheels of the car on the ground, the trailer attempts to move in one direction and the vehicle in the exact opposite direction.

After about half an hour of trying to negotiate a ninety-degree corner, I was completely exasperated. That was when the night security officer decided to launch a rescue effort. While he coached, I shifted and turned and backed up and pulled forward over and over, but the outcome was the same. The obvious solution, removing the car from the trailer, was not an option; the key to the vehicle was several hours away with my son-in-law.

The next option seemed to be to remove the small trailer from the rental truck. Hammering on the underside of the hitch did nothing to free it from the ball of the truck. Flashlight in hand, the security officer surveyed the north side of the hotel property and returned with what seemed like a viable proposal. I would need simply to pull the truck forward, over the curb at the end of the parking lot, make a left turn on the grass, drive the length of the hotel mostly on grass and partly on the sidewalk, and re-enter the parking lot on the west side of the property. I expressed some concern about potential damage to the lawn, which he kindly dismissed. It was now about 1:30 AM and, like it or not, he was fully invested in getting me to safe ground on the property. His appeared to be the most expedient solution.

While I pulled the truck and trailer forward and eased up over the curb, the security officer waved the flashlight ahead to identify the proper route to the parking lot. The plan seemed to be working, until we heard the grating sound of steel on concrete immediately behind the truck. The security officer discovered that there was insufficient clearance under the trailer for it to roll up over the curb. To complicate matters, the lawn area where the 12,000 pounds of truck was temporarily positioned had recently been watered, and the rear dual wheels were sinking. The wheels spun violently as I tried desperately to move the truck off the grass. By moving the gearshift first into drive, then quickly into reverse, I tried to rock the truck free. The more I tried, the deeper the dual wheels sank into the sod and mud; in moments the lawn was unrecognizable.

It was now 2:00 AM. As I looked back at the three-story hotel, I saw curtains pulled open. Hotel guests stared at what likely appeared to be some bizarre fraternity prank gone awry. After about fifteen more minutes of trying to move in either direction, I surrendered, and the security officer called a diesel truck-towing service.

The tow truck arrived about half and hour later. Climbing out of his rig, the tow truck driver stared quizzically at the stuck Penske, wiped his brow with his left forearm, and then uttered these unforgettable words: "Who is responsible for this mess?" By this time I was alone in the parking lot; the security officer was inside the hotel.

At times the accumulated weight of expectations of higher and higher results can lead us to feel that our tires are deep in mud, the trailer is high-centered, we can't go forward, and there is no going back. To make matters worse, we may have people gawking at us from the corporate office with a measure of delight, as they see us suffer the humiliation of trying to get our sales careers back on solid footing and headed in a positive direction. Sometimes even the most well-intended advice from people who operate within the sales territory can lead to missteps. Unfortunately, when the rescue party finally arrives on the scene, the agony of attaching a winch cable to your bumper can be excruciating, and the scars left behind will become fodder for water cooler stories for years to come.

At the hotel in Toledo, it was apparent to me and a lot of other people that I had lost all ability to move forward. I wanted to run and hide, but my fingerprints were on the steering wheel and my kid's belongings were in the back of the truck. The tow truck driver's condescension and ridicule and hotel patrons' disdainful scowls seemed like a heavy price for a brief lapse in judgment.

We forfeit the right to select consequences when we abdicate our responsibility as leaders. Fortunately for me, there was irrefutable evidence that I had lost all forward motion. For many sales professionals, it may not be quite so obvious.

Before we outline the essential components of the *Personal Leadership Model*, which is designed to provide the "winch and cable" for sales professionals who lack any serious forward motion, let's identify some key symptoms of Sales Paralysis.

Eight Symptoms of Sales Paralysis

Sales Paralysis is a state in which forward progress has either ceased or substantially subsided, or where there is a clear void between outcomes and the sales professional's individual potential. As with most common physical ailments we encounter in our lives, a viable diagnosis does not require all of the symptoms to be present. In some instances chronic symptoms in even one or two areas are sufficient to suggest corrective action.

An unwillingness to respond effectively to these symptoms can be terminal to a selling career. As later chapters will explain, without a sales model grounded in the notion of *Personal Leadership*, we may spend time and money treating symptoms ineffectively, while the solution languishes outside our frame of reference, and our sales revenue plummets to disastrous levels.

Sales professionals who exhibit these eight common symptoms are dangerously stuck and nearly always require some type of assistance to regain the forward motion.

Symptom 1: The Passion Is Gone

When I finally reached the refuge of my hotel room in Toledo at 3:15 AM, the last thing on earth I wanted to do was think about climbing into the cab of that rental truck and finishing the drive to Erie, Pennsylvania. There had been a sense of excitement during first few hundred miles of the trip, and driving the truck had been new and challenging and in some strange way moderately exhilarating. Now, as I sat in the quiet of my hotel room, all of that enthusiasm was gone. There was more than sufficient evidence to conclude that I lacked the skill and competency to drive this truck on a cross-country odyssey. There were at least fifty hotel guests who could stand as witnesses. I managed to finish the final five hours of driving, but it was painful. When I left the truck for the last time I sighed with relief. My desire to drive was gone.

Sales professionals who similarly lack passion for the work will shows signs of dried mud on the sidewalls of their tires, from spinning them without making measurable forward progress. In many instances, these are solid professionals with proven competency, but they have lost the personal exhilaration they once found in being engaged in the selling process. Realignment of sales territories, changes to compensation programs, and serious challenges in their personal lives all can contribute to this emotional "flatlining."

If sales professionals are unable to motivate themselves to produce excellent work, revenue numbers will fall, customers will be estranged, and the sales territory will soon be in need of serious repair. Motivation (or passion) is the engine that drives the human machine towards extraordinary achievement. When the passion is gone, it will only be a short time before the inevitable weeds grow and the territory will be a barren landscape of disenfranchised customers. A sales professional without passion is stuck, and, unless help is provided immediately, even a metaphorical winch and cable will be insufficient to hoist the salesperson back onto a positive track.

Symptom Two: Inattentive Listening

When I arrived at the hotel in Toledo and parked the truck in front of the main entrance, I had already passed the proverbial "point of no return." Even in that location navigating my way to the safety of the parking lot on the west side of the building would have been rather problematic. Certainly the associated damages would have been less, but the error in judgment had already been made. The map provided by the desk clerk marked the location of my room and also provided a broad view of the hotel property and the adjacent parking area. The fact that the parking lot did not circle the hotel was clearly visible. Because I did not pay attention, in a sense I was already stuck before I climbed back in the truck.

The inability of sales professionals to pay attention – to listen carefully — is an unmistakable sign of losing forward motion and is one of the most serious problems in our profession. It prevents the development of collaborative, high-trust relationships with clients that uniquely allow sales professionals to position their products or services to solve complex problems for their customers. Careful and attentive listening to verbal and nonverbal communication, born of a genuine desire to understand the customer's needs, is a hallmark of high-performing sales professionals.

Making product presentations without a careful customer need analysis makes no more sense than driving a fully loaded Penske rental truck onto a wet lawn in Toledo at 2:00 AM. Attentive listening provides the sales professional with a map of the property. By asking thoughtful questions and listening carefully to reasoned answers, the sales professional can avoid getting high-centered on the arrogance that accompanies inattentive listening.

Symptom Three: "Winging It"

In retrospect, my drive to Erie reflected both a tremendous lack of driving experience and a lack of respect for professional drivers and their skills. While I had briefly consulted a map, I had made no real, substantive preparations for the drive. The most serious thinking began during the first few miles of the trip.

I could have planned the trip in advance by identifying possible fuel stops, receiving information about highway construction delays, and making hotel reservations. I could have made a contingency plan with my son-in-law, in case we were separated. But absolutely none of this happened! I simply climbed in the truck, turned on the ignition, and began "winging it" across the country. The absence of any credible preparation was directly linked to the crushing embarrassment in Toledo two nights later.

I have seen far too many sales professionals who believed that "winging it" will somehow insure a safe arrival at the desired destination. Sadly, they set out on a course they think will lead them to the top of their profession, only to find themselves miles off course and mired in mud.

Sales professionals who neglect to stay current on industry topics, such as changes in market trends and technology, evolving customer attitudes and preferences, market price points and new product developments from competitors, are virtually doomed to have their careers bogged down and caked in mud, while others zoom by them in the fast lane. Sales professionals who are assiduous readers, who study the landscape of the industry, and who eagerly consume data about customers and competitors not only avoid the metaphorical pitfalls of concrete curbs and wet lawns, but also fundamentally differentiate themselves in the minds of their customers. They add value through their comprehensive understanding of issues relevant to product selection.

Sales professionals who enter a client's office without thoughtful planning and careful thinking about questions to be asked, problems to be resolved, product differentiation to be clarified, prices that need to be justified, or reports on previous commitments which need to be given will soon feel the soles of their shoes sinking in mud. Their truck makes it over the "curb" and into the office, but their propensity for winging it, as an unfortunate alternative to skillful preparation will leave them languishing in the mud.

Failing to prepare for client visits is boorish. It shows disrespect for customers and a lack of the self-discipline required for consistent success in selling. Generally speaking, sales professionals who adopt a pattern of inadequate preparation and planning end up so badly stuck that the only remedy is a change of careers.

Symptom Four: Lack of a Sense of Urgency

Motivated by a sense of urgency about problem-solving, a leader gathers solid, verifiable information about potential options and problems. It is a basic responsibility.

Looking back at that frustrating night in Toledo, I see failures on a number of levels. Most involve poor judgment and limited information. I was more interested in getting to bed than in carefully evaluating possible solutions to the problem. Better advice about releasing the trailer from the hitch of the truck would have been a way through the problem. But, rather than investigating that possibility further, I let a well-meaning young man with his own agenda of expediency dictate the outcome. I lacked not only a sense of urgency, but also a sense of interest in serious problem-solving. When urgency dissipates and attention wanes, there will generally be trouble on the road ahead.

One of the significant barometers to measure whether or not a sales professional has lost forward motion is evaluating that sense of urgency in responding to clients and company associates. A lack of urgency can manifest itself in failure to respond quickly to telephone calls, delays in answering requests for technical support, missed reporting deadlines, consistent tardiness to meetings, failure to fully engage during sales training seminars, repeated mistakes in data collection, or missing critical time windows for responding to customer requests.

By contrast, the ability to work with a sense of urgency about critical, time-sensitive matters is one of the most consistent character traits of top-performing sales professionals. Making informed decisions about which issues require a higher level of urgency is a matter of personal judgment. Personal judgment is always a question of *Personal Leadership*. Without a sales philosophy firmly rooted in *Personal Leadership*, a sales professional would be wise to have the telephone number of a good tow truck driver on speed dial.

Symptom Five: Contemplation of a Job Change

Standing in the parking lot of the Toledo Marriott Courtyard with my head down, contemplating the debris field in front of me, was a sobering experience. The energy I felt earlier in the day for delivering my cargo to Pennsylvania had completely evaporated, leaving behind a pool of self-pity and some mild rants of self-loathing. My lack of skill created a feeling of inadequacy about driving the truck that made any thought of finishing the project almost unbearable. The hotel patrons' pointed fingers were not something that inspired self-confidence. Though not written on paper, my letter of resignation was nonetheless indelibly printed in my heart. My career as a long-haul truck driver was over.

Even the most seasoned sales professionals make mistakes. Accidents and errors in judgment happen. Incessant rumination on mistakes can paralyze progress and lead us to believe that we lack the proper skill set to succeed in a given sales assignment. This erosion of self-confidence can lead us to formulate an exit strategy when we should be planning to succeed.

Marinating in thoughts of a better life in a new profession blunts clarity about pressing issues, shifts responsibilities to different shoulders, and depletes the oxygen that gives life to a current vocation. Operating day to day with one eye on the road ahead, while the other eye scans the landscape for new opportunities, is a perilous position. It is also a clear symptom of a sales professional who is desperately stuck.

Symptom Six: Feelings of Frustration

Waiting for the tow truck driver to arrive, I paced the parking lot and periodically stared back at the staggering site of a large yellow moving truck up to its axles in mud and sod. Only yesterday, the same patch of turf could have hosted a picnic while toddlers played nearby or provided space for some last-minute chip shots before a golf outing with old college friends. Tomorrow it would stand as a witness to misguided plans and poor preparation. In those solitary moments, when I could feel the piercing stares from behind partially-drawn curtains, my frustration was physically palpable. My palms were wet, and my stomach was wrenching. After all, I was just a dad trying to help my kids, and, to be quite honest, I didn't have time for this. One thing was certain: this would be the last time I would step forward for duty that included a risk of this type of undeserved outcome. At first I had been embarrassed; now I was just angry.

All of us, regardless of our chosen vocation in life, experience frustration. It is when we allow those feelings to take up long-term residency that our effectiveness in selling comes to an abrupt halt, and our forward motion slips into a backward slide. More often than not, sales professionals who lose forward motion while wallowing in frustration see themselves as victims, and not just of a single event. This frustration can lead to a paranoia that drains every ounce of positive energy from the mind of the sales professional.

Without an environment saturated by a sense of hope, sales professionals become impotent in problem-solving and obsessed by the injustice of circumstances seemingly out of their control. Sales professionals who carry the burden of chronic frustration wear an invisible mask which may not be seen, but will certainly be felt, by everyone they encounter. This frustration can have a crippling affect on product presentations, customer follow-up, and any collaborative work with customers or company associates. It will be manifested by a tendency to be inconsiderate of the opinions of others, a shortness of temper, and a deep sense of agitation. These are symptoms of stagnation in the selling process and of a sales professional who has miserably lost all forward motion.

Symptom Seven: Blaming Others

By the time I handed over my credit card to the tow truck driver, his curious and judgmental grin from an hour earlier had given way to a sense of weariness and perhaps even a modicum of compassion. For my part, as I scribbled my name on the credit card receipt, I could hear the first strains of whining bouncing around in my head. I told myself, "This was not my fault. There was no way on this planet that I would have even attempted a dash across the lawn without considerable coaxing." The pitch of my voice, at least in my mind, escalated until sleep finally muted the noise thirty minutes later. When I retold the story to family members, I accentuated the security officer's role in the decision and portrayed myself as more or less a victim of the unmitigated incompetence of a hotel employee. The deflection strategy helped for several days, until I realized that in a way I was still stuck back in Toledo, sinking up to my knees in mud of my own making.

Perhaps the single most obvious symptom of a sales professional being critically stuck is the sound of blame being systematically offloaded to customers, products, the corporate office, predatory competitors, economic downturns, or even the capricious nature of the weather. The shameful sound of a sales professional shifting blame to others is the emotional equivalent of dual wheels spinning without traction in ten inches of mud with a two-inch topping of shredded Kentucky bluegrass.

The complexity of professional selling in dynamic sales environments simply requires the leader, who has charge of the territory, to accept complete responsibility for all outcomes. Does this mean that there are no other complicit factors? Of course not. It means that, as the person responsible for revenue production in the territory, I can never evade my responsibility for final results.

As long as I cling to the notion that someone else is entirely or even partially to blame for failure, my forward progress is stalled. Sales professionals who are blinded by their own pride forfeit the valuable feedback that can change future outcomes, reverse territory trends, and rebuild sales careers. They remain stuck in an emotional cesspool that, if left uncorrected, will make even breathing a difficult process.

Symptom Eight: Low Energy for Problem Solving

Getting a 25-foot Penske truck stuck on the lawn at 2:00 AM required more than a single lapse in judgment. I had driven far too many miles in far too short a time to have been able to muster the energy required for some serious problem solving. A decision at the beginning of the trip to identify realistic benchmarks to pace the long journey may have produced a slightly different outcome. After two long days of travel, I was road-worn and anxious to get some rest. I was not in the best shape to wrap my head around the problem that needed my immediate attention.

Low energy for problem-solving creates a high risk of problems. Reflecting on that night in Toledo, I see how my own inability to seek constructive solutions exacerbated the problem. Emotionally, I was flying a white flag, and even someone else's best effort to rescue me couldn't avert the embarrassing outcome.

Professional selling requires an aptitude for finding solutions to complex problems. Even the most tangible products frequently are bought for intangible reasons. At a very basic level, professional selling is mastering the skill of creative problemsolving. The sales professional's ability to identify needs and fit the product into an appropriate solution-oriented context is an essential element of consistent success.

A solution-oriented mindset differs from a focus that is principally product-based in that solutions are always customer-driven and frequently involve sifting through complex layers of information that are not always easily accessible. Solutions generally demand critical and creative thinking, which itself becomes a clear benefit to the customer.

Despite the protests of legions of sales professionals to the contrary, productoriented selling is the standard operating protocol for the vast majority of sales transactions. It has a narrow, "product only" focus and pushes the solution discovery process into the hands of the customer. In essence, the sales professional abdicates to the customer's judgment the creative process of determining how the product solves problems and fills needs. In some instances desperate customers will wrestle with the product to find solutions. Usually they will not. Instead, they discard the product and dismiss the sales professional who refuses or neglects to engage in problem-solving. When the sales professional fails to think creativity and critically, the sales process is reduced to a simple discussion of price. When price becomes the sole determinant in product selection, the sales professional has lost all forward motion.

Eight Symptoms of Sales Paralysis
Score 1 - 10 (1 = Strongly Disagree   10 = Strongly Agree)

	YOUR SCORE
1. I am a highly motivated sales professional.	
2. I am an attentive listener.	
3. I prepare well in advance for every client meeting.	
4. I work with a sense of urgency.	
5. I do not spend time considering a change in employment.	
6. I don't waste time being frustrated.	
7. I do not blame others.	
8. I am energized about solving problems.	
TOTAL POINTS	

Figure 1-1: Eight Symptoms of Sales Paralysis

You could probably add to this list of eight common symptoms several others that signal a loss of momentum and cause revenue in the sales territory to stagnate, customers to become indifferent, and competitors to gain ground. All of these can in large measure be attributed to the sales professional somehow getting stuck. When this happens, the monthly sales report reads like the sound of wheels turning uselessly in the soft mud of a territory which otherwise shows sizable potential.

I think it would be helpful before we move on to the next chapter to take just a minute and assess what you were thinking or feeling as you read through these eight symptoms. Besides the obvious fact that you were grateful that it was me and not you driving the truck, did any of the eight symptoms sound familiar? Could you identify right now or at some point in your career with how these symptoms will negatively impact your ability to sell effectively? Was it clear to you how, when even one or two of these symptoms were present, it could be difficult for you to work at a very high level of productivity?

If you are not right now experiencing at least one of these symptoms, you are a bit unusual. I have found that most people in selling often show signs of several at once, and in some cases the symptoms can be so pronounced that forward progress can be a painful exercise every day. Let me just assure you that there is help available, and that I am confident that, as we move through this book, you will be encouraged that complete eradication of these symptoms can take place and that administering the antidote is almost completely in your hands. We will return to these symptoms periodically in the book to show how the six key selling skills, when powered by the *Personal Leadership Drivers* of *Vision, Character* and *Passion* can restore you and your sales territory to full health.

CHAPTER 2

Personal Leadership
The Defining Skill

PERSONAL LEADERSHIP is important in selling for the same reason it is important in every aspect of life: it leads to productive outcomes. The injection of *Personal Leadership* into any life experience promotes a sense of alignment with overarching goals, objectives and values. *Personal Leadership* allows a person to sift through a hundred pieces of irrelevant material and find one tiny morsel that will accelerate movement toward a clearly defined goal.

Personal Leadership in selling is the skill of defining the overall objective, developing a workable plan and then executing the plan at precisely the right moment and in the right way, to produce the desired result-maximum revenue production.

In nearly every instance where I have worked closely with a high-performing sales professional who is deeply invested in the notion of *Personal Leadership,* that professional's expectations for revenue production have exceeded my own. Where I have made the mistake of looking at revenue from similar territories to determine an annual sales goal, they have looked at their territories from an understanding of their own potential and have nearly always envisioned greater results. I have looked at product potential; they have looked at personal potential. I have effectively lowered the bar to the standard of median performance; they have effectively raised the bar to expect outstanding performance.

To understand the role of *Personal Leadership* and how it relates to important selling skills or practices like prospecting, client presentations, planning, etc., visualize in your mind all the parts of the automobile as the various skills required to make your territory productive. Now put a person in the driver's seat. That person represents the role of *Personal*

Leadership in mobilizing all of the intricate facets of the car to make it fully operational. The skills in the new model represent the parts. *Personal Leadership* is about the person driving.

Even car components, which are finely tuned to run at optimal levels, stand little chance of making it out of the garage without a driver, and on the road a driver makes split-second decisions about a wide assortment of different controls to move the car along a chosen path toward an intended destination.

Personal Leadership is about pushing the accelerator, tapping the brakes, adjusting the mirrors, dimming the lights, checking the tires, putting gas in the tank, and a hundred other things that allow the car to perform in a way that the goal of the driver is realized. *Personal Leadership* is about knowing what buttons to push and which levers to pull, at precisely the right time to produce the best possible outcome. It is about taking responsibility for arriving on time at your destination. The car needs to be a finely tuned machine, but even the best tires and the most powerful engine will never compensate for poor choices made by the driver.

As we move through this book it will be helpful for you to separate the *Personal Leadership* function from the basic selling skills required to be successful in the profession. The role of *Personal Leadership* – specifically *Vision, Character* and *Passion* – needs to become clear as it relates to bringing together all of the parts and pieces   of this complex vehicle to perform with all the expert precision of an Indy car.

Figure 2-1 *Personal Leadership* Drives the Selling Process

Vision, Character and Passion: The Three Competencies of Personal Leadership

What image comes to mind when you think about the most effective leader you have either worked with, voted for, studied or admired from a distance? It is almost certain that the person you are thinking about demonstrated a clear sense of *vision*, possessed a strong personal *character* and exhibited an infectious *passion* for the work. Keep this in mind as we introduce the concept of *Personal Leadership Drivers*. These are simply traits or competencies, such as *Vision*, which power a particular set of selling skills. Three drivers play a vital role in powering the *Personal Leadership Model*.

Each *Personal Leadership Driver* contributes in a distinct way to drive the selling process forward. In some ways the *Personal Leadership Drivers* represent the root of the selling process, and the skills are what grow above ground on the branches as illustrated in **Figure 2-2.** Most people can recognize the fruit, but they seldom consider the root system which sustains life. The root feeds the fruit. *Personal Leadership Drivers* provide the sustenance from which the skills of selling can be constantly nourished and fully implemented.

Vision. Have you ever looked at a piece of art, watched a motion picture, or listened to music that inspired you at some level? Maybe the color composition, the clever dialogue, or the melodic chords helped you think or feel differently about your life or your career? Perhaps it gave you a new idea for solving a problem or a needed lift to face a new challenge. Such things happen when we momentarily experience someone else's *vision*. Likewise, your own *vision* of your territory and your life should inspire and move you. The relationship between Personal Leadership Drivers and skills is shown in **Figure 2-3.**

This *vision* is not a dream. It is an understanding of the possibilities. It is a clear-headed assessment of a new reality, based upon reliable information. Creating a *vision* in professional selling isn't about spending more time in meditation. *Vision* is primarily quantitative; it begins with crunching some numbers, reading a lot of relevant data, mapping trends, monitoring forecasts, and becoming an industry expert about your product in your territory. From your *vision* you create an action plan for the next sales year.

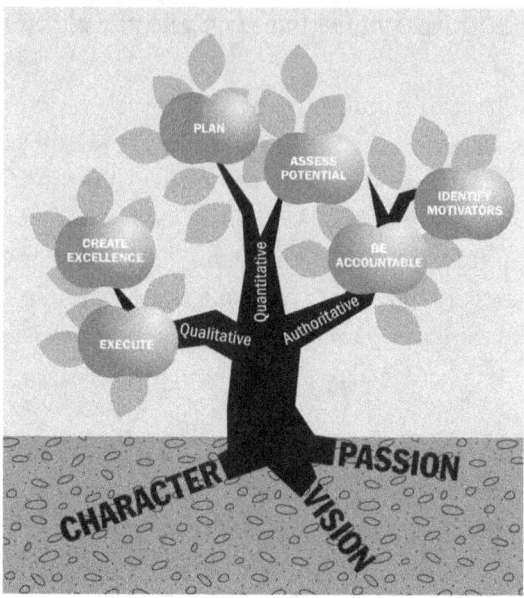

Figure 2-2: *What is a Personal Leadership Driver?*

*The term **Personal Leadership Driver** is a basic leadership competency that powers or drives the execution of a selling skill. The three **Personal Leadership Drivers** or competencies essential to success in selling are **Vision, Character** and **Passion.***

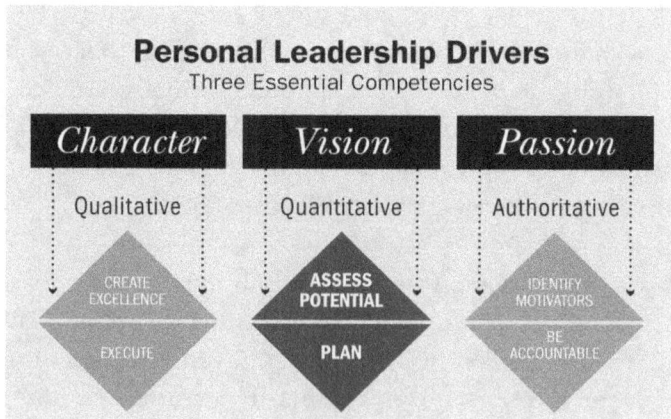

Figure 2-3: *Personal Leadership Drivers*

Regardless of what your experience with analytical work has been in the past, you are capable of doing this. I will provide you some simple steps later in the book. Without accurate and supportable information you will never chart a course that leads you to discover your potential as a sales professional and the potential of your product. Without such information you will not have a clear *vision*.

Every effective leader who I have known, or whose life I have studied, has had a sense of *vision*. During the Great Depression President Franklin Delano Roosevelt challenged the American preoccupation with fear and replaced it with a sense of hope. Winston Churchill proved that clearly connected words that inspire hope and fortify purpose can be as powerful as weapons of war. Martin Luther King, Jr., changed the course of a nation by persuading us that equality for all citizens is the highest aspiration of a free society. All three of these leaders had *visions* that, at times, no one else could see. Each changed the course of history.

The progress you make in building your sales territory may not compare with a historic piece of congressional legislation or rallying a people to fend off an invading enemy, but it can define your life's work. When measured on that scale, few things have greater weight. The more willing you are to study and understand your territory, your customers, your competitors, and your product, the clearer your *vision* of potential outcomes will become. That clarity will allow you to construct a plan which, fully executed, will make you feel like you have had your own "rendezvous with destiny."

Character. As a *Personal Leadership Driver* it is *Character* that propels you to do your best work. *Character* is most often considered a qualitative measurement. More simply stated, it is the quality of the work you produce. It really isn't about doing more or selling more than the rest of the associates on the sales team. It is simply working consistently within your ability in every aspect of the selling process. The experience of selling has to be more than the year-end numbers on the sales report. You are the only one who really knows whether or not your sales totals represent your best effort, which is nearly always an assessment of quality.

Character is what drives you to subordinate your self-interest, your commission, to the interest of the client. *Character* is what fosters trust, inspires confidence, builds loyalty, eliminates doubt, enhances credibility, adds value, differentiates products and ultimately produces collaboration. *Character* is always more important than products, when it is time to make a final buying decision. *Character* is who you really are when you get back into the car after a client presentation.

While I believe *character* is an indispensable part of success in selling, sales professionals as a group are often stereotyped as self-indulgent charlatans. So on one hand we can profess *character's* relative importance while simultaneously acknowledging on the other hand the dearth of *character* that exists in our industry. I have worked with sales professionals who have consistently produced respectable revenue numbers, but who never earned the respect of their closest peers. Successful sales careers have to be measured by something more than a relative comparison among members of the sales team. Personal and territory potential should be the final measurement of sales success.

Passion. It might be possible for a person with low *character* and an obscure *vision* of the territory to produce respectable revenue numbers, but lofty sales totals will never happen without a passion for the work. *Passion* is the fuel that drives all outstanding achievement. It is a compensatory *Personal Leadership* skill that can fill voids left by deficiencies in *character* and an imperfect territory *vision*. *Passion* is about making an authoritative statement about your work. It is about owning your destiny.

Passion is what drives long hours prospecting for new clients and keeps searing rejection from becoming defeat. As a *Personal Leadership Driver* it is *Passion* that pushes you to identify personal benefits from outstanding achievement and to reformulate those images into a viable fuel source that keeps your energy levels high day in and day out. *Passion* is also what drives you to be accountable for your goals, plans, and implementation strategy. Without a constant source of *passion* for the work, even the best plans and most productive territories will dry up overnight, even in the hands of capable professionals.

Selling is a tough business. Competitors are constantly trying to chip away at your market share. Customer attitudes and buying preferences fluctuate over time. The rapid change of technology accelerates the speed of innovation. And the changing global economy impacts the way your business is conducted. In this environment sustaining *passion* requires a constant "refueling" effort. Sales professionals who are effective leaders understand the role of passion and make conscious choices daily to keep the tank full, so the engine can run long and hard.

Before we examine how the three *Personal Leadership Drivers* power key selling skills at a day to day operational level in the territory, let's take a broader look to understand how these competencies will be required to reach your potential in selling.

Personal Leadership through *Vision:* Working "At the End of the Bar"

Selling is challenging work. Consistently achieving revenue goals can be exhausting and working carefully in alignment with your potential is a daunting task. It can feel like you are attempting to lift a heaving stone beyond your physical and emotional capacity. At times it can seem overwhelming, if not altogether impossible. It can be done. People around you are doing it. So can you.

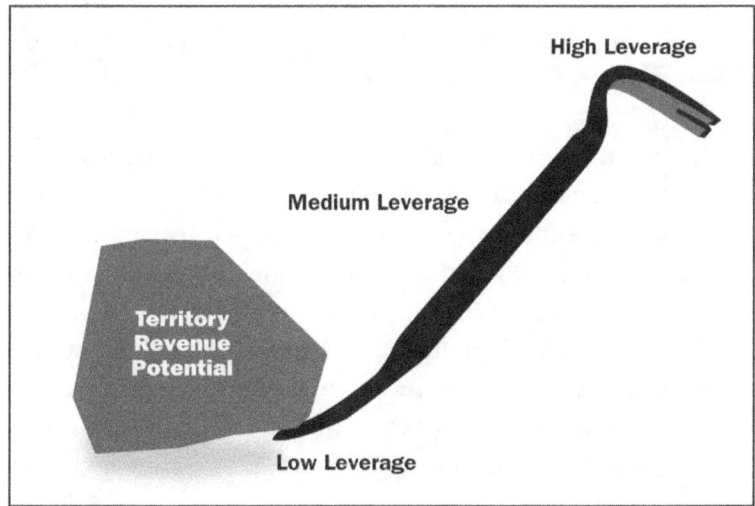

Figure 2-4: *Personal Leadership* Promotes Working at the "End of the Bar"

The large stone in **Figure 2-4** is shown being pried from the ground with a long crowbar. This illustrates how using a simple tool or lever and applying our own strength in a different way enable us to perform a task that may have been beyond our normal capacity. It is not about working harder or developing stronger muscles; it is simply about the correct use of a tool, which in most instances will permit us to exert less effort while producing a more favorable outcome.

Notice that the greatest leverage is always at the end of the crowbar. The closer your hands are to the stone, the more force you will have to exert on the lever. Conversely, as your hands move toward the end of the crowbar, your leverage increases, and the force required to move the object decreases.

Personal Leadership, particularly demonstrated by clarity of purpose or *vision*, is the ability to use the right tools in the right way at the right time to move the stone in the desired direction. It is about always working to keep your hands at the end of the bar. Some sales activities could be described as productive; others, perhaps, as important; and a few as absolutely essential. *Vision* enables you to understand the relative importance of different sales activities and allocate your time accordingly. This empowers you to constantly work to spend more and more of your time at the highest leverage point. You may not possess all the technical skills of other members of the sales team, but with a clear *vision* you can consistently apply downward pressure at a position on the bar that gives you the best chance to move the stone.

One of the veterans on our sales team sets a personal goal to make thirty customer contacts every day. When I first heard him say this at a sales meeting, I seemed to sense all the oxygen leaving the room, as new members of the team began gasping for air. At the same meeting another veteran reported that his weekly goal was forty hours of time with customers. This obviously included meetings where four or five customers might be in the same meeting for the same hour and a half. These sales professionals were equally certain that these daily and weekly goals positively impacted long-term revenue production. They had a clear *vision* of desired outcomes. Their personal *vision* helped move their hands towards the end of the bar.

About twenty years ago I was becoming increasingly exasperated by the poor sales totals from a member of our team in a large western metropolitan area. The market demand was clearly identified; our price position was moderately aggressive; and the supporting research suggested solid brand awareness among important customer groups, with decided preference for our product in two or three key market segments. Yet the sales totals year after year remained at approximately thirty-five percent of anticipated annual revenue.

This member of our sales team was a bright, capable professional with excellent communication skills, proven work habits and an above-average desire for achievement. During the course of our several meetings it was apparent that we were nearing a time when a personnel change would be required to move the territory forward. He was a competent sales practitioner with the wrong skill set who lacked any clear *vision* about his own potential and the potential of the territory. He could prospect, present, follow up and close; unfortunately he just could not find the right balance to do what was required when it was required.

All the essential elements of *Personal Leadership* can be learned, and the results can be breathtaking. This young sales professional went from being a consistent lowerthird producer to being at or near the top of the sales report within two years. That is the good news. The great news is that he stayed there for the next fifteen years. *Personal Leadership* demonstrated by a clear *vision* is about leveraging time, assets and resources to produce the greatest possible benefit. His *vision* improved in a short period of time and so can yours.

Personal Leadership through *Character:* Quality Decision Making

Consistent territory growth will never come unless you can consistently make good decisions in the midst of the crucible of selling. Making good decision is always a question about judgment. In the world of professional selling good judgment is nearly always about *character.*

With the clamor of customers, the corporate office, product deliveries, pricing concerns, tomorrow's presentation and today's prospecting needs swirling about you, can you make the best decision possible to produce the desired result? That is what sales professionals who implement *Personal*

Leadership do consistently and proficiently. That is what you must do to get your revenue number to a higher altitude.

Several years ago I was attending a client meeting with a member of our sales team in a large west coast city. He was an experienced sales professional who had enjoyed moderate to good success during most of his ten or more years selling our products. He asked me to attend this meeting in an effort to resolve some technical issues that he felt were negatively impacting the buying decision.

For the first twenty minutes of the meeting I simply listened to the interaction between my associate and about four senior managers who comprised the decision making team for the client. These were reasonable people who asked logical questions and seemed genuinely interested in resolving some inconsistencies about product use. The responses from the member of our sales team were laced with sarcasm and condescension. He was convinced that the client had an agenda to remove him from possible consideration, and he seemed resigned to extracting a pint of blood on his way out of the door.

I could sense the tension of the room escalating and in an effort to diffuse the rancor I asked our clients if we could take a short break. I then stepped into an adjacent hallway with my associate and we had a brief but memorable conversation about both the tone and substance of his message. I tried to persuade him that all the concerns raised were legitimate, and that until we dialed back the defensive rhetoric, the chance of this client making a favorable buying decision was about the same as me hitting a ninety mile-per-hour fastball.

Personal Leadership in any endeavor, and especially in selling, consists of making good decisions that are aligned with key strategic objectives. That type of discipline requires *character*. This member of our sales team was a solid revenue producer with good technical skills and a desire to improve. His intentions were good, but his judgment was poor. All the product training in the world would never have compensated for his inability to make good judgments about key issues at critical times.

Selling consists of making hundreds of small decisions every week. *Personal Leadership* empowers the sales professional with the ability to process every important decision through a filter. Your filter is largely an expression of your *character* as it relates to the selling process. It should consist of:

1. A basic belief or philosophy about customers.

2. Long-term strategic objectives for the territory.

3. Short-term revenue goals.

4. Standard practices or policies established by the company.

5. Personal beliefs, attitudes and values.

6. Previously established commitments.

7. The perceived value or yield rate of one activity or choice compared to another.

Let's assume for a moment that the seven items listed above comprise the framework or filter for processing information about important decisions. With this information providing the context for decision making, let's return to the meeting I described earlier. My fellow sales associate was responding to stimulus in the room that he interpreted as being argumentative or dismissive. He simply reacted in the same fashion he would if some careless driver cut him off in traffic. Leaders don't react to circumstances. They act only after processing all the relevant information through a filter of their basic attitudes and beliefs about their territory.

The more clarity you have about the filter, your *character*, the greater the possibility that the decisions you make will be consistent with the long-term objectives for your territory. It will also mean that your hands will move farther out near the end of the bar. In the new *Personal Leadership Model* it is *Character* that will power the development of two important skills that will improve the quality of your work and the consistent execution of your plan. Together these two skills will facilitate the process of good decision making.

Personal Leadership through *Passion:* Conducting Regular Diagnostic Work

Your ability to conduct real time self diagnostic work prevents the encroachment of the symptoms of Sales Paralysis. With these symptoms removed a serious discussion about personal and territory potential can take place. Self diagnosis is the "anti-virus" software for professional selling. It requires a healthy dose of *passion* to maintain constant vigilance to prevent the incursion of the "bugs" that can disrupt the selling process.

Our family has a cabin located in the mountains, about 8500 feet above sea level. During a normal winter the snow accumulation can range from 150 to 300 inches. Once, while traveling outside the country in the middle of January, I received a phone call from a person who was staying at the cabin. There was a "slight" water problem.

I have learned that, when it comes to homes in the mountains – and in the middle of a harsh winter – there is no such thing as a slight water problem. After separate diagnostic calls from two different plumbers, it was concluded that the problem was an inadequately sealed drain in an upstairs bathroom. This diagnosis involved cutting away the sheetrock while water dripped through the ceiling.

Concerned about potential water damage in the cabin, I spoke with the plumber from my hotel in London. I asked him if he was certain he had found the problem. His answer was one that I will not soon forget: "I am not perfect, but when it comes to troubleshooting plumbing problems, I am as close as it gets." He explained his investigatory work behind the drywall. His bravado worked. I traveled home comfortably with little or no anxiety about any further water problems.

Arriving at the cabin a few days later, I was surprised to see the water dripping on the tile floor near the entry area. I grabbed a flashlight and examined the holes left by the plumber. Then I decided to go outside. I soon found that there was a small ice dam pushing water through a pinhead-sized hole, resulting in a constant drizzle of water. With that fixed, the floor finally started to dry out.

The confident plumber was like many of us who work in sales leadership roles, who have seen "problems like this" a thousand times. We go through the motions of careful diagnostic work and prescribe a remedy based upon our experience. "Well, let's see, revenue is down, so you need to make more sales calls." Certainly that will stop the leak, right? Or, "Your contract totals are sluggish because your bidding activity is down; you need to make an effort to bid more projects this month." That will definitely get rid of those water spots on the floor. You may even reach for the guilt trip to plug the hole, saying something like, "You have just too much ability not to be producing more revenue. I suggest you do some serious thinking about whether or not you are fit for a career in sales." Nothing gets the water off the floor like a good shot to the solar plexus.

In the environment of selling we are measured weekly, monthly, and annually by clearly identified numbers that rarely lie. This is not a subjective performance review, where a clever manager with a penchant for creative writing can construct a different view of reality based on a number of occasionally conflicting factors. Poor sales performance is like the dripping of water from the ceiling that leaves a pool of anxiety on the floor for someone to clean up. I have been on the emergency response crew more than once, where my assessment could have sounded as brash and impudent as my plumber's words about his diagnostic prowess.

The steady dripping sound of water hitting the bucket is a common occurrence in most sales organizations. Sometimes we devise clever systems to empty the buckets more quickly by turning over the sales team or spending more time on technical product training, or perhaps implementing more systems of accountability. At times the water may disappear through evaporation caused by the heat generated internally in the organization. But the long-term solution is to identify clearly the entry point of the water. When that has been done, the buckets can be permanently retired.

When you have mastered this skill and discipline, self-diagnostics occur regularly, and remedial action is initiated at the first sign of water penetrating the outside wall. Sales professionals who excel in *Personal Leadership* as demonstrated by the constant *passion* to improve, cultivate the ability to assess potential breaches in advance and can mobilize a defensive strategy.

An Introduction to the Personal Leadership Model

The *Personal Leadership Model* is designed to provide you with the tools you need to achieve your potential as a sales professional. When your performance is in alignment with your potential the revenue numbers you produce will be at the highest possible levels.

The term "model" as it is used in selling or any other aspect of business is simply a tool to communicate clearly a process or strategy designed to produce successful outcomes. The *Personal Leadership Model* is a map that provides a graphic representation of how key skills become fully operational through the infusion of *Personal Leadership*, specifically *Vision, Character* and *Passion. Personal Leadership* is the *Defining Skill* because it controls how and when all the other six key skills in selling are executed.

The remaining chapters of this book will present a detailed examination of the six key selling skills that comprise the *Personal Leadership Model*. As shown in **Figure 2-5** the skills are compartmented into either Strategic or Tactical Work. Most sales professionals spend their time in Tactical Work and ignore the exponential gains that can only come from the skills in Strategic Work.

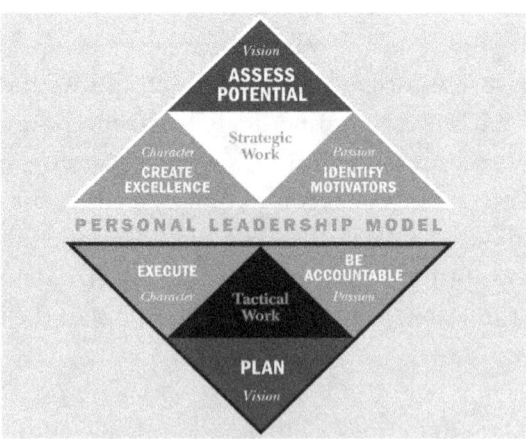

Figure 2-5: *Personal Leadership Model*

The skills in Strategic Work are more long term in nature and are designed to clarify potential, enhance the quality of your work and to develop a method to sustain levels of personal motivation for long periods of time. The skills of Tactical Work represent the operational strategy for the territory during the present sales year. It might help you you to think of Strategic Work as "preparational" and Tactical Work as "operational."

Only when Strategic and Tactical Work are fully executed will you be positioned to experience the type of sustained revenue growth that will lead to the full realization of your potential as a sales professional. You must learn to think strategically and work tactically.

Principles, Practices, and Skills:
A Short Course in the Language of Leadership in Selling

> ### DEFINITIONS
> **Understanding the Difference between Principles, Practices, Traits, and Skills**
>
> **Principle A:** a comprehensive and fundamental law, doctrine, or assumption **B:** a rule or code of conduct
>
> **Practice 1:** to do repeated exercises for proficiency **2:** actual performance or application **3:** a repeated or customary action
>
> **Skill** the learned power of doing something competently
>
> *From Webster's Ninth New Collegiate Dictionary*

Throughout this book I will use the terms principles, practices, and skills, and at times they may seem interchangeable. Please note that it is not my intent to use them as synonyms. I want you to understand principles, so that you can identify natural laws or proven assumptions that produce successful outcomes. I want you to understand practices, so that you can improve your proficiency in important skills. And finally, I want you to understand skills, so that you know how to achieve your potential as a sales professional.

An example from aviation illustrates the relationship between principles, practices and skills. A scientist named Bernoulli first postulated that the difference in speed of air moving across the top and bottom of an airfoil causes a difference in pressure, which creates lift. The growth of modern aviation can be tied to both understanding this natural law and strictly adhering to it. The Wright brothers tested their first glider near Kitty Hawk, North Carolina, in 1900 by correct application of this principle. NASA's Space Shuttle, while infinitely more sophisticated than the Wright Brothers' glider, utilizes the same basic principles of lift to return safely to earth from orbit. The key to understanding heavier-than-air flight is a basic knowledge of the principles associated with lift.

On January 15, 2009, U.S. Airways Flight 1549, departing from La-Guardia Airport in New York for Charlotte, North Carolina, struck a flock of birds shortly after take-off. Both engines failed almost immediately. The pilot, Captain Chelsey "Sully" Sullenberger responded to the emergency by safely landing the plane in the frigid waters of the Hudson River. All 155 passengers and crew escaped without serious injury. His wife later described her husband to the New York Post by saying, "He is about performing that aircraft to the exact precision to which it is made." That expression represents the very essence of skills being "the learned power of doing something competently."

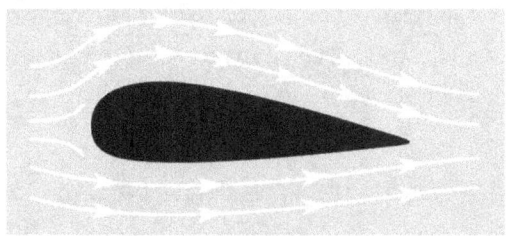

In the world of professional selling we are trying to create "lift" in our territories by moving revenue numbers closer to potential. To experience this upward movement of revenue, we first need to identify the governing laws or principles which create lift, and then practice the skills of selling with precision. Captain Sullenberger attributed this "routine" landing to the hundreds of hours of extensive training. Those hours are the essential practice that leads to highlydeveloped skills.

When principles are properly identified, it is much easier to design the necessary practices to produce the needed skills to insure that sales territories soar to new heights.

This book is not about learning merely to survive the constant sea changes in the world of professional selling. It is about understanding *Personal Leadership* and selling skills which will allow you to work at your highest possible level amid the ebbs and flows of a dynamic world economy and an increasingly competitive sales environment.

Much of what has been presented up to this point has been largely theoretical in nature. It is now time to move past the theory and directly into the actual practice. The transformation of your territory or your professional life will happen only with the consistent execution of six key skills and a rather large assortment of essential practices. The Eight Symptoms of Sales Paralysis are behind us, six new skills lie just ahead, and the role of *Personal Leadership* will cast a long shadow over every important aspect of the selling process.

PART I

Vision

THE REMAINING portion of the book will be divided into three parts, *Vision, Character* and *Passion.* I chose to present the six key selling skills grouped together with their corresponding *Personel Leadership Drivers* for the simple purpose of underscoring the role of *Personel Leadership* in professional selling. I think it will be helpful to have an image in your mind of where each skill fits in the *Personal Leadership Model,* but the overarching point is to understand how important *Personal Leadership* competencies make this skill fully operational in your life.

The following chapters could be called the "skills chapters." The skills form the fabric of the *Personal Leadership Model* and inject *Personal Leadership* into virtually every aspect of professional selling. These chapters are similarly organized according to the following basic framework:

1. **Identify the Principle.** This is an introduction of the primary principles, laws or assumptions that form the basic objective of skill development. Understanding the principle is important, but, remember, our objective is skill development.

2. **Present the Practices.** As we learned in an earlier chapter, practices are the repeated, specific exercises which enhance skill development. Skills are "learned power" that lead to optimum performance.

With this basic framework in mind, it should be easier to keep your orientation as we move through each chapter.

Principles define purpose, practices escalate skill development, skills lead to the infusion of *Personal Leadership,* and leadership will move your hands near the end of the bar. When your hands are consistently at or near the end of the bar, your revenue totals can only move in one direction ... up!

The next two chapters explain the skills which are powered by the *Personal Leadership Driver* known as *Vision. Vision* is the leadership competency that allows us to see the future and plan accordingly. It demands that we carefully examine opportunities in front of us and inside of us. It is about constantly considering the possibilities created by a changing market and adapting accordingly. In the world of professional selling vision is found in how you do two things. The first is assessing potential, and the second is translating your territory assessment into the operational sales plan for the territory. Great territories and great lives both begin with a sense of *vision*, and that *vision* leads to a plan.

CHAPTER 3

Assess Potential
Inward Capabilities and Outward Possibilities

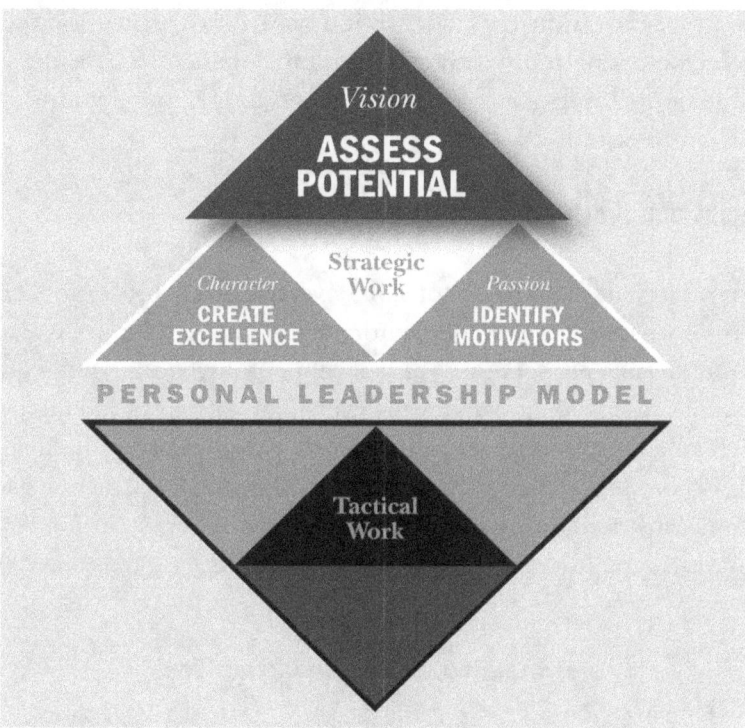

Figure 3-1 Assess Potential: The *Vision* Component of Strategic Work

THE FIRST TIME I met Jay Smart, I was a freshman in college, and I had recently been hired to fill an entry-level position on a production line in his manufacturing business. His product was an upscale line of folding partitions. It was interesting work, but, the way I looked at it, the product line was narrow, and the market seemed small, with limited growth opportunities. What I soon learned was that the gulf between what I could see and what he could see was roughly similar to the space between the north rim of the Grand

Canyon and Tranquility Base on the moon. My eyesight was fine. His vision was superb.

Jay Smart's experience with the product, his understanding of the market and his passion to create exceptional work were all molded together into a unique vision. He could see how the integration of emerging microprocessor technology and the complexity of fire protection regulation could define a new high-growth market segment. This vision shaped his growing company for much of the next thirty years and established it as the industry leader in innovative fire protection technology. *Vision* most naturally flows from minds opened to consider all the available opportunities as it assesses potential. Jay Smart's mind was always open to potential.

Principles and Practices in Assessing Potential

Bear in mind that the purpose of skill development in professional selling is to create what we have called territory "lift," which will move you toward optimum revenue production. This concept was introduced in the previous chapter, in a discussion about how heavier-than-air flight becomes possible through adherence to a governing principle and the correct application of a skill. When skills are aligned with natural laws or fundamental assumptions and reinforced by repeated practice, we can generate the *learned power* to move sales totals to their highest possible levels.

Principles, Skills, and Practices

Principles (*laws or assumptions*): A. We work according to our perception of potential; improved clarity about potential improves performance. B. Small gains in personal performance can produce big gains in revenue production. C. Long-term thinking prevents short-term setbacks.

Skill (*learned power*): Assessing Potential

Practices (*repeated exercises for proficiency*): 1) Make a Personal Assessment. 2) Implement a Self-development Program. 3) Conduct a Comprehensive Market Assessment. 4) Ask the Right Questions. 5) Use Metrics to Determine the Mission.

The three principles which support the skill of *assessing potential* are as follows: First, we tend to work in relationship to our perception of potential, either our own or the perceived potential of the product in the territory. Second, even small gains in personal performance can produce substantial gains in revenue production. And third, our ability to look and think in the long term prevents the short-term stumbling that results from preoccupation with less productive activities.

By clarifying potential we can generate lift by reformulating our perception of potential. Working in alignment with potential requires an ongoing effort to construct a clear and reliable view of our potential and our product's potential in the territory. Similarly, as we elevate our personal performance, we often experience disproportionate gains in revenue production. Finally looking at and thinking about the long term allows us to initiate plans and strategies which will help us move closer to our potential and keep us away from distracting and timewasting activities that can consume us when our focus is on the near term.

This chapter will teach you the skill of *assessing potential*. The practices will be based on two exercises that will prompt you to ask pressing questions to challenge your basic assumptions about your perception of potential, and to examine specific ways to elevate your performance. These exercises are in the form of templates which should be used every year as you prepare your annual territory sales plan.

Principle A. We Work According to our Perception of Potential; Improved Clarity Improves Performance

Our overall perception of the potential in front of us governs how we work. This basic principle shapes the framework of the skill of assessing potential. The more clarity we have about our own personal potential and the potential for our product within the sales territory, the better prepared we will be to design an operational plan that will lead us to higher revenue production.

Contrary to what many people believe, much of the work of creating *vision* in professional selling is analytical in nature. I had to learn how to activate this *Personal Leadership Driver* of *Vision* by developing some new skills in quantitative analysis; I will show you how this is done. Remember, this new model is about moving away from some aspects of your past behavior and learning new skills that will dramatically change your future.

I have found that the work involved in *assessing potential* is generally the most difficult for sales professionals. Not surprisingly, it is also the least likely to be done. This skill requires you to think inwardly, as you assess your own potential, and work outwardly, as you read and analyze critical data to find information about new opportunities for your product in the territory.

This is not really a difficult skill; it is just a *different* skill. Suppose you learned to ski when you were young and recently decided to try snow-boarding. It can seem very uncomfortable at first, but probably not from the inherent difficulty of the new skill. More likely, it is the difference from skills you have mastered before that causes you to hesitate and feel awkward.

Assessing potential is generally a quantitative activity. It involves numbers, trends, forecasts, ratios, and other important analytical tools. These will give you a view of your territory that will be like a razor-sharp image from the lens of a high-definition camera. In the business of professional selling, the more comfortable you become with processing numbers, the more likely you will be to have a firm handle on emerging trends and opportunities that will shape your territory in the coming years.

I will offer some specific guidelines to focus your attention on areas where data collection will be helpful in constructing your new *vision* of the territory. Some of these guidelines may not be precisely relevant to your product or industry, but, if you will allow yourself to think broadly about the concepts and to understand the basic framework of gathering market intelligence, you will be well prepared to implement this skill fully in your territory. When this happens, you will start to see your territory with new eyes. You will have developed a clear *vision* of new opportunities.

No More Curves

Two assessments are integral to the *Personal Leadership Model,* and both will be discussed in this chapter. The first is a comprehensive personal assessment to evaluate individual potential and your commitment to work and to perform consistent with your own talents and abilities. The second is a comprehensive study to determine the sales territory's over-all revenue potential. Both assessments play an important role in your work as a leader. With this information in hand you can best assess how to allocate available resources, such as time and money, to improve deficiencies and better position your product to respond to underdeveloped opportunities.

Nearly all sales professionals claim to be "goal-oriented." Goals are important to achieving annual objectives; however, they rarely involve the type of critical thinking and analysis required to answer the basic question of potential. Lacking a clear assessment of personal and product potential, one can simultaneously stand at the head of the class and be the biggest underachiever in the room.

The simple truth is that without supportable, reliable intelligence about both individual and market potential, sales performance will always be evaluated on a curve. That works for a lot of people, but those who yearn to achieve a measure of personal greatness in their lives must cast aside the curves and face the reality of absolutes, where both product and personal performance are concerned. The shining gold of plaques and statues fades over time. The fulfillment of living and working on a level consistent with gifts and talents never dims.

The Difference between Sight and Vision

Creating a sales plan is a tactical effort that incorporates the best critical thinking currently available. Creating a *vision* is a strategic effort that incorporates the best critical thinking about what the possibilities will be tomorrow. Both are essential to success. A well-conceived sales plan can produce consistent, incremental revenue growth. A well-conceived *vision* can produce exponential personal growth. A plan for the territory measures outcomes relative to past performance. A *vision* for the territory measures the absolute realities of potential and ignores past performance.

As you read through the next few paragraphs in this section, try to differentiate between *vision* and sight. Try to sense and feel how a *vision* is relevant to moving both you and your territory closer towards full potential. Sight is an invaluable asset for most of the activities we enjoy in life. On the other hand, *vision* will be required if you really want to make quantum leaps in revenue production. When it comes to producing big sales numbers, there is simply no substitute for developing a clear sense of *vision*.

Sight allows us to see the present. *Vision* allows us to see the future. Our eyes are windows to the world as it is. Our minds are the gateway to the world as we would like it to be. Sight distinguishes light, color, motion and a landscape of visual subtleties. *Vision* sees potential, possibilities, dreams, hopes and fondest aspirations. Sight takes place in real time. *Vision* takes place in the human mind. Sight can be enhanced by a surgical procedure designed to reshape the eye. *Vision* can be enhanced by a procedure of similar precision designed to reshape thinking.

The story of Helen Keller reminds us that it is possible to be a person of great *vision* without being able to see objects in front of you. However, the debris field of bankrupt companies also reminds us that it is impossible to see the potential in front of you without having a clear sense of *vision*. People who climb great mountains in life depend on their ability to construct a clear *vision* of possible outcomes. People who are defeated in their attempted conquest of tall summits walk in others' paths, but may fail to see for themselves. Those who see only falls and failures live with limited *vision*. They acknowledge only the reality of risk, while ignoring the ecstasy of reward. They choose to walk through life with their eyes open and their minds closed.

Sight comes to most of us as a gift and requires little thought. *Vision* comes only after excruciating thought. Looking at a mountaintop requires very little effort. Creating a path to the mountaintop demands maximum effort. Sight is innate, instinctive and commonplace. *Vision* is uncommon. Sight is a physical trait which most people enjoy. *Vision* is a mental trait that relatively few people ever learn.

Vision is about foresight, not about eyesight. It requires the discipline to learn, to study, to analyze trends, to ask thoughtful questions and to listen to reasoned answers. *Vision* is about identifying potential and creating a map that will lead to optimum outcomes. *Vision* is not only an elevated view of a task, but an elevated idea that inspires a person's best work.

The most distinguishing aspect of *Personal Leadership* is the ability to forge a unique *vision* of realistic outcomes. Leaders who possess the skills to manage a crisis are readily available. Leaders who can see far enough ahead to avoid market downturns and seize burgeoning opportunities are seldom available.

Developing a sense of *vision* in any responsibility is a learned behavior. It requires looking up while others around you are looking down. It requires the voracious consumption of forecasting data to sense the nuances of shifting marketing trends and customer preferences. A sense of *vision* begins by asking insightful questions, not by reciting logical answers. The creation of a *vision* compels a person to discover both external and internal potential.

Sight allows you to see the best performance in others. *Vision* allows you to work to the best performance in yourself. Does your *vision* of the future inspire your best work?

Practice 1: Personal Assessment – Creating a Clear Vision of Your Potential

Vision is about foresight. The more clear your *vision* becomes, the better you understand the gaps that need to be filled between where you are today and where your can be tomorrow. *Assessing potential* is really the process of clarifying the gaps. Once the gaps have been defined, the formulation of a strategy to plug the holes becomes much easier. Most of us in selling seem to have a lot of clarity about what we do well, while being almost ignorant about our shortcomings. Let me illustrate this for you with a short exercise.

Take out a sheet of paper and make two columns, with numbers from one to ten in both columns. At the top of one column write the word "strengths"; at the top of the other column write the word "weaknesses." You'll be listing both in a moment.

Personal Assessment

I. Identify Weaknesses
List five specific areas that you need to improve as a sales professional

1. _____
2. _____
3. _____
4. _____
5. _____

II. General Self-evaluation Exercise
Score 1 - 10 (1 = Strongly Disagree 10 = Strongly Agree)

	YOUR SCORE
1. I am technically proficient in every aspect of the products I represent.	
2. I consistently set and achieve goals in my territory.	
3. I write an annual sales plan for my territory.	
4. I implement my sales plan by integrating it into weekly planning sessions.	
5. I have a regularly program of self development designed to improve my overall effectiveness as a sales professional.	
6. I consistently monitor industry trends and forecasts that may impact my product.	
7. The revenue produced in my territory is consistent with the revenue being produced by other sales professionals in similar territories.	
8. I regularly seek feedback to improve my ability as a sales professional.	
9. I work to stay current on all recent changes to my competitor's products.	
10. I have a well conceived long term strategy for my territory.	
TOTAL POINTS	

Find a place where you can work privately and undistracted for a few minutes; in order for this to work, you need to time yourself. Allow yourself only two minutes per column. Are you ready?

Get started. Come back in four minutes . . .

So how did you do? Let me guess. If you are like most of your fellow sales professionals, your list of strengths filled up quickly, but you struggled to find even three or four things to write in the weaknesses column.

I can predict this typical response because I have asked the question hundreds of times in interviews, and it is the most common response from applicants for new sales positions.

Do you think for a moment that, if you were to ask a world-class athlete in any sport to describe their weaknesses, they would fumble around trying to piece together a response? The most successful athletes do repetitive diagnostic work on their weaknesses and allocate a great deal of time to strengthening their areas of vulnerability. Why should you work any differently?

In a later chapter on another selling skill, learning to plan, we will be identifying various components for inclusion in your annual sales plan. I suggest that, as you work on your annual plan, you develop the habit of conducting a careful personal assessment. This document is only for your review, but it is important to have it in writing. Knowing your strengths is useful; understanding your weaknesses is essential.

Practice 2: Implement a Program of Continuous Improvement

Working to improve your deficiencies is a high-leverage activity. It is a practice that will assist you in working toward your own potential as a sales professional. The Personal Assessment reveals areas of improvement. A continuous improvement program is an operational plan specifically designed for you to elevate important proficiencies that will lead you to higher levels of performance.

Many of the so-called professions require annual certification or the completion of continuing education credits for renewal of federal, state, county or associationissued licenses. These continuing education programs provide a measure of insurance to clients and the general public that professionals are current in standard industry practices, new technology and regulatory changes that may impact the services they provide. Many industries provide accreditation programs to certify sales professionals in basic aspects of their profession. These programs can be comprehensive where the technical elements of certain products are concerned, but they are rarely sufficient to insure continued professional development.

To be effective, the practice of continuous improvement works very much like your annual sales plan. It is based on a comprehensive need analysis, conducted as part of the *Assessing Potential* component of Strategic Work. If you carefully analyze your own strengths and weaknesses as a sales professional, you can, first, identify your potential and, second, create a map or a plan to move you closer to that potential. This is essentially what you are doing with your territory. You identify opportunities for growth and write a plan that will move you closer to new revenue opportunities. An annual continuous improvement program should accomplish the same purpose on a personal level.

Industry-sponsored programs are great, and in many instances they provide a means to address some of the deficiencies that separate you from your optimum potential as a sales professional. However, if you do a careful and thoughtful personal analysis, you will find that your deficiencies as a sales professional will not be satisfactorily addressed by additional technical information about the industry or your product. Most of the inhibitors to sales success are non-technical in nature and thus require non-technical solutions. The key to an effective continuous improvement program is thorough personal need analysis. Once this is in place, designing your own program will be relatively easy.

If you are serious about achieving personal and professional potential, you must be serious about improving. Effective self-development programs don't need to be overly ambitious undertakings that pull you away from the pressing demands of managing a territory. They do need to be consistent. Consider for a moment how different your revenue production would be if, during every week of your professional career, you had learned one new thing or perhaps acquired one new skill that would improve how you work. The accumulated weight of this type of improvement over time would be extraordinary. So would your sales results.

Your ongoing effort to improve is not just a matter of how you work and plan. It is a matter of how you think. Once you embrace a philosophy of continuous improvement, you will find it to be not only enjoyable, but, for the most part, remarkably simple. You can recapture some down time while driving by listening to topical programs, reading books on subjects that are relevant to your own personal needs, or making plans to attend seminars periodically throughout the year.

The process of continuous improvement requires very little time; costs are minimal; and the yield can be exponential. If you do not currently have a well-conceived self-development program that addresses your specific needs as a sales professional, creating one could provide the accelerant you need to put your personal and professional potential within reach. Here is a suggested exercise to guide your planning.

Annual Self Development Program Plan

I. The 5 areas that, if improved, would have the greatest impact on my ability to work more closely to my potential as a sales professional are:

1. _____
2. _____
3. _____
4. _____
5. _____

II. The activities I will conduct to improve my proficiency in the 5 areas that need improvement:

	Daily	Weekly	Monthly
1. _____			
2. _____			
3. _____			
4. _____			
5. _____			
6. _____			
7. _____			
8. _____			

Principle B. Small Gains in Personal Performance Support Big Gains in Revenue Production

The second basic principle or assumption that supports the skill of *assessing potential* is the idea that, as we improve our personal productivity, we quite often experience disproportionate gains in revenue production. *Assessing potential* is the process of conducting a thorough assessment of opportunities, so that our territory sales plan can identify goals and strategies specifically designed to capture emerging revenue sources.

There is not a linear relationship between gains in personal perform-ance and the resultant impact on revenue production. It is possible that a ten percent gain in personal performance could produce a fifty per-cent gain in revenue production. In some instances the relationship can be almost exponential.

In the early nineties I hired a young sales professional to work in a large east coast market. He brought to this new position the finest technical qualifications of any person I had ever interviewed. He seemed motivated, his experience suggested that he had great self discipline in maneuvering projects through complex sales processes, and his communication and presentation skills were well above average. He seemed destined to have great success and a productive career with our products.

Over the next three years his sales numbers put him in the bottom third of our sales team. He was frustrated, I was disappointed and there was no obvious solution in sight. He and I had a serious conversation about his future, and I explained as clearly as possible that I sensed he was spending too much time analyzing the market and competitors and ru-minating about lack of support from the team at the corporate office. I tried to persuade him that the solution to the sagging revenue numbers would likely be found by an internal assessment of what he was or was not bringing to the table, rather than by consuming valuable energy obsessing about external market or customer support factors.

That conversation took place twenty-four years ago. Within a short time his own personal assessment (even though it wasn't called that at the time) revealed that he was spending needless time on activities that would not impact revenue production. With his own assessment in hand he began the work of re-engineering his method of selling. In other words, he started to exert a higher level of *Personal Leadership* in his approach to professional selling.

Within a matter of twelve months his revenue grew 57 percent. In twenty-four months that total went to 162 percent. At the end of five years his annual sales revenue had increased 429 percent. It stayed in that revenue range for the next ten years, and he became one of the most productive members of our sales team.

A few years ago at one of our sales meeting I heard him tell the experience of our "personal assessment meeting" to other members of our sales team. I was surprised that he described with great clarity the content of the meeting. The most interesting aspect of his brief recollection was how he viewed this short session as a transformative moment in his career.

My guess is that the changes which produced rather spectacular results were far from earth-shattering. They likely would not have turned a lot of heads at a sales meeting. For him these small changes in personal productivity, gleaned from the type of personal introspection that comes from a sincere desire to change, to improve, accounted for only a ten to fifteen percent difference in how he conducted business. Not surprisingly, the results turned a lot heads, mine included.

If you will pursue clarity about your own deficiencies and weaknesses with the same zeal that you chase a six-figure contract, you will uncover some important areas to work on in the coming year. Your potential will never be fully realized until your weaknesses are fully discovered.

The process of moving closer to your potential is largely about eliminating or substantially improving your weaknesses as a sales professional. You will never be able to begin this journey without a clear and comprehensive personal assessment.

Practice 3: Conducting a Market Assessment

Conducting a comprehensive market assessment is designed to identify opportunities and reveal vulnerabilities. Remember, we are looking for ways to make even small gains in personal performance, which will lead to disproportionate gains in revenue production. Every territory has undiscovered opportunities. So does every sales professional. This practice of conducting a market assessment will be invaluable as you learn the skill of *assessing potential*.

I would suggest that you conduct both a personal assessment and a market assessment near the end of your sales year. The personal assessment can be done relatively fast. The market assessment is considerably more labor-intensive. It is not necessary to complete these assessments in any particular order. Just make sure you complete them.

Developing a clear and concise territory market assessment can be tedious and even rather labor-intensive. It requires research and analysis. It usually requires you to read unfamiliar source material. In some instances there may be costs associated with collecting the verifiable metrics you need for an accurate snapshot of the territory.

These are the most frequent barriers to entry. They prevent many sales professionals from conducting the reconnaissance they need to fully evaluate opportunities in the territory. There is a clear linkage between completing this work and achieving optimum revenue potential in any market.

Many believe that data collection is not justifiable in terms of increased short-term revenue production. But to omit data collection is usually to perpetuate a status quo which is content with merely nominal revenue gains and with underperformance by members of the sales team. Without an absolutely clear *vision* of opportunities in the market, mediocrity flourishes. We wouldn't tolerate airlines allowing their planes to take off without diligent attention to weather conditions, aircraft maintenance checks and local air traffic. Yet in most of our professional lives we ignore the gathering of critical information which may significantly impact our ability to achieve take-off speed and get airborne.

Ignoring important information in any aspect of our lives can lead to hazardous consequences.

Shortly after our oldest child graduated from high school, we took our entire family to Kauai for a week-long getaway. My wife Michele and I could see the changes coming in our family and realized that this might be the last time we would have such an experience together with all our children. The weather was spectacular, and the kids enjoyed being together. To this day it is a family vacation we all reminisce about.

On about the second day of our trip, we were enjoying a day at the beach not far from our condo. Michele and I were standing together about twenty yards from the shoreline, absorbed in conversation, while the children played, swam, built sand castles, and occasionally tormented each other. The beach was not overly crowded, so it wasn't difficult to track the whereabouts of our youngest two children, who were eight and eleven years old at the time.

I don't remember how it happened, but I can still recall the sudden burst of panic. Our two young children, who were floating on a boogie board together, drifted quickly away from shore. They held on tight to the board and to each other, but it was apparent that they were in trouble. Neither was wearing a life jacket, and they were not strong enough swimmers to make it to shore. Wearing only shorts and a t-shirt, with no shoes, I did the only thing a desperate father could do. I ran frantically into the surging ocean.

Fortunately there was a reef that permitted access to the area toward which the rip tide was pulling them. Without the reef, a more sophisticated rescue effort would have been required. I ran as far as I could across the reef, dove into the water, and swam a short distance to retrieve the frightened kids. By this time the adrenaline was pumping through me so hard that I don't even remember how long it took to reach safety back on the beach. About ten minutes after our safe return, the pain in my feet became excruciating. The blood-soaked sand was a painful reminder of the razor-sharp coral of the reef.

There were signs posted in the area, warning of dangerous rip tides. A closer look at activity on the beach would have confirmed an air of caution shared by nearly everyone who enjoyed the sun and water that day at the beach. We were so anxious to have a great time together that we failed to be watchful for potential dangers lurking beyond the shoreline. My absorption in conversation and inattention to our surroundings could have resulted in more serious complications than badly cut feet. Thoughts of those potential complications cause me dread and discomfort to this day.

Most sales territories today feature the tugs and pulls of dangerous rip tides and sharp coral reefs that can disrupt our lives and imperil the long-term security of our careers. But it is not just dangers that require our vigilance; it is also surging opportunities that ebb and flow with the rising tides. When our heads are down, as we focus on the next contract, it can be impossible to read all of the signs that forecast danger and foretell important trends rolling toward shore.

The market assessment practice in Strategic Work gives you the ability to keep your head up while the sand is shifting at your feet. It allows you to feel the winds of change billowing at your back without cutting your feet, as you try to make up for time lost while you were absorbed in well-meaning and productive activities. Sales professionals who clearly see the territory in front of them anticipate future opportunities. They keep their shoes on when rip tides are in the area. They are prepared to meet safely the changes of a dynamic market that brings waves of new challenges and opportunity when they are least expected.

About 25 years ago, our company had no method in place to gather the accurate market intelligence needed for a market assessment. Without a clear read on realistic market opportunities, I was left to make relative judgments about both potential revenue numbers and the performance of members of our sales team, based upon year-end sales reports. As we slowly started to collect this data, most of us who were responsible for directing long-term strategy were gasping for air. Our best projections about market revenue potential were under-reported by at least sixty percent. In the following years, the foundation of a comprehensive market assessment influenced virtually every tactical decision that was made. The planning that resulted from this new insight into the market was a major force behind a period of sustained revenue growth that lasted twenty years.

Conducting a market assessment is a bit like finally succumbing to an ultrasound to identify the source of some nagging abdominal pain. Without a clear view inside the belly, you may make a host of assumptions that have little or no basis in reality. You will likely spend time and money attempting to mollify symptoms that remain a persistent nuisance. One simple test may dictate the appropriate course of action to alleviate the pain. The more clear and reliable the information, the better the chances will be for complete amelioration of the discomfort.

The market assessment portion of *Assessing Potential* is the critical lab work that constitutes the final diagnosis, the annual sales plan. Leaders recognize how this kind of information affects most of the tactical decisions about the territory. Sales professionals who are committed leaders get the lab work done first, to insure the best possible treatment to keep the territory healthy.

Practice 4: Ask the Right Questions

The gathering of current and relevant market intelligence is the bulwark of a sales philosophy grounded in strategic thinking. And while Strategic Work includes at least two other important skills, *assessing potential* in your territory is foundational to a sales career that pushes the limits of optimum revenue production.

The two other skills of Strategic Work support the sales professional's quest to realize personal and product potential. Excellence in professional selling should never be measured in relative terms. It ultimately is found in the congruence of ability or potential with actual performance. The same can be said of revenue potential for any given market area. The best measure of performance is not comparison to other members of the sales team or even to previous years' revenues. It is measuring our performance against the market potential for our product, based on an accurate market assessment.

Not surprisingly, *assessing potential* can be unsettling for some people. It can expose the weaknesses of previous sales plans or confirm the need to expand the sales team in the territory. Consequently, many sales professional assume that generating serious and well-researched analytical data is the corporate marketing team's domain and is beyond the scope of their primary charge to support business operations through consistent revenue production. This misguided assumption will invariably result in underperforming sales professionals and under-producing sales territories.

The overarching question to be answered by the skill of assessing potential is simply, "What?" More specifically, "What is this territory's potential, and what is my potential as a sales professional?" Good, clear, supportable answers to these pressing questions are the first step toward a coherent and workable sales plan. If we can't answer, or refuse even to ask, these basic questions, measurable progress in the territory will be a painful pursuit.

I always enjoy seeing high-performing sales professionals scratch and claw for new information and greater insight about territory sales potential. They don't assume that products or markets are static and impervious to change. They don't assume that they already have the best available information about new opportunities that may exist around them.

Assessing potential is a process, not a one-time occurrence. It is a way of thinking about how you work in the sales environment. As a sales professional you are working in the field regularly, probably daily. You meet with customers, review technical information about product requirements, respond to client questions about your product and construct a viable value proposition of the benefits of choosing your product over an array of competitive options. These activities form the rudiments of basic market intelligence gathering.

Your close proximity to customers provides you with valuable insight about changing market conditions, price pressures, emerging technology which may impact product demand, ideas to encourage innovation, and information to alleviate concerns about customer support. In many respects, you should be oneperson reconnaissance team, constantly gathering critical market intelligence from key sources in the field. This information is then recorded and corroborated with other sources; then it is actionable. Field work is only one method of conducting a broad market assessment, but its relative importance must not be minimized.

Principle C. Long-Term Thinking Prevents Short-Term Setbacks

The notion that long-term thinking prevents short-term setbacks is the third and final principle associated with the skill of *assessing potential*. It is based on the assumption that, as we look and think long-term, we are better positioned to anticipate both problems and opportunities and thereby to initiate a better response strategy. Long-term thinking is driven by a sense of personal *vision* and executed by the skill of *assessing potential*. Effective leaders work in the present and think in the future.

Market assessment's focus on long-term thinking, planning, and analysis is at least part of the reason why Strategic Work forms much of the foundation of the *Personal Leadership Model*. This practice encourages information gathering, to give a clear view of the sales territory and to influence the Tactical Work in the territory sales plan. Sales professionals who think strategically anticipate new opportunities and can mobilize a quick response. This heads-up view of professional selling also helps prevent costly and even embarrassing mistakes.

A few years ago I visited a large customer in Hong Kong. We communicated electronically in advance of the meeting, and I received some clear information about topics that needed my preparation prior to the long journey to Asia. I carefully reviewed all the material for the meeting, collaborated as needed with others from the company about issues to be discussed, and arranged for a hotel that was only a few miles from the client's office. I also prepared a three-by-five card with the address of the client and the name of the building in both Chinese and English, to prevent a foreseeable problem with the language barrier.

The meeting was scheduled for 10:00 AM, and I was told that the location of the office was only about fifteen minutes in traffic from my hotel. It had been a couple of years since I had visited this office in Hong Kong, but I was confident that I would recognize it when I was in the right area. At 9:30 AM I went down to the lobby of the hotel. My taxi was waiting outside. I handed the driver the card with the address of the building in both languages,. We left with ample time to allow for even the most congested morning traffic in Hong Kong. As the car pulled away from the hotel, I saw umbrellas opening in the hands of passing pedestrians opening almost in unison, as rain began to fall.

It had taken only about ten minutes to arrive at the address on my note card. The taxi driver seemed a little perplexed, and nothing about the area seemed at all familiar to me. He pointed to the building that corresponded to the number shown on my address card. I paused only momentarily, then stepped out of the cab and into the pouring rain. I still had fifteen minutes to arrive at the office, and I hoped to stay somewhat dry in the process.

I clearly was not in a business district. The narrow street was lined with small markets, and the buildings were apartment complexes. With a clock ticking away in my mind, I stood with my suit soaking. There were no English speakers in sight, and there was probably not a cab for blocks. I had just traveled halfway around the world for a meeting with an important client, and not only was I going to be late; I would be a dreadful sight by the time I arrived.

In the weeks leading up to the meeting in Hong Kong, I essentially had my head down, doing all the necessary work, preparing to answer questions and resolve problems, and fine-tuning my short presentation. I had carefully prepared the address card for the taxi driver, but I had failed to confirm the address with the customer. The address in my contact file was incorrect, and I ended up very wet and very late for a very important meeting.

I was standing on a street in a foreign country, without any real ability to communicate, with rain dripping from my head, and consumed by a sense of hopelessness. In our profession we can have a similar experience without traveling to Hong Kong for morning appointments in the rain; gaps in our thoughtful planning can leave us with wrinkled suits and cold feet.

Assessing potential requires asking all the pertinent questions in advance, analyzing the answers, and then planning our day accordingly. We can grind through a task list with laser-like proficiency, but if the real opportunities in the territory are a few blocks or a few miles away, we may arrive late, poorly dressed, and incapable of having a coherent conversation. A strategic mind is preparation-al and anticipates problems and asks all the right questions in advance – and it always carries an umbrella.

Practice 5: Use Metrics to Determine the Mission

If we were mountain climbers leaving base camp on our way to a summit, we would probably want to know some important data about the journey ahead. The condition of the terrain and the technical difficulty of the climb would likely impact our preparation. Up-to-date weather forecasts and climate conditions might influence the timing of the climb and the clothing we would select. Elevation changes would be an important consideration. Finally, the expected time to reach the summit and return would determine food and water supplies and the start time for the climb. All of this information will affect the safety and success of the climb.

Collecting relevant data about market conditions, customers and competitors helps us identify a clear and direct passage to the top of our mountain, and key metrics provide a baseline to measure performance. They also add color and detail to the picture of the sales territory that grows out of our ongoing reconnaissance. The sales professional does not need to pore over page after page of analysis to create the clear *vision* needed to move the territory forward. However, there are some fundamental measurements with which each member of the sales team should be familiar, to help identify opportunities and potential problems. A viable *vision* that inspires *passion* and commitment can be created only in an environment saturated by clarity. Familiarity with tools for assessing overall market potential enhances that clarity.

It is one thing to learn to think strategically (long term-preparation-al) and an entirely different matter to have in your hands all the tools to facilitate strategic planning. Sales professionals must be willing to ask for support from the corporate office and to assume a fair share of responsibility for compiling this data in their territories. It is not uncommon to see sales professionals who operate on modest budgets and with little or no analytical support from the corporate office implement rather unsophisticated, yet surprisingly reliable, methods of data collection. When a commitment is made to conduct a regular market assessment, noticeable gains can be made with readily available information. The following are the basic tools used to measure and *assess potential* in your market:

◆ Actual Market Revenue

◆ Market Share Analysis

◆ Market Revenue Potential

◆ Market Forecasting Information

◆ Brand and Market Awareness Levels

◆ Customer Identification

◆ Industry Changes

These seven key market indicators are basic methods of measurement that should constitute the framework of your annual market assessment. Some of these numbers may prove impossible to obtain. Others may be impractical, due to time constraints or financial considerations. But give this your best effort. Learning to conduct a regular, comprehensive market assessment will clarify opportunities and dictate much of the operational strategy included in your annual sales plan.

Actual Market Revenue. This is a simple number: the total revenue produced in your market during the previous twelve months. This should include all possible competitive alternatives purchased during this period by all customers. This can be difficult to track down. Industry associations are generally the most useful source of reliable information on aggregate revenue production. If your products are competitively bid, you will already have a number that will be a useful starting point, to which you can add allowances for work not included in your bid totals.

Getting your arms around the actual market revenue in your territory is a vital part of thinking strategically. Actual market revenue establishes the order of magnitude of the project ahead.

Market Share Analysis. Knowing the actual market revenue and your product's revenue allows you to make a simple calculation to determine your market share. Your market share is your product sales as a percentage of the actual market revenue. While this may be a simple calculation, what it represents should not be dismissed. It provides you with the best overall assessment of your relative position in the marketplace.

Market Share Analysis

$$\frac{\text{Actual Product Sales}}{\text{Actual Market Revenue Production}} = \text{Market Share}$$

A low market share could suggest a number of different things that may influence your sales plan for the foreseeable future. The market share alone cannot tell you, for example, why a product with superior benefits and priced nominally above the median range market price point suffers from an abysmally low market share. This requires intuitive analysis which is best provided by the person in the field who is in closest proximity to the customer – that is, the sales professional.

How will our interpretation of the market share data influence the strategy we design for the territory? Let's consider as a simple case study of a company with solid product benefits and competitive pricing, but a low market share. The market share itself cannot tell us what it means. That analysis must come from the analyst on the ground.

This exercise is designed to illustrate how raw data collection alone, without informed analytical thinking, may not help us to develop a viable strategic plan. Without additional information, either of these interpretations of the market share ratio may be reasonable, but the two lead us in much different strategic directions..

Option One: Poor selling. This product's sales manager may decide that the low market share results from marginal levels of product visibility among customers. The assumption is that low visibility equates to an insufficient number of customer contacts. The remedy may include more sales calls among target customer groups. If customers are not buying it must ultimately be the responsibility of the sales team!

Option Two: Predatory Competitors. The low market share may be attributed to predatory competitors infiltrating the market with deep discounts. This might lead to a retaliatory response that will drive prices and margins even lower.

With additional data collected by the sales professional in the territory, we may reach a totally different conclusion about the low market share. For example, suppose that the sales professional reports regular contact among key target customer groups and no noticeable change in market price points among competitors. The conclusion is that while the company boasts certain key product features to justify modest price differences, customers remain unmoved. They do not see those features as justification for a higher price, so they don't buy.

The interpretation of the data is nearly always more important than the data itself.

In this example the data collection combined with on-the-ground analysis supports the need either to refine or reposition the product features as customer benefits, or to eliminate or modify the features in such a way as to permit more competitive pricing. There is no substitute for effective data analysis performed by capable and experienced members of the sales team.

Market Revenue Potential. This number can be a moving target. Assuming your products have not reached market saturation, it is possible to use relevant statistical data from other territories and make accommodation for differences in market size. It may be possible to find a sales territory in your geographic region with a similar economic and demographic profile that has a high market share. With some basic adjustments to accommodate differences in market size, this number can be used as a baseline to assess market potential.

Among all the data you might collect, this number deserves some time and attention. The more thoroughly you consider all the relevant factors which influence your product's overall market potential, the better you will be able to approximate your product's revenue potential. If you don't already have good information, I suggest that you start by reviewing historical data about market share in other territories, coupled with total market revenue.

Identifying a solid and supportable market revenue potential (MRP) is an essential part of building a long-term strategy. For example, if your MRP is three times your existing sales volume, it is unlikely that traditional approaches that are designed to produce incremental increases in revenue will have the desired impact on sales production. A ten percent increase may sound good during an annual review, but it may not reflect realistic market opportunities.

The incremental sales mentality that encourages members of the sales team to think in terms of seven to twelve percent increases is largely based on continuing the same practices and processes, just doing them better and faster. A sales initiative designed to move quickly towards

MRP must look beyond streamlining established processes and consider new methods and practices not presently included in the existing sales model. This will require a more strategic approach to revenue production. A clear assessment of MRP will drive the strategy.

Market Forecasting Information. You should be able to describe what the projected growth in your territory's total revenue will be for the next year and for the next three to five years. There are vast resources of market intelligence generated by government agencies, financial institutions, trade associations, newspapers, trade publications and some private sources. Most general information is available without cost and can be readily accessed on the Internet. If your product is sold to different segments of the market, it will be important to track projected growth in each segment to identify emerging trends.

Sales professionals who carefully monitor industry trends and forecasts by reading from a variety of different sources are much better positioned to modify the sales plan in order to avoid foreseeable reversals or exploit new opportunities. Regular conversation with customers about changing market conditions may also help you construct a clear and accurate picture of your marketplace. Asking good questions, reading industry published material, and staying constantly alert to any source of information that may provide insight into your market will enable you to see your market with the clarity needed to create a viable *vision* for the future.

Brand Image and Awareness. In larger organizations most of this type of productspecific information will likely be provided by the corporate marketing team. Ongoing market research is an invaluable tool. Identifying opportunities will help the sales team and also will influence customer opinions about products. If you don't currently have access to this type of information for your sales territory, I suggest two options. The first is to work with your corporate marketing group to design a brief customer survey that will provide information about overall brand awareness among key customer groups in your market. The survey should also drill further into relevant attitudes and general customer perceptions about your product and its relative position to competitors.

Second, if corporate marketing support is not available to you, I strongly suggest that you consider hiring a local independent research firm to assist you. The random sampling of even a small number of customers can provide vital insight to important strategic issues. If you prepare the survey and provide the customer list, the project can be completed at an affordable rate. The information provided by even small quantities of research can save large amounts of time and money. It also can eliminate much of the guesswork and speculation about customer attitudes that can lead to misdirected sales efforts.

Research is vital in developing a comprehensive view of your market. While such research is not commonly a function of the sales team, skillful sales practitioners employ the information it provides in both long-term strategic planning and daily tactical work in the territory. Once territory benchmarks for brand awareness levels have been established, repeating the survey every two or three years will provide useful ongoing information about your strategy's effectiveness and the execution of your sales plan.

Customer Identification. Most sales team members can readily print lists of key customer groups from their contact files. It is wise not only to log all pertinent contact information, but also to track customers based upon revenue generated from year to year. More specific account information may also prove relevant to your business. For example, with some customers there may be more than one point of contact for final buying decisions. One person in an office may regularly purchase your products, while another person in the same office still prefers a competitor. Keeping an up-to-date and accurate record of buying decisions within individual customer offices may be an important reference tool as you evaluate important goals for the next sales year.

When products have multiple uses, it will be important to monitor customers' buying decisions by specific product use. A single customer may provide substantial revenue each year, while using the product in a narrow range of applications. When all the relevant market intelligence is gathered, it may be reasonable to conclude that the best opportunity for revenue gains will be found in mining the existing customer base for opportunities to broaden product use.

You should have intimate knowledge about your customers. This includes not only the politics of the customer's decision-making process, but also the two or three reasons why your product is repeatedly selected. Where a collaborative relationship exists, a customer is generally willing to share information about critical factors in product selection. In the absence of trust, it is reasonable to assume that your product will be vulnerable to substitution by the next sales professional that walks through the door and offers a lower price.

Compiling statistical profiles of key accounts is a fundamental part of effective territory management. Perhaps the more provocative questions for customer identification are, Who are the largest potential customers in your market that are not currently buying your product, and why? Answer these questions well, and the likelihood of hitting your expanded revenue goal next year will take a sizeable leap forward.

Customer identification in your marketplace requires that you meticulously collect information about a group of qualified customers whose purchasing or product selection profiles align with your product and company. The first phase of this effort is writing a profile to qualify key customer groups. This information is constantly rolling around inside the head of most sales professionals. Put in on paper, refer to it periodically, and modify it as needed. You need a clear idea of what type of new account you are looking for. Otherwise, the old Chinese proverb may apply: "If you know not what harbor you seek, any wind is the right wind."

The second phase of customer identification is matching potential new accounts with the established profile and ranking them according to the magnitude of the potential opportunity. This process of writing, sorting, and making value judgments based on revenue potential is a *Personal Leadership* skill. Outstanding sales professionals perform this function in an almost intuitive way. They sort and process information, constantly seeking ways to leverage time and resources to pursue the greatest potential opportunities. The sorting process's effectiveness is diminished if there is not absolute clarity about outcomes. Consequently, it is not unusual to find sales professionals who work harder but consistently produce less revenue than colleagues in the same organization who have better *Personal Leadership* skills.

Market Assessment Summary

I. Actual Market Revenue (The total revenue for all products, including yours, that was sold during the previous 12 months) _____

II. Market Share Analysis (This is the ratio of your sales volume as a percentage of the *Actual Market Revenue* identified above) _____

III. Market Revenue Potential (This is a realistic estimate of what the total revenue your product can produce annual within a five year period.) _____

IV. Market Forecast (Provide a brief summary of the best available forecasting information for your product/industry for the next 12 months)

_____

_____

_____

V. Brand Awareness Levels (Identify responses from key customers in the following areas. The blanks should be filled with percentages)

    a. Very familiar _____%

    b. Somewhat familiar _____%

    c. Recognize the name only _____%

    d. No familiarity _____%

VI. Customer Identification (Current buyers)

    a. Current Buyers _____

_____

_____

    b. Potential Buyers (The Top 10 Accounts buying a competitive product) _____

_____

_____

    c. Potential Buyers not buying your product or a competitor _____

_____

_____

VII. Industry Changes (A brief summary of the industry and an identification of potential changes that may influence product demand)

_____

_____

_____

_____

Trends related to environmental responsibility have been gaining momentum for several years. This is the type of issue that needs careful attention to fully assess the impact of future market demand. The annual sales plan should address this topic.

In most selling environments you will have the benefit of regularly hearing the customer's voice. Over time this saturation of customer perceptions about product features and benefits, coupled with attitudes about changing marketing conditions, should shape your organization's new product development agenda. Research and development projects designed to improve the company's competitive position will nearly always benefit from a clear understanding of both changing market conditions and the customer's reaction to these changes. Members of the sales team who consistently track industry trends and customer opinions can be valuable contributors to new product iterations and line extensions which will influence revenue generation in future sales cycles.

Constancy in establishing and employing clear methods of measuring and assessing the market allows you to dismiss "pie in the sky" illusions and embrace a reality where the sky is the only limit to revenue potential.

Assessing Potential and the Eight Symptoms of Sales Paralysis

What we have defined as Sales Paralysis can damage careers in selling and undermine the sales professional's ability to produce sustained revenue growth. Near the end of each chapter on the six key selling skills, we will conduct a short analysis of how the individual skill contributes to the eradication of Sales Paralysis.

Symptom	Impact	Comments
The Passion is gone	HIGH	A clear Vision of sales potential re-kindles a passion and commitment.
Winging it	HIGH	Potential inspires purpose. Purpose accelerates the creation of a plan.
Lack of a sense of urgency	HIGH	Urgency evaporates without clear benefit. Vision identifies potential.
Feelings of frustration	HIGH	Vision inspires hope. Hope breathes new life and removes frustration.
Low energy/Problem solving	MEDIUM	A strong vision of potential opportunities can elevate energy levels.

The skill of *assessing potential* plays a significant role in reducing or eliminating five of the eight pernicious symptoms. In four of five cases it could be argued that the skill can have a high impact. *Vision*, the *Personal Leadership Driver* connected to this skill, is largely responsible for this change.

Vision clarifies opportunities and underscores the personal benefit of high performance levels.

I suggest that you include both assessments provided in this chapter in your annual sales plan and update them at least annually. An assessment of your potential and the potential of your territory should be an ever-expanding *vision* of how changes in your abilities and the factors influencing product demand in your market evolve over time.

Assess Potential: Foresight not Eyesight

Assessing potential is a vital part of developing a clear and viable *vision* or mission for the sales territory. That *vision* should provide a picture not just of the existing condition of your product in the marketplace, but also of future opportunities. The *vision* we create of the territory shapes the annual sales plan and the identification of key goals. Accurate and reliable information also inspires a greater sense of confidence in realistic outcomes. A clear *vision* of possible outcomes kindles the desire that naturally leads to great outcomes.

Effective leaders create, shape, and inspire a shared sense of *vision* among all stakeholders. In many cases the *visions* that inspire us initially seem out of reach. As more information confirms the legitimacy of the *vision*, we warm to and ultimately embrace the proposition. Early in President John F. Kennedy's administration, he challenged the country to put a man on the moon by the end of the decade. It was bold, clear and scientifically supportable. The *vision* of one man mobilized the energy, talents, resources and commitment of a nation to pursue a goal worthy of its best effort.

The leader's *vision* has enormous power. This was true in the quest to land a man on the moon and begin the exploration of outer space, and it is also true of more down-to-earth missions involving complex products in our own space. First and foremost, it is *vision* that inspires us. *Personal Leadership*'s power to determine the success of any product in any territory begins with the type of creative *vision* that comes from a complete market assessment.

Constructing clear and inspiring *visions* of desired outcomes is not the exclusive domain of people like Martin Luther King, Jr., John F. Kennedy or Winston Churchill. Nor are great accomplishments limited to people like Michael Jordan, Bill Gates and Oprah Winfrey. The vast majority of sales professionals have the ability to create the inspiring *visions* that lead to outstanding achievement. It can be done. It is less difficult and more fulfilling than most sales professionals imagine.

If it is possible for us to create a clear and inspiring *vision* for a product in a territory, and if the associated benefits have the potential to roughly approximate a lunar landing, then why isn't it done? I see at least three reasons.

First, most of us are driven by process. We become skilled technicians on the ground, contributing parts and expertise to the building of the lunar module. We are trained and retrained to focus on customers and to be mindful of predatory competitors. Product sales cycles require vigilant attention to the horizon. We constantly rebuild the dynamic pipeline with new business. Sales reports are produced monthly, quarterly, and annually to help us evaluate performance. These activities and the associated environment foster a mindset that is deeply invested in short-term, tactical thinking. We overlook the long-term, strategic thinking that is critical to the seemingly ethereal notion of creating a viable territory *vision*.

Second, many compensation plans push us into a short term, tactically-oriented sales philosophy to meet pressing financial needs. A long-term, strategic approach to selling seems like a luxury we cannot afford.

Third, professional selling literature and organizational training programs seldom, if ever, emphasize the role of basic *Personal Leadership* skills in achieving long-term success. It is generally assumed that the soft topics of *vision* and mission are left to the senior leadership team at the corporate office. You may have printed copies of the company mission statement in your office, but the notion of creating a powerful *vision* for your own territory, based on reliable metrics and ongoing market analysis, can seem as far away as the moon.

Perhaps the most distinguishing element of the *Personal Leadership Model* is the relative importance of key leadership skills. Learning to internalize the key skills of *assessing potential, creating excellence* and *identifying motivators* can help you take the lead in producing territory revenue totals which previously seemed impossible. If we can agree that these are skills leaders must have to move organizations forward, why would you think things are different for you in trying to move your territory forward?

Jay Smart developed the ability to see something very few people see. He understood his product, the market, customer attitudes and the industry, and he anticipated changes. The amalgamation of those traits provided him with a keen sense of *vision*. If you will take the time to look inward and better understand your own potential as a sales professional, and then look outward to examine the opportunities that exist for your product in your territory, a new *vision* of opportunities will start to take shape. The emergence of that *vision* will equip you with the foresight to push your revenue totals to levels only a few people dream about.

The Relationship of Principles and Practices in Developing the Skill (*"Learned Power"*) of Assessing Potential

Principle A. We work in relationship to our **perception** of potential.
> Supporting Practices:
>> 1. Conduct a Personal Assessment
>> 2. Implement a Self-Development Program
>> 3. Ask the Right Questions
>> 4. Conduct a Comprehensive Market Assessment

Principle B. Small gains in personal performance can produce big gains in revenue production.
> Supporting Practices:
>> 1. Conduct a Personal Assessment
>> 2. Implement a Self-Development Program
>> 3. Ask the Right Questions

Principle C. Long-term thinking prevents short-term setbacks.
> Supporting Practices:
>> 1. Ask the Right Questions
>> 2. Conduct a Comprehensive Market Assessment
>> 3. Use Metrics to Determine the Mission

CHAPTER 4

Plan

Committed and Flexible

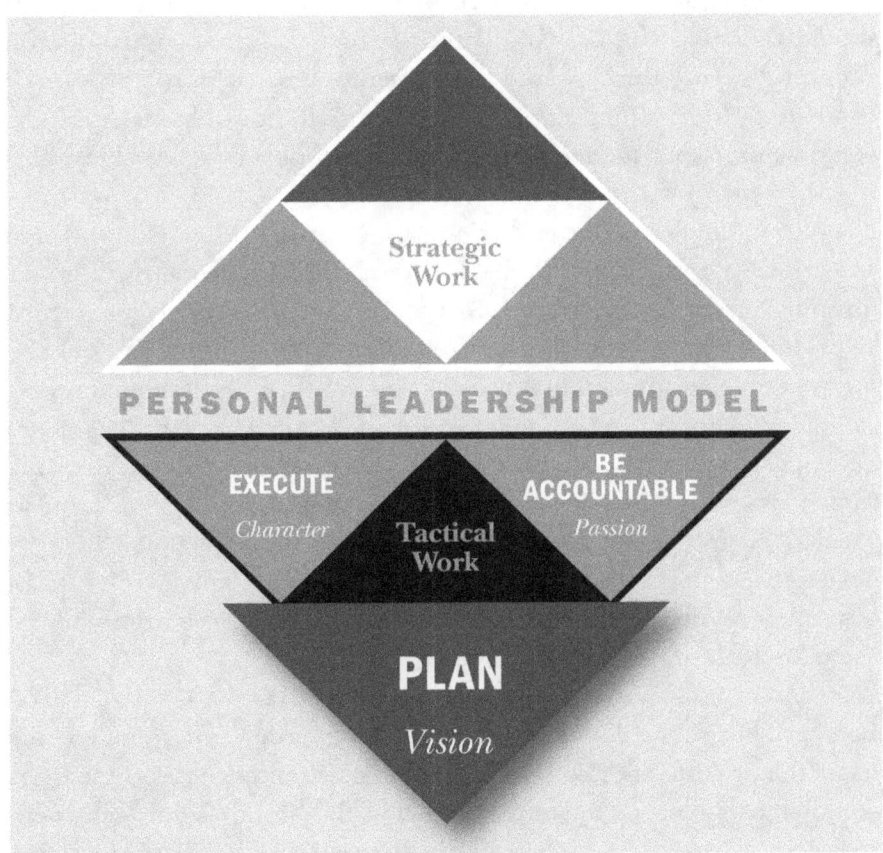

Figure 4-1 Plan: The *Vision* Component of Tactical Work

PLANNING IS CONSTRUCTING a map through the territory that will lead to the realization of market revenue potential. The more effort you apply to creating the map, the less effort you will need to expend on the actual journey. *Planning* is not just about arriving safely at a desired destination. *Planning* is also about taking preemptive measures to insure that, despite all our hard work and dedication, we don't inadvertently get lost along the way.

The second skill that shares the *Personal Leadership Driver* of *Vision* is learning to *plan*. As you will notice from the graphic, this skill is part of Tactical Work in the *Personal Leadership Model*. As you read through the following story, think about the role of effective *planning* as it relates to navigating through your territory during the sales year. The *plan* is not only designed to lead you toward the realization of your goal, but it should also help you to avoid detours which sap time and resources. Careful *planning* that is based in the reality created in the process of conducting a thorough market assessment will not only make the experience more productive, but also make the journey more enjoyable.

Every person should have a friend like Ben Banks. His emotional constitution is an extraordinary blend of court jester, raging adrenaline junkie, and self-assured CEO. He is a zealous proponent of "working outside your comfort zone," and he ambitiously seeks to foist that philosophy upon unsuspecting family, friends and company associates who wander unguarded into his office. Several years ago he made a proposal to me that put me so far outside my comfort zone that it would have taken an F-14 Tomcat traveling for an hour at Mach 2 just to get me within cell phone range. Even then I might have needed an international authorization code to make the call. In other words, my comfort zone was somewhere on the other side of the planet, figuratively speaking.

Ben has been scuba diving in Palau, regularly jumps out of helicopters to ski the pristine back country terrain of Wyoming and Montana, has completed numerous technical climbs in the Teton region and spent six weeks at base camp preparing for an assault on the formidable K-2. He drives a yellow Porsche Carrera, while I drive a white mid-sized sedan. Outdoor risk-taking for me usually means playing from the tips at my golf club. You get the picture.

When Ben proposed that we take a transcontinental bicycle trip from Canada to Mexico, a distance of 1,985 miles, in nineteen riding days, what was going through my middle-aged mind, as you can probably imagine, was, "Are you nuts?"

The entire odyssey of pedaling a bike the length of the west coast turned out to be one of the most exhilarating experiences of my life. For some strange reason I found the rarified air outside my comfort zone easier to breathe with each passing mile. The stunning views of the Pacific Ocean, adorned in every imaginable shade of light and color and enhanced by windswept skies and glistening orange hues of the setting sun, would be impossible to describe adequately. We survived torrents of rain in the Ho River Valley, an encounter with bicycle thieves in Monterey, and the thunderous roar of hundreds upon hundreds of logging trucks as we made our way south along the Pacific Coast Highway.

One day we made our way into the town of Point Reyes Station north of San Francisco. Normally we rode side by side, so that the levity of conversation could ease the pain of the occasional climb. This day was no different.

The route took a hard right turn at the top of a steep grade as we entered the town. I coasted to the bottom and turned my head to check the distance between Ben and me. He wasn't there. I waited. Five minutes turned to fifteen, and still he did not arrive. Thinking he might be at the top of the grade, I rode back up the hill. There was absolutely no sign of him. After another fifteen minutes I decided to retrace the route back to a point where I was sure we were together. He was still nowhere in sight.

At this point I had to make a decision, since neither of us was carrying a cell phone. I guessed that somehow, as we descended the grade, he had turned early, found his way to Highway 1, and was now riding hard, thinking I was ahead of him. An hour separated us, but what was even more disturbing was that I had the map. The route across the Golden Gate Bridge was perhaps the most circuitous part of the entire ride. Due to the convergence of interstate highways, an abundance of local knowledge is needed to navigate the path to the bridge, to avoid ending up on a freeway. Some of the cycling paths are poorly marked dirt trails and side streets. The journey to the bridge would be virtually impossible without a map with clearly marked directions.

Ben was in better shape than I and a naturally stronger rider. I later learned he had indeed found his way back to Highway 1 and rode hard, assuming that the Pacific Coast Highway would ultimately get him to the Golden Gate Bridge. What he didn't know was that the highway would lead him through the mountainous stretch of road through the Marin Headlands. After some challenging climbs over a period of several hours, the road narrowed, traffic increased and he surrendered. He was able to find a cab that took him to a rental car office, and for the balance of the afternoon he went in search of his cycling buddy.

Even the most experienced sales professionals, who work hard and seem to understand the landscape, frequently get lost in their own territories and spend hours upon hours pounding away at rugged terrain. They may never find safe passage to the bridge that will carry them to market revenue potential. The precise location of this bridge is different territory to territory. Only after you compile extensive local knowledge will you be able to connect all the unmarked trails and obscure paths in a way that will insure safe arrival at your destination.

Ben was working plenty hard, and his failure to reach the bridge had nothing to do with his overall fitness level. Even his positive attitude and engaging personality still left him grinding away, mile after tortuous mile, in the mountains. He had a good idea where the bridge was relative to his position, but navigating in unfamiliar territory without the benefit of precise directions nullified any chance of reaching the bridge.

On the other hand, for me the journey was quite uneventful, except for losing my good friend and cycling partner. Using the map and the directions made my ride to the bridge simple, with little or no traffic congestion. With the map the experience of maneuvering through a complex metropolitan area, where all major roads were pinched to one bridge, was amazingly easy.

Like every other map you use, well-conceived sales *plans*, formulated from tireless analysis and the tedious work of assessing potential, can reveal the location of all available routes to your desired destination. The yearly sales *plan* requires the sales professional first to select the desired destination, then to map out a route, choosing among several different possible routes. This selection will be influenced by your local knowledge, which is your basic understanding of the territory's needs, along with available assets and resources at your disposal.

Most long trips require some modification to the planned route, based on new information about road construction, weather problems, or traffic jams. These changes require that we promptly *react* to changing circumstances. At other times we simply *act*, because new opportunities appear that were not previously known. For example, we might take a detour from the planned route to take in a scenic point of interest or to visit family or friends in a nearby town. Sales *plans* work the same way. They should be designed to be sufficiently flexible to allow us to *react* to changing market conditions that may make the chosen outcomes un-desirable, while also permitting us wide latitude to *act* aggressively to pursue new opportunities in the market.

Principles and Practices in Developing the Skill of Planning

Principles, Skills & Practices

Principles *(laws or assumptions)*: "The quality of a person's life is in direct proportion to their commitment to excellence, regardless of their chosen field of endeavor" (Vince Lombardi). A. Excellent work produces excellent results. B. Creating excellence begins with a strong desire to produce outstanding work. C. Improved competency improves the prospect of creating excellence. D. People of character naturally build collaborative relationships.

Skill *(learned power)*: Create Excellence

Practices *(repeated exercises for proficiency)*: 1) Work to develop collaborative relation-ships. 2) Work with the expectation of positive results. 3) Produce consistent quality. 4) Work to improve your sales ability and add value to your customers. 5) Understand customer needs and communicate clearly. 6) Think of the sales transaction in terms of customer benefit. 7) Consistently do your best work.

Don't underestimate the power of creating a viable map. It will keep you from getting lost. In this chapter we will learn more about creating the type of map that will keep you from pounding away for needless hours in difficult terrain, with no clear view of your goal in sight. Speaking of maps, here is a brief look at what to expect from the remainder of this chapter:

- *Planning* Makes Dreams Possible; Dreaming Is Not *Planning*. (Principle)

- Well-Conceived *Plans* Produce Highly Productive Outcomes. (Principle)

- *Planning* Should Be Both Committed and Flexible. (Practice)

- Make *Planning* Empowering with Clarity of Content. (Practice)

- The *Plan* Must Be Written. (Practice)

- The *Plan* Should Be Simple. (Practice)

- *Planning* to Create Your Future. (Practice)

- Implement the Seven Essential Components of the Territory Sales *Plan*. (Practice)

- Design the *Plan* to Accommodate Change.

The principles provide a reason for us to develop a skill. The practices simply teach us the methods to improve our proficiency in the specific skill. The *Personal Leadership Model* is grounded in skill development. It is the skills that you will need to make sweeping changes in how your work. The skills will be easier to implement if you understand the principles and repeat the practices outlined in each chapter.

Principle A. Planning Makes Dreams Possible

Are you a planner or a dreamer? Do your *plans* take shape on paper, or do they exist only in your mind? Have you plotted a specific course to the top of the mountain, or are your eyes fixated on the summit? Dreams create delicious images of desired outcomes. *Plans* provide workable maps that lead us to realize our greatest aspirations. Dreams *describe* to our minds what we would like to do. *Plans inscribe* in our minds how we can get there.

Dreams are whimsical and fleeting. They pass through us while we are passing time. *Plans* are specific and measurable. They become part of us and allow us to make the most of our time. Thoughts stored only in the mind are like dreams; they suggest only what we *might* become. *Plans* are thoughts stored on paper after critical, analytical scrutiny. They are a reliable prediction of what we *will* become.

People who dream but fail to *plan* imagine the view from the summit, but never leave the base camp. People who dream and *plan* meticulously chart safe and passable routes to the summit and live their lives in the exhilaration of the climb. Dreams can give us a brief glimpse of the future through creative imagination. *Plans* allow us to savor the present by identifying the path to a lofty destination and our current place on that path.

A failure to *plan* is a failure in Personal Leadership. Leaders know that outcomes worthy of a person's best effort require precision *planning* and consistent execution. Leaders who imagine ambitious endeavors, but refuse or neglect to construct workable *plans* and commit them to a readable form, spend much of life tilting at the imaginary windmills of life and wading in the frustration of lost opportunity and squandered potential. Leadership is a call to action. A call to action is a plea to define a path. Careful *planning* clarifies the required action while illuminating the most desirable path.

Dreams are images of what might be. *Plans* describe specific activities to create what will be. Dreams come and go like the wind and require little thought. *Plans* are firm and unshakeable, like mountains, and demand considerable forethought. All of us dream. Few of us *plan*. If your *plan* to maximize your potential only exists in your mind, you are a dreamer, and your future is very much in doubt. If you have a dream that is formulated into a *plan* of action that enumerates goals, timetables, and a system of accountability, there is no life endeavor out of reach, and your future will never be in doubt.

People who only dream and fail to *plan* indulge themselves in a common quest to escape the realities of a life under-lived. People who dream and consistently *plan* immerse themselves in an uncommon quest to pursue the realities of a life well lived. Dreams are an essential part of all human achievement. They can generate needed lift as we climb to higher elevations. *Plans* are equally essential. They provide the ballast to steady our pace, enhance our focus, and fortify our will as we work daily to walk the path to a place some people only dream about.

Constructing a great building starts with a dream. The dream provides the building's form, color, texture, and general appearance. But before the first spadeful of ground is turned or the first ton of concrete poured, every aspect of the building takes shape on paper. Architectural drawings provide a detailed map for the builder. Interior elevations vividly portrayed in multiple views and comprehensive specifications for glazing, lighting, and every other design component provide the owner with an advance look at the completed project. Why should building a life be any different?

Planning is purposeful. It requires a sense of *Vision* of desired outcomes and an understanding of realistic obstacles. We must consult the *plan* regularly, or we risk being lost along the way. *Plans* do not confine us; in large measure they define us. Dreams tell us which summits can inspire us to achieve our greatest potential. *Plans* plot the course that makes even the tallest summit seem conquerable.

Are your dreams for the future supported by careful *planning* today?

Principle B. Well-Conceived Plans Produce Highly Productive Outcomes

Several years ago, a member of our sales team had an idea for growing his business in a large western city. I had heard similar ideas in the past, and, to be quite honest, I was not overly enthusiastic about reconsidering our position. He persisted, and I finally capitulated and allowed him to attend a meeting with the senior sales leadership team and formally present his plans for expanding revenue in his territory.

I still remember the look on the faces of the senior sales leaders as he finished the presentation and left the room. The incredulity that had filled the room at the beginning of the meeting had evaporated in the heat of a well-constructed *plan* for revenue expansion. He acknowledged past failures from similar ventures, provided a clear synopsis of why these strategies fell short of revenue projections, and concluded by outlining specific, measurable goals and plans, within the framework of an implementation timetable. Costs were explained in detail, and projected revenue streams were justified by concise and well-supported market research.

Not only did he receive the financial support to expand his territory; he made a strong case in the process for the persuasive impact of well-conceived *plans*. He took a group of entrenched sales leaders who were dubious about the prospect of appropriating funds to expand the territory, and within a half an hour had all of us confident and enthusiastic about his chances for great success. Effective *plans* not only create a map; they can also create a sustainable level of confidence. In short, learning to *plan* effectively is another way to infuse *Personal Leadership* into the process of selling. Well-conceived *plans* invariably lead to highly productive outcomes.

The territory sales *plan* identifies every possible productive activity to move the territory toward revenue potential. *Planning* is a quantitative activity that should include measurable goals; these become the key benchmarks used to assess performance. The more precise, specific and measurable the goals are, the more likely it is that the outcomes will be in line with objectives for the territory.

Planning is territory mapping. The map is intended not just to identify customers and competitors, but also to define a specific path to highest possible revenue total. *Planning* should be done in the context of maximizing outcomes for the given time period. It is propelled by the *Personal Leadership Driver* of *Vision*. Assessing potential and *planning* are bound together through the creation of a *Vision* for desired outcomes that include personal and product potential. Because they share the same *Personal Leadership Driver*, the process is similar, even though the actual practice is different.

Practice 1: Planning Should be both Committed and Flexible

Juxtaposing *committed* and *flexible* may seem a bit odd, since the notion of flexibility might suggest a lack of total commitment to the operational *plan*. Nothing could be further from the truth. The practice of allowing for flexibility merely acknowledges that we live and work in dynamic environments, where change is a frequent occurrence. It is possible to be 100 percent committed to a *plan* for the territory, while retaining the ability to sift through new market intelligence, which may indicate that some tweaking or modest retrenching is in order. You must be committed first and flexible second. As you become more involved with strategic work, the combination of being rigid and committed on one hand and supple and flexible on the other will begin to make sense.

This rigidity is grounded in the notion of ownership of the *plan* and a deep sense of responsibility for revenue produced in the territory. You write it, and you own it. At the same time, since Strategic Work is an ongoing process, we need to allow ourselves to be influenced by new information and ideas. Rigidity and flexibility are essential qualities in any territory sales *plan*.

Strategic and Tactical Work operate in tandem, like the two hemispheres of the brain. They perform separate and distinct functions, often simultaneously. Being fully engaged in Strategic Work generally requires a change in thinking, while becoming fully engaged in Tactical Work typically requires a change in how you work. They are purposely compartmentalized in this book in order to accentuate the differences. In practice they overlap to the point that there may be no conscious recognition when you move from Strategic to Tactical Work and back again. The key is learning how to think more strategically and work more tactically.

As you learn to spend more time in Strategic Work, you will experience an almost constant flow of new information and ideas about how you can do things in your territory with improved effectiveness and greater efficiency. Consequently, there is need for a measure of flexibility in the territory sales *plan*, to accommodate new information about changing market conditions, customer attitudes about your product, the integration of new technology or a competitor's enhanced position.

As a rule, a careful, if not necessarily exhaustive, effort to assess potential substantially reduces the likelihood that you will need to make radical changes to the *plan*. In any case, the need for flexibility should never become an excuse not to prepare a well-conceived *plan*. In most cases the adjustments that are made during the sales year will be modest and will not dramatically change the practices planned to move you closer to your annual revenue goal.

A critical aspect of every sales *plan* is your overall level of commitment. If you do not believe that the programs, activities and goals in your *plan* will lead to the desired objectives, the *plan* will have no more power to move you closer to your territory revenue potential than reading *Popular Mechanics* will have on improving your golf game. If you write a sales *plan* primarily to assuage the pressing demands of the senior sales leadership team, and not principally to increase your own personal investment in territory, you may as well save yourself the trouble and work instead on that great American novel you have always wanted to write. At least your children might enjoy the novel.

We'll consider these elements of the *plan* in more detail, later in this chapter.

Practice 2: Make Planning Empowering with Clarity of Content

Tactical Work in general is about the implementation of high-leverage activities. Nearly all of these can be quantified in some fashion. For example, prospecting time is easy to break down into the number of hours per day or per week. This important sales function could also be measured by the number of new customer contacts per day, per week or per month. The number of product presentations is something you can quantify. Be specific. Your numbers should reflect your careful analysis of what the territory needs and where the opportunities are, not just to satisfy the sales leadership team or your own ego.

The new customer contact portion of your *plan* should name names, if you sell products where that type of customer identification can realistically be made in advance. This is a conscious effort to recognize that all customers are not the same, and that time allocated to sales calls may vary in value among potential customers. In other words, this is the portion of the *plan* that has both quantitative and qualitative characteristics. It is quantitative, because you have identified the number of new contacts for a specific time frame. It is qualitative, because you are making a value judgment about which customers provide the greatest opportunity for growing your business in the territory.

Planning is an enabling, empowering and at times uniquely validating exercise in critical thinking about the outcome of future events. The actual experience of *planning* happens *today* and deeply engages you in influencing the revenue results of *tomorrow*. It is empowering and enabling, because the simple act of *planning* gives you a canvas on which to paint in vivid color what the future will look like. When all the requisite preparation of assessing potential is complete, you become the artist, painting with the resources and assets available on your sales palette, and creating a result that uniquely reflects your own skills and talents. *Planning* is an act of personal empowerment, because it allows you to say, "This is what I will do in my territory." That statement can be both validating and liberating.

The liberation comes from not being harnessed by the constraints of past performance. Thoughtful *planning*, conducted after assiduous investigation of overall market potential, can eliminate boundaries and give a sense of freedom to move in new directions. The validation comes to most sales professionals from the affirmation of their own intuitive sense that both they and the market are capable of more. The process of assessing potential provides the window through which you can see both your own and the market's potential. Looking out this window causes heads to nod, because the research validates what most people already know: "I can do more, and the territory and the product can produce more."

If this work of art, your *plan*, is something you create, and its composition is unique and original to you, your territory, your product and your customers, the process of committing it to canvas (or paper) can also be validating, because it is an example of your best work. In a sense it becomes a sales and marketing masterpiece that says more about you and your potential, your desire, your ambition and your hopes and dreams than any other single thing in your professional life. Your actual revenue number from last year may be spectacular, relatively speaking, but it is not likely to inspire you again this year. In fact, it may only add weight to an already overloaded backpack, as you start your assault on the new sales year's summit.

Practice 3: The Plan Must Be Written

The *plan* you prepare must be written. I have found too many sales professionals confess to be consistent planners, but the *plan* never takes form on paper. It resides in the inner sanctum of their brains. You must completely engage your mind, but the *plan* must emerge from your mind in a tangible, readable format. If your *plan* has not been recorded on either paper or electronic media, it does not exist! The neurons in your brain are far too changeable and lack sufficient power to implement an effective method of accountability. The process of transferring ideas to written form itself adds depth and clarity, while increasing the level of personal ownership. *Personal Leadership* requires that all *planning* take written form.

The process of writing your *plan* compels you to be rational. It is largely an exercise in rhetorical or persuasive writing. In essence you are preparing a brief for a judge, recommending a particular outcome in an important case. The case is your professional life, and your role is both arguing for the petition and hearing the plea. If you learn to think critically about your territory and develop the skill also to think strategically about potential outcomes, while at the same time engaging your rational mind in the process of developing a viable *plan*, you will find that writing your *plan* will be the annual experience in which you will feel the greatest measure of connection to your work and your future.

If you have not made writing a short territory sales *plan* part of your regular routine, you are in good company, including most of the sales professionals I have worked with over the years. They nearly all talk about a *plan*, but only a very small minority conducts this annual planning session consistently. *Planning* is a high-leverage activity. It is one of those unique experiences that, with even a small investment in time, preparation, and rudimentary analysis, can help you to take large steps forward in your territory.

The *plan* itself doesn't need to be a lengthy composition. It just needs to be well composed, with clear goal statements, timetables for implementation and specific statements about *what* you will accomplish, *how* you will accomplish it and *when* you can reasonably expect the *plan*'s activities to be fully accomplished. Nearly every session of actually writing your *plan* will exceed your expectations. It's as if the wiring of the brain is somehow connected to your fingertips. Engaging both together frequently produces results that were not available to your conscious mind until you began to write.

Successful organizations develop *plans* and take meticulous care of the implementation process. *Plans* inspire confidence and create a sense of organizational unity around shared objectives. *Plans* provide a map that marks a specific course to a desired destination. Still, the lack of consistent planning by front line members of the sales team is nothing short of an epidemic. Writing a *plan* that inspires confidence in a selected route leading to market potential is the easiest way to move yourself up the mountain and into the thinner air of outstanding achievement. It also prevents you from getting lost in the busy shuffle of low-yield activities.

Practice 4 : The Plan Should Be Simple

The call for simplicity should never be a reason to promote mediocrity. *Vision* is the *Personal Leadership Driver* behind creating a territory sales *plan.* In the *Personal Leadership Model* we generally associate vision with quantitative analysis. Much of the work of the sales *plan* is rooted in the type of critical thinking that results in quantifiable numbers. The most obvious example is the annual revenue goal, but this also applies to budgets, general market forecasting information and almost all of the individual sales activity goals, which routinely ask for some number to measure performance.

In the end the *plan* will be judged by the quality of its content rather than its quantity of written pages. The planning process fairly screams for your best work. If you intend to write your own symphony in the selling profession, your own original work that uniquely describes who you are, put the notes on paper during the planning process. Performing it comes later, but the grandeur of the piece and all of its harmonic elements come to life in the planning phase.

I understand the notion of "keeping it simple." The push for simplicity is an imperative that should cast a shadow over most of our sales activities, to keep us away from making the selling process more complex than it has to be. In the planning process, simplicity is found in seeking alignment. Everything in the process should be about one or two primary objectives; all goals, strategies, plans and programs should support those objectives. The *plan* should be based on producing revenue, and virtually every other piece of the *plan* should support this overarching objective.

Many interpret "keep it simple" as a mandate to marginalize, minimize and, in many instances, default to the easiest possible means of achieving compliance. A sales *plan* for your territory could be fifteen pages of clear, concise, even simple thinking. Or it could be one or two pages, with none of the clarity about direction that encourages simplicity. The *plan's* organizational content and its overall clarity about how completing specified goals will produce the targeted revenue number are much better indicators of simplicity than the fact that you were able to keep your *plan* shorter than three pages.

How long should your *plan* be? That depends. In fact, it depends upon so many different variables that it would be impossible to design one template that would apply to a wide range of products, organizations, customers and individual market conditions. The *plan* should be written for you, so in the final analysis you will know when you have an operational strategy in place that captures all the essential tasks to hit your revenue number for the next year. If the annual planning process is something you undertake for yourself, the length of the *plan* is unimportant, provided that it leads you to discover, and contains your description of, how you intend to achieve your goal this year.

Practice 5: Plan to Create Your Future

Your sales *plan* is your autobiography, written in advance. It describes in rich color, with consideration of even the smallest details, the peaks on which you will stand at the end of the year. Your mind surges with confidence in the outcomes, because of the clarity and specificity of the *plan*. Through the planning process you have envisioned the desired destination and have combined that vision with a course of action. This has allowed you to assume complete ownership. Personal ownership of a *plan* undergirds outstanding achievement. Taking ownership is also an act of *Personal Leadership*.

Planning itself is creating. If you cannot create in your mind and commit to paper your dreams as a sales professional, in the form of a viable *plan* of action, outstanding achievement will always remain out of reach. Inevitably, over time you will find that people around you – some who are less gifted, others who don't seem to work as hard – move up the mountain faster and reach heights that to you seem virtually unattainable. Effective *planning* is the great equalizer in professional selling. Members of the sales team who *plan* well, consistently execute the *plan*, and regularly hold themselves accountable will always seem like overachievers. The truth is that *planning* doesn't result in *over*achieving. It simply keeps you from *under*achieving, from working below your potential.

Practice 6: Implement the Seven Essential Components of the Territory Sales Plan

Everything we have discussed in this chapter up to this point has been about preparing you to begin the work of writing an action *plan* for your territory. Our primary objective with the *plan* is to address the two governing principles we discussed at the beginning of this chapter. First, to make your dreams for your professional life and your sales territory possible. And second, to design a well-conceived *plan* that will give you the best possible chance to produce favorable outcomes. If you will *plan* consistently, you will literally feel your hands slide further along the handle of the bar. With your hands positioned near the end, prying up even some of the more entrenched boulders in your territory can become commonplace.

The list below is a short summary of key components of effective sales *planning*. It is not comprehensive. You may find that other elements are needed for your territory and your product, to provide a clear map of viable routes for the coming year. These are merely suggested minimums. You are the best person to draw the line, when it comes to defining acceptable maximums.

Annual Revenue Goal. This goal is the overall revenue number to which you are committed for the next sales year. Formulating this revenue goal depends on the work of assessing potential, as discussed in Chapter 3. If the market assessment is current, identifying an achievable revenue goal should be a fairly simple task, even though it is the centerpiece of your sales *plan*.

There is a tendency in the annual *planning* process to place too much emphasis on the revenue produced in the territory in the past year. Last year's revenue is one element of the forecasting equation, but it should not cast too long a shadow over your *plan* for the coming year. *Planning* and setting a goal for revenue production that is based too much on last year's numbers invariably produces incremental results. Exponential gains come from a deep commitment to executing all three skills of Strategic Work.

We saw earlier that the primary *Personal Leadership Driver* in planning is *Vision*, which is largely quantitative in nature. *Vision* powers both assessing potential and the *plan* itself. This essential *Personal Leadership* skill helps you sift through piles of data and determine which elements are essential, as you construct, first, a clear and realistic vision for your territory, and then an achievable *plan*. Professional selling is ultimately about the revenue that is produced in your territory. The whole purpose of *Vision* in the *planning* process is to force you to think critically about potential outcomes and identify a goal that you believe in. A revenue number that is based on solid quantitative thinking and analysis will not only inspire your best work (create excellence), but also help you more confidently visualize desired outcomes (identify motivators).

While it is true that *Vision* drives the creation of the revenue goal, as in all of the components of the *Personal Leadership Model*, the other *Personal Leadership Drivers* should have a voice. As a rule, the more important the function, the greater the role all three *Personal Leadership Drivers* should play in the final outcome. And since revenue production is the basic performance criterion by which most sales professionals are evaluated, it could be argued that the development and achievement of this single number is the capstone of both Strategic and Tactical Work. Ask yourself, how will *Vision*, *Character* and *Passion* influence your goal number?

It takes *Character* to select a number that exceeds the reasonable expectations of your peers and senior sales leaders. The overwhelming tendency is to default to an easier number, to minimize the pressure you feel for the coming year. Perhaps this is the reason that most sales professionals, even in the face of solid empirical data to the contrary, select goals that neither require nor motivate their best work. This is where mediocrity gains ground in most organizations and within most individual sales professionals.

It should be obvious that *Passion* is vital to any significant achievement or life endeavor. The more fully your subconscious mind accepts your goal and the corresponding implementation strategy, the greater success you will have in producing sustained levels of motivation over long periods of time. Motivation is fueled by thinking about desired outcomes. The more challenging realistic outcomes are to you, the more success you will have in describing the benefits to your subconscious mind through sensory-rich images.

I might be able to trick my subconscious mind in to believing something that is patently absurd by suspending my rational conscious mind for a short period of time. Day in and day out, however, such trickery diminishes the process, and you lose credibility with yourself, simply because you know that the images you are creating are not based in the real world. You may get a short-term bump in adrenaline, but your long-term success will be frustrated. Your *Vision* of desired outcomes must be grounded in credible thinking, or it becomes little more than passive daydreaming. The more you believe in yourself, your product, and your market, the greater success you will have in stimulating your subconscious mind with the sort of image that will fuel the steep climbs ahead.

Sales Goals and Implementation Strategy. If the annual revenue goal is the heart of the sales *plan*, the goals and strategy section is the mind. This is the operational portion of the *plan*. It will contain much of the detail of what you intended to do and how you will achieve your goal. Just about every other aspect of the sales *plan* is a prelude to developing key elements that will propel you toward your annual revenue goal. The revenue number alone, particularly if it challenges your best work, will rarely be sufficient. It needs the support of a well-conceived *plan* of action.

Writing clear and concise goal statements that are supported by a short description of how the goal will be achieved allows you to design a strategy for achieving lofty revenue goals that will inspire your best work. I suggest you start by writing bullet points for each of the goal statements. Once these are in place, you can provide a logical explanation of how that goal will be accomplished. Where possible, include specific numbers of hours, contacts, etc. This will help you later on, as you implement a process for holding yourself accountable. If you are committed to completing all aspects of strategic work, writing the goals and implementation strategy section of your annual sales *plan* will be an exhilarating experience.

I'd like to dispel at least one common sales myth. Sales goals, despite their projected grandeur, have little or no power to move people forward. Goal statements are fundamentally inert, which is why they seldom if ever actually work. Goal statements without well-conceived action *plans* are like campaign promises without supporting legislation. They make good sound bites but rarely effect real change. A goal statement is a promise you make to yourself. For you to be persuaded that the goal can be achieved, there must be a clear, concise and supportable action *plan* describing how it will be achieved. The more measurable components you can include in the implementation strategy, the more lift your *plan* will generate toward the goal. In short, the power in goal setting comes not from the goals themselves, but from viable, workable plans that describe specifically how those goals will be achieved.

The development of specific goals should flow naturally from assessing potential, which you did to reveal growth opportunities in your market, and also to identify weak points in your current product positioning or key customers' perception of product, price or benefits relative to the nearest competitors. Assessing potential creates a snapshot of the territory from the stratosphere. Properly done, it reveals both the peaks and the valleys between you and optimum revenue production. The peaks stand out vividly; they are burgeoning opportunities for revenue growth. A clear *Vision* of these possibilities helps stimulate the inspiration that will sustain you on the difficult climbs. But do not become so preoccupied with visualizing your ascent up the mountain that you ignore the valleys.

The market assessment is purposely designed to reveal the soft underbelly of your work in the territory. Your annual sales *plan* should also address pressing issues that distract your customers from making buying decisions. These can be technical support issues, lead times, warranty concerns, unresolved regulatory compliance problems or a simple lack of clarity about your current product offering. The peaks in your market assessment require offensive maneuvers, while the valleys are generally more defensive in nature. Both are essential to long-term territory growth.

Before we look at some specific examples of goal statements and short implementation strategies, please note that this portion of your sales *plan* doesn't need to be exhaustive to be effective. In most cases ten to fifteen specific goal statements that are mined from your market assessment work will be sufficient. I suggest that you spend a few days before you write this section of your *plan* just reviewing the data collected from your market assessment, and think deeply about your territory and the past year. Once you can frame in your mind what is needed to move forward, you are ready to map the critical path up the mountain. This critical path is simply a representation of essential things you will need, and need to do, to achieve your goal this year.

When you are ready to start the work, I suggest you make this process as easy and painless as possible. If you have prepared correctly, it shouldn't take too much time, and you will find the writing of goals and strategies to be one of the easier and more enjoyable experiences you have each year.

Here is how I have done it for about thirty years. I simply take out a sheet of paper or open a blank page on my computer and start writing. I don't stop to analyze or critique anything I have written. You may remember an exercise like this in "free writing" from your freshman English class in college. When I start to get stuck between goal statements, I know it is time to stop. I review the list to insure that all pertinent points have been covered, and then I leave it alone for several hours, maybe even a few days.

SALES GOALS

1. More prospecting hours this year. Maybe 5 hours or more.

2. Presentations. How many? Possibly one a week.

3. Self development — what can I do to improve my technical skills?

4. Competitor knowledge. I need to know more about all of my competitors.

The act of returning to the list of goal statements is generally quite revealing. I nearly always find that the initial exercise in free thinking has produced some ideas that were not obvious to me before. When I allow myself to let go and write without inhibition, I actually learn something new about either myself or my territory. For me, over the years, the most effective part of setting goals is *writing them*.

It is part analytical and part creative. If you prepare by consuming all the pertinent data in advance, then let that information simmer for a few days, and finally engage your mind in free thinking about possibilities, you are likely to discover some interesting things you can do to move your territory forward.

To help you get started, here are some sample goal statements, combined with short implementation strategies. This is not a comprehensive list, just an attempt to help you get started. I realize that these goal statements and implementation strategies may not apply to your product and market, but the concepts may be useful, once you have adapted them to your circumstances.

1. *I will complete five hours of prospecting work every week.* I will achieve this by starting every day with a minimum of one hour of such work *before* retrieving voice mail messages or responding to email. I will keep a log of my hours. When I am out of the office, I will

make up the prospecting time on other days, so that my weekly total is never less than five hours.

2. *I will make fifty presentations to new customers within my target contact group.* I will make one product presentation every week to a new customer in my key target group. These are customers who should be buying my product, but currently are not. These presentations will be scheduled at least two weeks in advance. I will allot time each Monday morning to keeping my presentation schedule current.

3. *I will actively follow up on every potential contract closing.* To accomplish this goal this year, I will keep a record of all potential new orders on a spreadsheet, with contact names and phone numbers. I will make calls for a minimum of one hour per day or until I have made a minimum of fifteen customer contacts. I will keep a written log of time spent and the number of contacts made each day.

4. *I will remain committed to strengthening relationships with my top 25 key accounts.* I will do this through fifteen hours of key customer contact work each week. (A onehour meeting with three customers equals three hours of contact time.) I will keep a written record of time spent with key customers. I will use this time to resolve problems, clarify new product developments, receive feedback about past performance and better understand and assess future needs. My primary objective will be to underscore the notion that   no one else is as committed to earning their business and as capable of keeping it as I am.

5. *I will respond to every customer inquiry promptly.* When I am working in the office, I will return every phone call within an hour. When I am traveling, I will return every phone call within an hour after the end of an appointment. I will respond to every e-mail message on the same day. Urgent messages will receive top priority and will receive a follow-up call within fifteen minutes.

6. *I will improve my overall technical proficiency with my product and those of the nearest competitors.* I will spend a minimum of two hours per

week studying my product and my competitors' products. This year I will make an audio recording of important technical information about my product to which   I can listen to while traveling in my car. I will also make a separate recording of competitor information. During the first month of the year I will review the information to be covered and make the audio recording. During the remaining months I will review the material repeatedly. I will keep a written log of hours spent completing this goal each week.

7. *I will become a better-informed resource to my customers by having a broad knowledge of my industry.* To complete this goal I will be enroll in two separate one-day courses and complete one additional online class. I will also read at least one book on an industry topic and read an industry publication each month.

Writing goals and implementation strategies is an acquired skill. If you simply clench your fist, grit your teeth and compose some pithy goal statements to complete an assignment, you will find, if you haven't already, that these statements will have little power to move you. Goal statements need to create powerful images, and their corresponding implementation strategies need to give a measure of confidence that the goal is achievable, if you follow the strategies.

The practice of goal setting quite naturally flows from the three skills in Strategic Work, fueled by the three *Personal Leadership Drivers*. Sales professionals who repeatedly demonstrate the three key competencies of *Personal Leadership* recognize that it takes *Vision* to see the future and to understand their product's potential. They also know that *Character* compels them to produce excellence, which drives them always to seek their greatest personal potential. Finally, they know that, without *Passion*, dreams die of natural causes, and even well-conceived plans fade over time.

Setting goals and designing workable strategies is a *Personal Leadership* imperative. It is also a practice that will lead you develop proficiency in effective *planning*. Leaders know that high-leverage work is where the bulk of their time should be spent. Leaders know that the practice of goal setting is the ultimate high-leverage experience.

Evaluation of Goals from the Previous Year. Every *plan* I have prepared for the past twenty or more years contains one section that simply evaluates the previous year's performance. I prefer to list each goal separately, then report in a paragraph or two whether or not this goal was satisfactorily accomplished. At the top of the paragraph, adjacent to the goal statement, I list a letter grade in a capital letter. This grade provides me with a simple, at-a-glance evaluation of the previous year's progress.

> GOAL: To complete 5 hours of prospecting weekly
>
> GRADE: B+
>
> I started the year averaging about 4 hours a week using the Weekly Progress Report, but during the last half of the year my weekly totals dropped to around 3.5. This is an area that I need to spend more time on again this year.

Including this in my *plan* each year has influenced my thinking to such a degree that I find myself periodically giving myself midterm grades, too, at least in my mind. As I review the *plan* and evaluate specific goals, the letter grades begin to take shape in my mind. Over time I have learned that a day of reckoning will eventually arrive, and I inevitably feel more determined to take the necessary steps to insure that my grades will be acceptable, even though the individual goals and my corresponding evaluations are usually for my eyes only.

This annual evaluation of sales goals generates a surprising amount of power. It engenders a higher level of consciousness about goal achievement, while promoting the regular integration of activities that lead to completing each goal into weekly and monthly planning sessions. If you learn to do this consistently, you will find it to be one of the most helpful and satisfying aspects of preparing your annual sales *plan*.

Market Forecast. It is impossible to write an effective sales *plan* without a clear forecast of market conditions for the coming year. Driving through the Rockies in winter can be a precarious experience. A map with a selected route is good. A map with a selected route and updated weather conditions is much better. The market forecast portion of your *plan* is the sales equivalent of having information about current weather conditions for your drive this year. The more clarity you can provide about trends for your product, the more confidence you will develop in your ability to set a course leading to lofty revenue production.

Many industries have subscription-based services that provide comprehensive market trend analysis, as well as both longand short-term forecasts for your market. Some of these subscription-based services may be a bit too pricey for your budget. The most credible low-cost alternatives are generated by industry associations. Trade publications can also be consulted; annual editions may provide important economic forecasting information. I have also found the local office of the U.S. Department of Commerce useful in providing good supplemental market forecasting information. In many instances, a key word search on the Web will yield more than enough material to clarify and quantify expected market conditions for your sales environment in the coming year.

Your market forecast establishes the context for your *plan*. This information should not be limited to aggregate spending, but should also include any other factors which may impact customers' product selection decisions in the coming year. Increased governmental regulation or consumer demand, influenced by growing concern about the environment, are examples of topics that should be addressed in the market forecasting section of your sales *plan*. The market forecast is a snapshot of the territory from above cloud level. The clearer the image, the more successful you will be in designing a route away from potential trouble and toward potential opportunities.

Competitor Analysis. The inclusion of competitor analysis in your sales *plan* helps you in a couple of different ways. First, it forces you to remain current about product development changes implemented by your competitors during the past sales year. Second, having a clear understanding of your competitors' relative strengths and weaknesses will influence your selection of a strategy in the goal portion of your *plan*. The best practice in this section of the *plan* also includes a general assessment of how your customers are responding to key messages delivered by your competitors about their products.

We have already discussed the notion that collaboration is the process that leads towards product selection and represents the highest level of interaction between a customer and a sales professional. Your ability to be a skillful collaborator will be diminished if you are not current on a broad range of industry topics, including the intricacies of your nearest competitors. Over the course of a long selling season, your customers need to learn to trust you as a person who is competent about standard industry practices and the subtle differences in products among competitors. In planning viable routes, you must have the best information available about your competitors, in order to avoid the occasional minefield.

Knowing the relative strengths and weaknesses of your product, compared to your nearest competitors' products, will enable you credibly to position your message in the minds of your customers. Your message is simply your conviction of how your product uniquely addresses the customers' specific needs. If you are not driving this message in your market, your competitors will, and you will find yourself in an uncomfortable, defensive posture much of the time. The more you have to defend your product, the more your voice sounds whining and shallow. Neither attribute inspires customer confidence.

The selling high ground is always found in uniquely positioning the product in the context of customer needs. This effort is an ambitiously offensive undertaking. A well-conceived *plan* is an offensive tool for shaping customer perceptions of you and your product. A clear analysis of your nearest competitors will prove invaluable as you craft your primary message for the coming sales year.

Budget. In a sense the annual budget for your territory is the oxygen supply needed to sustain life for the coming year. Far too often, sales professionals mistakenly assume that most of the challenges in their territories could be either resolved or substantially mitigated by spending more money. In fact this simple assumption could be a major barrier that prevents sales professionals from moving territories toward optimum revenue production. The solution is rarely found in a simple mandate for more money.

Budgets in nearly all sales environments will always be a scarce resource. Thoughtful *planning*, built on a foundation of critical thinking and analysis, will solve most budget conflicts. A commitment to leverage available resources through wellselected plans and programs provides the best opportunity for revenue growth. In my thirty years of experience, I have yet to find a sales professional who could not improve his use of available resources to better position the product to grow revenue in the territory. Without a commitment to complete all of the elements of Strategic Work which are designed to reveal market opportunities, it will always seem that there is not enough money to do what is needed to reach the annual revenue goal. The truth is that most territories could use more *planning* and less money. As a profession we suffer from anemic planning, not from under-funded programs.

Budgets are an integral part of the *planning* process, but preparing an annual budget is more than writing down a number for projected annual expenses. Each goal and corresponding strategy we select must include a cost component. Consequently, planning is a tandem exercise of determining the coming year's high-leverage activities that align with our market assessment, and the allocation of available financial resources to put these plans in motion. Writing a *plan* for the territory and preparing a budget need to be done simultaneously.

With the possible exception of the annual revenue goal, the ratio of the total cost of selling to the total revenue generated in the territory is the most critical measurement of overall sales effectiveness. A lower cost of selling ratio essentially suggests a higher yield rate. Sales professionals who are conscious of both revenue production and cost control nearly always produce high yield rates. As a rule, sales professionals with high yield rates are among the best-compensated people in the selling profession.

Reports. Your annual sales *plan* should be a repository of every piece of data relevant to your sales effort. While its essential component is the yearly operational strategy that drives you toward your revenue goal, it can also be a collecting pool for important reports that you generate over the course of each sales year. I like to compile an appendix section in each yearly *plan* with information that I update yearly, for ease of reference. For example, a simple sheet with a compilation of annual goals and corresponding revenue numbers is an important collection of historical data not only about your territory, but also, more importantly, about your career.

The appendix of your sales *plan* is also a good place to put your market assessment. This binds your market reconnaissance work to your yearly *plan* and makes it easy to retrieve. It is also a constant reminder of the need to continue gathering important data about market conditions within your territory.

Some of the other reports I like to include in the annual sales *plan* are these:

◆ Top 25 customers

◆ Top 25 largest contracts during the past year.

◆ A product application analysis

◆ Sales awards received

◆ Self-development programs completed

For the most part, these are reports you already compile and will require little or   no additional work. With these documents in place, I put a card stock cover on the front and have the document spiral-bound. During my career these annual sales *plans* have traveled over two million miles with me. They always finish the year with tattered edges, torn pages, margin notes, food stains, and a generous amount of yellow highlights. This is the one document I "never leave home without." It is a single-source reference guide for every significant aspect of selling for the next twelve months. Later, this year's *plan* will become the template for next year's *plan*. Year after year, the *plan* is easy for me to navigate, because all the documents are located in essentially the same places.

It never occurred to me, when I started preparing this annual report, that it would become an interesting reference about key sales initiatives, a record of important goals and their achievement or a timeline for product penetration. I did not intend it to be a historical document, but the hundreds and hundreds of pages of simple annual sales *plans* I have accumulated during my career provide a much better account of my career than my mind can.

Annual Territory Sales Plan

Table of Contents

Practice 7: Design the Plan to Accommodate Change

Change is inevitable in every sales year and within every sales *plan. Plan* for it. Weekly planning sessions, where you review goals and strategies to insure their alignment with the territory's current needs, are one simple way to manage change. More will be discussed about this type of *planning* meeting in a later chapter. Let's face it: most selling environments are dynamic. Change occurs rapidly, often monthly and occasionally weekly. Your sales *plan* must be equally dynamic to allow you to respond appropriately.

Thinking strategically and working tactically allow you to call the appropriate audible as you discover shifting trends in the market. Strategic Work is a continuous process that requires the constant ingestion of market information, which ultimately impacts the *planning* component of Tactical Work. The annual sales *plan* represents a precise moment in time and summons all the best available market intelligence about your territory. Rapid market changes may render your best thinking from a month ago irrelevant. Don't discard the map. Just adjust the course to suit new information about the selling environment. If you use the rapidity of change as an argument against planning, your anticipation of future change will likely paralyze you when it is time for decisive action.

Assemble the best *plan* possible to start the year. Be committed to the overall objectives and implementation strategies. Adjust the *plan* and the corresponding activities as you process new information about your territory, customers, and competitors. This will mean writing new goal statements and corresponding strategies. The fluidity of your *plan* will be in direct proportion to the dynamic nature of the market in which you are selling. Accommodate change by incorporating a device in your *plan* to review, revise, amend and discard various elements as needed. Whatever you do, be sure to *plan* for change.

Planning and the Symptoms of Sales Paralysis

Writing a territory sales *plan* is an essential *Personal Leadership* skill. *Planning* demands research, careful analytical work, assessment of new opportunities, and willingness to accept responsibility for past failures or shortcomings in the territory. It is tedious and time-consuming work. The one constant I have observed in over three decades in selling is that sales professionals who learn to *plan* exert a measure of control over outcomes in their territories. In fact, leaders actively seek opportunities to control and influence the achievement of important strategic objectives in the territory.

If writing a territory sales *plan* is new to you, you may find it to be the most productive practice you incorporate in your territory each year.

The *plan* transcends the writing of simple goal statements and includes an operational strategy that is in line with the long-term potential of the territory, as revealed by your work in assessing potential. The *plan* becomes your territory map for the current sales year.

Symptom	Impact	Comments
Winging it	HIGH	Well-planned territories have a clear sense of direction.
Lack of a sense of urgency	MEDIUM	Planning reveals opportunities. Opportunities are always urgent.
Contemplation of a job change	LOW	Well-planned territories inspire confidence. Why look elsewhere?
Feelings of frustration	LOW	A cohesive strategy adds clear direction that soothes frustration.
Blaming others	MEDIUM	No reason to pass blame when you are fixated on solving problems.
Low energy for problem solving	HIGH	Less reason to pass blame when you have a map in hand.

Planning is powered by *Vision*. As a rule, when *Vision* is involved, its implications for selling are widespread. You will notice from the summary above how writing the sales *plan* impacts the Eight Symptoms of Sales Paralysis. This skill exerts more influence on enhancing the sales professional's productivity than any of the three skills of Tactical Work.

An Elevated View of Planning

Vision is fundamentally, but not exclusively, quantitative in nature in both Strategic and Tactical Work. The analytical work results in measurable territory benchmarks. As you may remember from an earlier chapter on assessing potential, the end result of all the data crunching is to produce some key numbers that will allow you to measure progress toward optimum revenue production.

The planning portion of Tactical Work reflects in many ways the market intelligence gathering component of Strategic Work, with a few notable differences. *Assessing potential* gives a broad view of the market, allowing you to see clearly opportunities for revenue growth over a period of several years. *Planning* is a much narrower view and is designed to outline a specific strategy to move the territory toward realistic goals. To be effective, both *planning* and assessing potential must include quantifiable elements, so that progress can be measured over time.

You must *plan* to measure progress in a wide range of relevant sales activities in the territory. The more you *plan* specific and measurable components, the more likely you are to succeed in the skills of Execution and Accountability. Revenue production is always measurable, but it may only tell you your position on the mountain relative to other climbers. That is an important number, but it will never be enough; knowing your precise elevation tells you little, if anything, about the height of the mountain.

The summit's elevation is something you should determine before you start the climb, by assessing potential. You will also need information about the terrain ahead and specific data about safe passage routes to the summit. Reliable, up-to-date weather forecasts will impact your route selection *(plan)* and your rate of progress (timetable).

The Role of Vision in Assessing Potential and Planning

It is important to remember that in the world of professional selling *Vision* is about foresight, not eyesight. It is anticipatory, forward-thinking and opportunityseeking. It requires a willingness to crunch numbers in search of new opportunities and hidden potential. Sometimes the most important discoveries are found within yourself.

Vision is an enabling power that provides a glimpse of what your territory can be and what you can become in the profession of selling. The impact of *Vision* when applied to the skills of assessing Potential and *planning* can provide a powerful combination to propel the revenue production in your territory to new heights. *Assessing potential* provides a clear view of opportunities. *Planning* provides a workable strategy to bring those opportunities into reality. Two different skills powered by the same *Personal Leadership Driver.* They share similar characteristics and produce different but equally important outcomes.

The skill of assessing potential is part of Strategic Work because it is oriented toward elevating personal performance within the territory. As you recall, the three skills of Strategic Work are performance-based and will assist you in working closer to your ultimate potential as a sales professional. Tactical Work is more operational in nature, and the associated three skills have a more product-based approach to the work of the territory and revenue production. I hope you are starting to visualize how the reallocation of time into the three skills of Strategic Work offer the most significant opportunities to make noticeable improvement in your work in professional selling.

Time spent in all of the six skills, but especially those in Strategic Work, quite literally moves your hands farther and farther to the outer reaches of the bar; this enables you to exert downward pressure on the lever, to move the stone that represents the overall potential of your territory to higher and higher levels. Leaders allocate time wisely. Strategic Work is always a wise allocation of time because it is rooted in the singular objective of improving your ability to work at a level consistent with your greatest potential.

The chapters that follow will repeat the same basic organization. They will consist of an introduction of the *Personal Leadership Driver*, a brief review of principles and practices, and discussion of workable tools to aid in skill development.

The Relationship of Principles and Practices in Developing the Skill (*"Learned Power"*) of Planning

Principle A. Planning makes dreams possible.
Supporting Practices:
1. Make the planning empowering with clarity of content
2. The plan must be written
3. Plan to create your future
4. Implement the seven components of the sales plan

Principle B. Well-conceived plans invariably produce highly productive outcomes.
Supporting Practices:
1. Planning should be committed and flexible
2. Make planning empowering with clarity of content
3. The plan must be written
4. The plan must be simple
5. Implement the seven components of the sales plan
6. Design the plan to accommodate change

PART II

Character

CHARACTER is the second *Personal Leadership Driver*. A careful assessment of the overall quality of your work relative to your potential is probably the best measurement of how well this driver is being deployed in your professional life. In this section we will be looking at how character influences the skill of *creating excellence* in Strategic Work and the skill of *execution* in Tactical Work.

Once we have developed a clear *vision* of potential outcomes for our territory, a person of *character* will act in accordance with the new view of reality. It is much easier to capitulate to incremental thinking. Growing your territory by a nominal percentage year over year is what dominates most of the sales planning in professional selling. Most people can produce nominal gains and never really explore the far and frequently untapped reaches of their own potential. This book is about changing your thinking from nominal gains to exponential gains. That will only happen when you first activate a sense of *vision* in your life and then have the courage or *character* to act accordingly.

Character is a *Personal Leadership* imperative because it is distinguished by the overall quality of the work you produce relative to your potential. Can you begin to understand how the actual process of working in alignment with your potential moves your hands near the end of the bar? If you are doing your best work each day in executing the sales plan that was conceived out of a clear *vision* for the territory, your life will be absorbed in high-leverage work. You will start to feel that enormous stone getting lighter, as it rises higher and higher towards the full realization of your potential. *Vision* and *Character* working together provide power to move the stone.

We learned from the previous chapter that assessing potential is understanding more about what needs to be done. The second skill in Strategic Work, *create excellence*, defines how that work will be done. *Excellence* in professional selling is doing your best work every day, every week in each sales year to reduce the gap between your potential and your actual performance.

Creating excellence is always about *Personal Leadership*. It consists of having the judgment to do the right things at the right time with the right people in the right way. No aspect of the *Personal Leadership Model* is more directly reflective of who you are as a sales professional than this skill.

Effective leaders manifest *character*. So do outstanding sales professionals. Trust is foundational to every customer interaction and builds strong support teams at the corporate office and with the companies your represent. *Character* is not just about the quality of relationships in your life. I have seen a lot of high-character people who had very short careers in selling. *Character* is also about the ability to execute well-conceived plans.

CHAPTER 5

Create Excellence

Optimum Outcomes

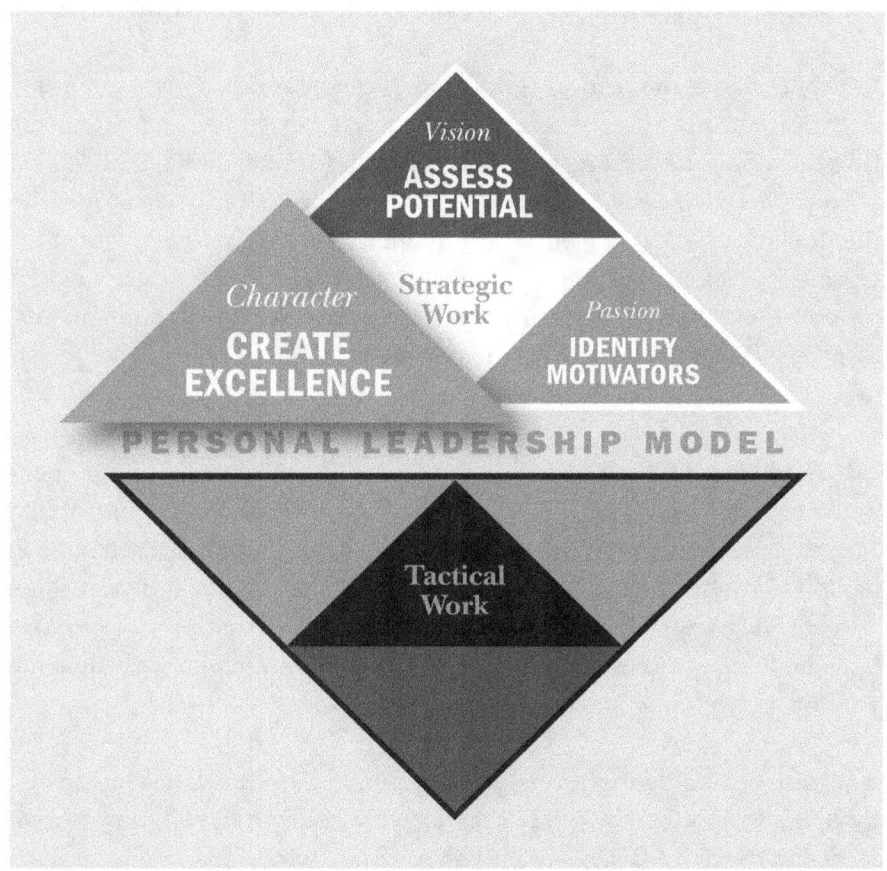

Figure 5-1 Create Excellence: The *Character* Component of Strategic Work

MY OWN mental image of *excellence* consists of dust mops, cleaning supplies, toilet paper, green grass and a man with khaki pants, short-cropped hair, and keys dangling at his side. What he created in his professional life has been my own personal quest for the past three decades.

Art Peterson was not a typical high school custodian. He was a spit-and-polish Marine sergeant who cleaned schools with the impassioned determination of a politician on the stump. Many men at his age and in his line of work punch the clock, pick up the paycheck, offer a conciliatory nod to the principal and count the days to retirement. Art was not that kind of guy, and anyone who ever worked for him either learned that lesson very quickly or gladly opted to seek employment elsewhere. Art knew only one way to clean and maintain a building. He never used the terms *excellence* or *best practice*, but his example of shiny floors and pristine windows is still the first thing that comes to my mind when those topics are discussed.

Sweeping floors and painting door frames can be relatively innocuous job skills or mundane life experiences. My university experience taught me the language of business, along with essential skills for functioning in the world of corporate finance and marketing. A few years working as a janitor under the tutelage of Art Peterson taught me that *creating excellence* is about integrity. It is about living and working in such a way as to insure the best possible outcomes. In the final analysis, true *excellence* is matching our performance to our potential, whether we are cleaning floors or selling leading-edge products.

Art could have been content with mediocrity, and nothing in his compensation program would have changed. For Art it was never about the money. He was a man who was hard-wired to do his best, regardless of the task at hand. He took what some might consider a simple job and produced an outcome that was simply exceptional. Art understood that *creating excellence* is about being your best, and that becoming your best requires challenging your own beliefs about your potential.

The skill of learning to *create excellence* is simply about working consistently to your own potential. In this chapter we will begin by defining what it means to *create excellence*, so that you can start to develop in your mind a clear image of what *excellence* looks like in your territory. Then we will look carefully at three aspects of *creating excellence:* desire, competency and character. Each of these sections will contain several different ways for you to evaluate your performance. You will also find some personal assessment exercises to help you in the evaluation process.

The simple images of polished floors and pristine windows remind me of what *excellence* looks like. At the end of this chapter you should have a better understanding of specific things you can do as a sales professional to create and sustain *excellence* in your territory.

Principles and Practices for Creating Excellence

In this chapter we will examine four basic principles, laws or underlying assumptions that will assist your progression toward acquiring the skill of *creating excellence*. Three of these principles will be presented in detail with the outline of seven practices that will accelerate skill development.

In many respects Vince Lombardi captured the essence of this principle when he said that "the quality of a person's life is in direct proportion to their commitment to *excellence*, regardless of their chosen field of endeavor." Art Peterson was a high school custodian, but the quality of his life and particularly his ability to influence others was elevated above the mundane tasks of cleaning classrooms because of a consistent commitment to produce quality outcomes.

Principles, Skills & Practices

Principles *(laws or assumptions)*: "The quality of a person's life is in direct proportion to their commitment to excellence, regardless of their chosen field of endeavor" (Vince Lombardi). A. Excellent work produces excellent results. B. Creating excellence begins with a strong desire to produce outstanding work. C. Improved competency improves the prospect of creating excellence. D. People of character naturally build collaborative relationships.

Skill *(learned power)*: Create Excellence

Practices *(repeated exercises for proficiency)*: 1) Work to develop collaborative relationships. 2) Work with the expectation of positive results. 3) Produce consistent quality. 4) Work to improve your sales ability and add value to your customers. 5) Understand customer needs and communicate clearly. 6) Think of the sales transaction in terms of customer benefit. 7) Consistently do your best work.

Character is the *Personal Leadership Driver* that powers this skill. It is located in the domain of Strategic Work because of its influence on enhancing overall performance levels of your work as a sales professional. As we will discuss later in this chapter, developing the skill to *create excellence* is driven by a willingness to work in alignment with your own talents and abilities. It requires *vision* to understand the potential for your product in your territory, but it will require *character* to forge a resolve to move in a new direction that will require some risk. It will require bigger plans, perhaps some sweeping changes in work habits and some new thinking about strategy development. It will also require some courage to believe that your assessment of the market and of your own potential are worth exploring.

Principle A. Excellent Work Produces Excellent Results

Many of us are programmed to think of *excellence* in terms of life achievements, but there is a distinct difference between achievement and *excellence*. Achievement in sales is nearly always measured by external factors, such as revenue goals, annual growth in territory sales totals, market share performance, or perhaps the attainment of a revenue number that substantially exceeded the established annual sales goal. *Excellence*, on the other hand, is nearly always an internal process. It is about the sales professional's commitment to explore the limits of personal potential. It is about fulfilling the possibilities of individual capacity and living with a sense of integrity, honoring that personal capacity regardless of external pressures to accept and even applaud lesser outcomes.

What is Excellence?

Webster's Ninth Collegiate Dictionary 1 : The quality of being excellent **2 :** An excellent or valuable quality

Thomas Edison – There's a way to do it better... find it.

Ralph Waldo Emerson – There is always a best way of doing everything.

Seneca – It is quality rather than quantity that matters.

George S. Patton – Always do more than is required of you.

Albert Einstein – Try not to become a man of success but rather try to become a man of value.

Booker T. Washington – Excellence is to do a common thing in an uncommon way.

All of the statements at the right describe, and in many respects define, what *excellence* means in our lives. In the specific context of professional selling I would like you to consider the following four descriptors as key elements of the overarching principle that *excellent* work produces *excellent* results.

- Consistently do your best work.

- Work to improve.

- Know your potential and work towards it.

- As a professional, demonstrate the key elements of having a desire for *excellence*, competency, and character.

A commitment to professional *excellence* is one of the defining attributes of leadership in selling. A leader seeks out new opportunities by carefully monitoring the horizon, then methodically crafts

a *vision* that will lead to the realization of those opportunities. Effective leaders in the selling profession expect more of themselves and clearly understand that the ultimate judgment of accomplishments worthy of celebration will come from themselves.

The quest for professional *excellence* begins with a clear understanding of how desire, competency and character will influence any effort to push the limits of personal and professional potential.

Practice 1: Work to Develop High-Trust Relationships

If there is one constant, one absolute in the emotional and psychological makeup of the outstanding sales professionals I have known, it is their unwavering commitment to live and work in such a way as to inspire confidence in their *character*. *Character* always trumps competency. A sales career that is deeply invested in *creating excellence* must unequivocally be built on a foundation of strong personal *character*. No level of technical competency can compensate for a weak *character*.

Sales professionals are frequently parodied in American popular culture as fast talking, flamboyant, charismatic people who possess the verbal skills to charm a snake from a bottle, while separating a destitute widow from her last dollar. Professor Harold Hill in Meredith Wilson's acclaimed musical, *The Music Man*, is the quintessential con man masquerading as a salesman. His scam is to persuade parents that he can teach musically challenged kids how to play instruments. He promises to form a band and accepts pre-paid orders for instruments and uniforms from unsuspecting and rather gullible parents. With payments in hand and no orders ever placed, he slips quietly out of town and on to his next easy mark.

It would be nice to blame Hollywood producers for the distrust many people feel toward sales professionals. But the tale of Harold Hill resonates with audiences not because it is fanciful, but because portions of it are authentic.

A sales training program that does not emphasize *creating excellence* as the primary means of creating high-trust relationships with customers is the educational equivalent of Harold Hill leading a chorus of "Seventy-six Trombones" to increase product demand in fictional River City, Iowa. If trust is not established as the focal point of all customer interactions, the selling process will eventually collapse on itself. And if you fail to work with integrity in all interactions with your customers, any attempt to build trust will dissipate faster than the bellowing notes of a trombone on a windy night.

Make no mistake, customers are intelligent people who seek to make informed decisions about products that add value, solve problems, provide measurable benefit and meet budget constraints. Outstanding sales professionals respect their customers and recognize that the quality and constancy of their character determines their ability to develop high-trust, collaborative relationships. They eschew duplicity and recognize that a significant factor in product differentiation in their customers' minds will be the character and competency they consistently demonstrate.

Sales professionals who exploit customers for personal gain will eventually be exposed, and the damage is nearly always irreparable. If you learn to consistently forgo personal gain in an effort to better represent your customer's interest you will position yourself to receive a windfall of goodwill and trust that will pay dividends for a long time. Sales professionals endowed with great character understand that selling strategies designed to coerce, manipulate, spin, or otherwise control the selling process are short-term tactics that may produce orders, but will never produce long-term customer loyalty.

Principle B. Creating Excellence Begins with a Strong Desire to Produce Outstanding Work

As we move through this section, I will introduce to you two important practices that support this principle. Following each of the principles, there will be information on two associated practices. Please make careful note that buried in the information presented are several other rudimentary practices that are essential to skill development. And while I have not listed the practices separately, they are summarized in the short self-evaluation exercise at the end this section. This pattern will follow for the next two sections.

Please review the information carefully to guide your work on executing the practices.

What does it mean to *desire* to *create excellence* ? The dictionary definition may describe most of us, "To long or hope for, or to express a wish to." I have found in the world of professional selling that it takes more than a longing or a wish to propel performance to the higher echelons of productivity. Of all the references to desire listed at the right, the expression by Sir Thomas Fowell Buxton seems the closest to the application of desire in professional selling. Desire must consist of "energy – invincible determination."

Now that we have established common ground on this topic, let's consider a few more pertinent questions. Where does a desire to *create excellence* come from? Is it embedded in your DNA, or do you breathe it in at the corporate office? Do you grow into it over time, or does the longing for *excellence* live only in the hearts of the young? Do socioeconomic factors influence your desire for *excellence* ? Do political systems play a role? Is there a linear relationship between level of education and desire for *excellence*? Can a person who has been estranged from *excellence* for a lifetime embrace it at last and feel new passion for *excellent* personal performance?

What is a Desire for Excellence?

Webster's Ninth Collegiate Dictionary 1 : To long or hope for **2 :** To express a wish to **3 :** Conscious impulse toward something that promises enjoyment or satisfaction in its attainment **4 :** Longing, craving

William James – Events are influenced by our very great desires.

Mirabeau – Nothing is impossible to the man who can will.

Johann Wolfgang Von Goethe – He who is firm and resolute in will molds the world to himself.

Abraham Lincoln – Always bear in mind that your own resolution to succeed is more important than any other one thing.

Walter Lippmann – Ignore what a man desires and you ignore the very source of his power.

Sir Thomas Fowell Buxton – The longer I live, the more I am certain that the great difference between men, between the feeble and the powerful, between the great and the insignificant, is energy – invincible determination – a purpose once fixed, and then death or victory.

Robert Collier – Mind is all that counts. You can be whatever you make up your mind to be.

Walt Disney – All our dreams can come true – if we have the courage to pursue them.

My observations over many years spent monitoring the performance of hundreds of sales professionals suggests only a couple of definitive conclusions: External forces can impact short-term gain, and internal forces can produce long-term change. The external factors, such as monetary reward, recognition and security, will undeniably influence job performance. However, increased job performance does not necessarily translate to an increased appetite for personal and professional *excellence*.

Desire is not motivation. Desire is the conscious selection of course of action. Motivation is what moves us to follow that desired course. Desire is a rational choice made by the conscious mind. Motivation is the domain of the subconscious mind; it is the human energy allocated to achieve a desired result. Since the subconscious mind does not evaluate the conscious mind's rationale, the mental inputs which fuel motivation may or may not be rational.

Using a GPS navigational system to select an intended destination could represent desire. The GPS system will provide a map, along with a detailed list of actions required to reach the final destination. Clarity about outcomes is essential fuel for motivation, but a vision or map alone is rarely sufficient. The consistent *creation of excellence* will require both the map to the intended destination (the desire) and a reliable engine (motivation) in the car. A well-conceived desire is essential to producing motivation; however, as we will see chapter 7, steep mountain passes in the route ahead may require high-octane fuel; its production requires more work. There will be much more on this topic in chapter 7.

A desire to *create excellence* may be influenced by the external "hardware" around us, but for the most part it seems to result from "software" changes that originate in our minds. While I don't profess to understand the cause-and-effect nature of this complex mental and emotional predisposition that seems almost to propel people into orbit, I have gathered a few clues, indicators that tell whether or not the internal wiring is in place that will encourage a desire for *excellence* to continue to grow.

In the balance of this section we will be examining different characteristics of sales professionals who exhibit a desire to *create excellence* in their work. After you have reviewed this section on cultivating a desire for *excellence*, take a few minute to complete the self-assessment exercise before proceeding to the next section.

Practice 2: Work with the Expectation of Positive Results

Sales professionals with a strong desire for *excellence* have clarity about their intended destination, and they expect positive outcomes. They recognize that detours occur in the journey, along with the occasional flat tire, transmission repair, fender-bender and unforeseen weather delay. Setbacks and slowdowns are as much a part of professional selling as is the exhilaration of closing large contracts. A clear understanding of road conditions permits flexibility, allowing modification of short-term expectations. A strong desire to excel not only identifies the intended destination but helps to generate the map.

Sales professionals with a strong desire for *excellence* are unflappable. They refrain from incessant whining about competitors, because they understand that, when market conditions are replete with formidable product alternatives, the resulting competition inevitably produces better products, better prices, better deliveries and stronger and more capable product representatives. Sales professionals who are passionate about *excellence* enjoy and even thrive on competition. They respect worthy opponents, because they know that the constant pressure to improve raises their own level of performance.

I enjoy facing challenging market conditions with members of a sales team who are optimistic by nature. These are upbeat people; they smile a lot and have great senses of humor. As a general rule, people who face challenges expecting positive outcomes seem to be more creative. They are better problem-solvers, and they inspire confidence in other members of the sales team.

For most of three decades my company had provided a line of proprietary products nominally below the radar of a group of natural competitors. We dominated a certain market niche and experienced steady year-over-year revenue increases, while preserving our margins. Without any advance warning, a large competitor suddenly introduced a knock-off, and in the process created a buzz in the industry and in the minds of members of our sales team. Some of the sales team seemed angry and even feared eroding market share, plummeting prices, and reduced commissions. Other members of the sales team responded much differently. They were energized by the challenge, resolute about moving their territories forward, reconciled to increased competition, and confident of their own ability to succeed. To make a long story short, both groups were basically right about their respective outcomes.

The desire for *excellence* directly correlates to your ability to visualize positive outcomes, regardless of circumstances. With a solid desire in place, that mental image can produce enormous personal energy as it is received by the subconscious mind. It works like coal in a boiler, producing enormous heat. The foundation of all great achievement is this heat, this personal motivation, sustained by a constant desire.

I have also found that sales professionals who expect positive results are some of the most enjoyable people on the planet to work with. I know what you are thinking. You have worked with or for countless people who have achieved a measure of success in their lives, but were the most cantankerous, ornery, arrogant, condescending and consistently difficult people you ever met, right? So have I. Success in and of itself is not and never will be *excellence*. This discussion is about pursuing *excellence*. Successful outcomes are always the natural result of seeking *excellence*. Too often we mistake noteworthy achievement for success; achievement can occur in the absence of genuine *excellence*.

Excellence is reaching your potential in every aspect of your life. It is not a single life event or recognition for some important corporate initiative. Success and personal achievement only mark the path to the summit you seek. If you mistake success itself for the summit, you will be filled with the lingering discontent that comes with squandered potential. You may hear the applause, but in your heart you will know that your best effort still remains within you, unrealized.

Sales professionals with a desire for *excellence* are people of high character. It takes character to walk the steep and winding path to your own potential, especially when the siren calls of success beg you to stop your climb and revel in your own achievement. It takes character to keep climbing above accepted industry and cultural norms for success, in pursuit of something few people can understand. People of character keep walking, because they alone know that the realization of their own potential can never be defined by anyone other than themselves.

People who desire *excellence* respect others and demonstrate genuine interest in and concern for those with whom they work and associate, because this attitude is indicative of solid character.

Could this be a false positive? Can you find people who are wonderfully pleasant, kind, nurturing, supportive, and attentive to others, but lack an inner orientation toward *excellence* ? Absolutely! However, when you consider all of the other markers, I believe that it is highly unlikely to find a person of character, who possesses a strong desire for *excellence*, who is unpleasant to work with. The character required to produce *excellence* runs contrary to the brash impudence that is sometimes associated with people who have merely achieved success.

The expectation of positive results propels a person's willingness to take on difficult and challenging tasks. In my career I have worked with far too many people who seem to be guided by this simple question: "What is the least I can do to accomplish this task satisfactorily?" Sales professionals with a desire for *excellence* see the same task but respond differently. Their question is more like this: "How can I perform this task in the best possible way?"

The difference between these two questions can seem small, but the difference in respective outcomes is rarely small. Sales professionals who operate with the second mindset create a lot of positive energy for problem solving. They think critically and originally. They use available resources and constantly seek input from mentors and associates.

Sales professionals of character are energized by challenges that may completely overwhelm those of weaker character. Both may seem confident about the outcomes. Both may be right.

Like life, selling consists of certain tasks and responsibilities which may or may not be aligned with our own talents and attitudes. The level of success most of us experience in any endeavor will depend on how well we do the tasks that are naturally difficult for us, rather than how we excel at the tasks which are naturally easy.

I have observed many sales professionals who possess natural talent for presenting and teaching, but who lack the self-discipline to prospect consistently and to do the tedious follow-up required to close orders. One of the most naturally gifted presenters I ever hired failed miserably in selling, because of an unwillingness to develop proficiency in the more mundane tasks of the profession. Selling requires discipline and proficiency in a wide array of skills. A willingness to perform even mundane tasks consistently is one measurement of a person's desire to *create excellence*.

In most instances, sales professionals who work and think expecting positive results exceed expectations of the sales leadership team. Sales professionals with a desire to *create excellence* weave a distinct pattern into the fabric of their careers. They are able to stitch together various pieces of their lives, which have diverse shapes and sizes, in such a way that all the pieces seem to fit together. Something as pedestrian as a letter to a client may have the same feel as a keynote speech to a large group of customers. The commonality between two tasks is in the quality of the work.

People passionate about *excellence* seldom compartmentalize their lives. Because they focus on the standard of *excellence* in all facets of their lives, once they find the right pitch, they tend to produce notes of a similar tonal quality whether they are prospecting for new clients, completing reports for the corporate office or conducting annual planning sessions for their territory. The pattern repeats itself. Unfortunately, the same is generally true for members of the sales team who languish in mediocrity.

A move toward *excellence* requires a change in thinking; the change in thinking begins with desire.

Exceeding expectations generally requires consistently producing your best work in every situation. It is a simple concept, but the effort rarely goes unnoticed.

Once, early in my career, I was traveling west from Washington, DC, on a flight out of what is now Reagan National Airport. The person sitting next to me was a distinguished-looking gentleman, who appeared to be in his late fifties or early sixties. An hour or so into the flight, we began talking about various topics. This ultimately led to an in-depth discussion of his professional career.

His name was Milton Barlow. For many years he had worked as a senior officer for the Marriott Corporation. He told me how J. Willard Marriott had recruited him out of college to work in a business that consisted of what he described as "root beer stands" and the rudiments of a small hotel chain. His story was fascinating, and his enthusiasm for being involved in the transformation of a company from a fledgling startup to a worldwide industry leader was captivating.

As we neared our destination, my thoughts turned to my own career. By every definition my twenty-something mind could imagine, this man represented the success I sought. Surely he could provide some insight, some novel idea, some insider formula that would accelerate my own journey in the same direction.

So I asked the question. It sounded something like this: "What one piece of advice could you give to me that you have learned over your many years in business that contributed the most to your success?"

At the time his answer seemed unremarkable. Thirty years later, his response still echoes in my ears. "Just do your best," was his reply. "In any situation, regardless of the task, do your best. If you can do that, success will never be far away." Working to exceed expectations is simply about doing your best. Doing your best is a reliable indicator of your desire for *excellence*.

Having a desire for *excellence* is commonly associated with an ability to work with a sense of urgency about important matters. Knowing which tasks need effective and immediate responses requires the deployment of the sales professional's skill and judgment as a leader. The vast majority of issues confronted in a given day may not fall into this category. It is when more urgent issues periodically surface that the quality of the response will display the sales professional's desire for *excellence*.

There are some issues that simply need action right now, not in fifteen minutes, and certainly not when you get back to the office tomorrow morning. They demand that you stop what you are doing and mobilize intense concentration to respond appropriately. The need for immediate action may make you uncomfortable and require you to face a potential conflict. But the surest way to make an urgent problem worse is to show a complete lack of urgency in responding to it.

Sales professionals who desire *excellence* make consistently good judgments about pressing problems. They are undeceived by matters that masquerade as vexing problems needing immediate corrective action, which threaten to drain us of valuable time and energy, but in the end are nothing more than agenda-driven diversions manufactured largely out of self-interest.

Sales professionals who are deeply immersed in the work of the territory stand as vanguards, keeping careful watch over all-important matters that may impact customers or company associates. As a rule they anticipate outcomes and reliably forecast potential trouble spots. This vigilance in the territory, coupled with judicious questions, can usually unmask the impostors that would otherwise take hostages and sap valuable time.

I have also found that there is an interesting relationship between a desire for *excellence* and a willingness to learn, to accept feedback and to be teachable. Sales professionals who genuinely desire to produce *excellence* learn from every available resource. They are the most engaged people at sales meetings and training seminars, and they ask good questions and take careful notes. They seem to have an insatiable appetite for information about the product, the customer, the industry, competitors, and the profession in general. They are hungry to learn and will welcome assistance and training from any available source.

Teachable sales professionals are easily identified. During the initial hiring process, they come to the interview with pages of questions about the product, the company and the position. Through their insightful questions, they conduct their own interview. They scratch and claw for more and more information. They are resourceful people who have the ability to learn even in environments that are not well equipped to provide training and support commensurate with their expectations.

Sales professionals who have learned to be teachable want feedback about their performance. They seek coaching to improve presentations, prospecting methods, new promotional methods, contract closings, and follow-up. They ask for feedback for the purpose of improving their performance, not to elicit praise. They are the quintessential tinkerers, always standing in front of the mirror of their professional lives, looking for ways to improve and ideas that will yield even slight gains in performance.

Teachable sales professionals find ways to learn from just about every circumstance and every interaction. They are able to sift through the irrelevant aspects of underperforming associates' professional lives and learn when others off-handedly dismiss. They are seldom, if ever, satisfied with present methods. They operate with a basic belief that there are better ideas to be discovered and ample room to improve.

Sales professionals with a strong desire to *create excellence* are eager to learn and are repulsed by the intransigence that stifles personal growth. By nature they are positive, and their genuine humility about personal improvement is often infectious in an organization. In almost every instance the sales professionals who consistently produce exceptional work are also the members of the sales team who are most receptive to new ideas and improved methods, even when they require the surrender of deeply-entrenched formulas that have been successful in the past. These are professionals who are progressive and proactive, who respect change and work well in dynamic sales environments.

Practice 3: Produce Consistent Quality in Your Work

Sales professionals who desire to *create excellence* diligently work through every detail of important client meetings in advance. They anticipate questions, prepare for the inevitable objections, and consider legitimate methods to resolve misunderstandings or confusion about product performance. They prepare to respond meticulously to any follow-up questions or assignments at the beginning of the client meeting. When you leave after a well-prepared meeting, the customer is confident of your ability and respects the professionalism with which you responded to questions and provided workable solutions to problems.

Consistent preparation for each client meeting is a major hurdle for most sales professionals. Over time one may begin to assume that there are only small differences between customers. That assumption can lead to meetings that focus on product performance and not on identifying customer needs. Preparations for every client meeting should to be made in the context of the customer's unique needs. If you can't identify the differences in needs from one customer to the next, rest assured that your competitors will.

For most of the past thirty years a large communications technology company has visited me to review our annual plan and discuss the integration of their information products into our business. Their presentations vary little from year to year. They are monologues punctuated by well-prepared graphics depicting the results of recent national surveys which show their market leadership. Such presentations work well at the annual shareholders meeting, but fall flat in one-on-one meetings with customers.

A chasm divides this company from us, their customers. Far too often these wellmeaning product representatives seem incapable of either swimming across the channel or even inflating a raft. I need help in growing our business, and they have important information products that could make help us develop new markets or expanding existing ones. While I need their products, what I really want is twenty minutes of their time spent trying to understanding our business, so that they can propose some viable and affordable solutions. They come to each meeting well prepared to discuss new product iterations but they are ill prepared to assist me in using their products to solve pressing problems in our business.

The key to being well prepared for meetings is your preparation to discuss your product in the specific context of your customer's needs. This is difficult, and it requires a greater commitment of time than preparing for a mediocre meeting. Sales professionals who have a passion to *create excellence* have the uncanny ability to see their own product from their customer's perspective. This skill gradually develops as the sales professional gets to know the customer and develops the ability to recite all the critical factors influencing that customer's product selection and buying decisions. Sales professionals who are well prepared for each meeting have *excellence* within their grasp.

I have also found that a strong desire for *excellence* produces a strong commitment. Sales professionals who are committed to goals and objectives for the territory find ways to accomplish the difficult tasks that can make the difference between success and failure, and very often account for the small margin between a good year and a great year. Being committed requires a person to follow through on obligations and promises, even if those promises are made to oneself.

Constancy in honoring commitments is an integral quality of great leaders. Leadership subordinates self-interest to a commitment to others. Sales professionals who are effective leaders identify clearly defined objectives and have the self-discipline to execute all the tasks necessary to achieve the stated goals.

Sales professionals who refuse to keep commitments to themselves find it easier to justify breaking commitments to customers and associates. A decision to *create excellence* frequently requires you to break old habits and to develop new skills that will push you closer to your potential as a sales professional, while moving your territory closer to optimum revenue levels. This is not an easy process. For most of us the starting point is a willingness simply to walk daily in a direction that leads to honoring commitments and realizing all significant objectives.

Too often sales professionals rationalize blatant disregard of commitments on the grounds that they are nonessential elements of success in a territory. True, the territory plan is a fluid document that needs constant revision as new information becomes available. But this should never justify off-handedly dismissing commitments. Honoring a commitment of any kind is a clear benchmark of a person's desire to *create excellence*. It is impossible to sustain a long-term pursuit of *excellence* without a strong personal resolve to keep commitments.

For some sales professionals prospecting can be a tedious task. While no one would dispute its importance to building a strong and vibrant sales territory, it is not a task that comes easily for most people. The constant flow of new customers into a territory is vital for most sales professionals. The outstanding sales professionals I have observed make a specific commitment each week to allocate a designated amount of time to this important sales practice. These members of the sales team become consistent revenue leaders, not because of an innate love for prospecting, but rather through the simplicity of their resolve to honor a commitment to meet   a specific objective.

It is normal to gravitate to tasks we enjoy, and to those which more closely align with our natural skill set and talents. It may also be normal to avoid doing things we find less desirable. But a desire for *excellence* is not normal. For most of us it is counterintuitive. It may require more effort than leaders of the sales team reasonably expect. It may require longer hours on difficult tasks and more time spent developing uncomfortable skills than most sales professionals are willing to offer.

Excellence is about realizing potential – first yours, then the territory's. Only keepers of commitments will manifest the desire necessary to optimize both.

I find that one of the distinguishing characteristics of outstanding sales professionals is their ability to listen. Good listeners are able to engage all of their senses in the experience of listening. They are vigilant seekers of information.

I am frequently amazed by people who have learned to be good listeners. They seem to have an innate ability to listen not just with their ears, but with their eyes and their heart. It isn't something they have been trained to do. It is a natural ability, born of a genuine desire to learn and understand another person. They hear subtle inflections in the tone of a voice. They interpret shifting posture. They understand the implications of eyes that refuse to make direct contact. They process all relevant information and make sense of it. They hear words, but they intuit intent.

During the 1992 presidential campaign there was a constant barrage of questions to incumbent president George H. W. Bush about the sluggish condition of the

U.S. economy. In one memorable moment of the nation's first ever town hall-style presidential debate with challengers Bill Clinton and H. Ross Perot, President Bush lost concentration. In doing so he underscored a nagging perception about the sitting president: he was out of touch with the lives of the American people. His response was clear and on message, but his actions left millions of viewers aghast.

What he said was, "Of course you feel it when you are President of the United States; that is why I am trying to do something about it." What he did was glance at this watch, as if bored. His voice tried to persuade the public that he understood the problem; his eyes betrayed him. Very few who were watching missed the point.

Not all messages are so blatant. Most are subtle, hidden behind the mask of compliance and the pretense of goodwill. Even today presidential historians differ on whether or not George Bush's ill-timed glance at his watch cost him a second term, but most agree that it harmed his campaign.

While the interaction of sales professionals with customers will not dictate the course of the free world, it will nonetheless have an unmistakable impact on revenue generated in the world of an important client. The message may not be as clear as the downward glance of eyes at a wristwatch, but it is likely that during every meeting there will be subtle yet important clues communicated in ways other than the spoken word. The attentive sales professional that detects and understands these clues is more likely to end up on the happy side of the sales equivalent of a landslide election.

Listening is about learning and understanding. Sales professionals who desire *excellence* are passionate about improving, receiving feedback, and understanding any new idea that could help them to maximize their personal potential. A person's skill in listening is one barometer by which to measure desire. Listening reflects the intent of the heart. Without complete alignment of heart and mind in the pursuit of *excellence*, listening will be little more than a manipulation technique used to advance an agenda. Seekers of *excellence* eschew manipulation, and the only item on their agenda is becoming their best. They listen to understand the needs of those they serve and to identify ways to make needed improvements. When one listens with this intent, powerful progress can be made toward any goal.

The ability to ask good, relevant, insightful questions is a common trait of sales professionals who desire *excellence*. A mind full of probing questions is akin to a heart filled with a desire to listen intently. Both share an almost singular need to gather more information. Good questions are the natural result of a desire to peel away layers of misconception and doubt. Asking good, relevant questions to move the discovery process forward in a meaningful way is like holding up a lantern in a dark room. Thoughtful questions illuminate conversation and bring unresolved problems to light, so that viable solutions can be offered.

The ability to ask simple, precise, probing questions that are not combative, to be illuminating but not intrusive and inquisitive without being petulant, depends mostly on intent. Given enough time in even the simplest conversation, our questions ultimately reveal our real intent. Skilled sales professionals, who possess broad competency in the industry and a deep understanding of customer needs, employ questions as naturally as a rancher uses a rope or an electrician uses a voltage meter.

Probing questions designed to explore the client's needs more fully are as essential to selling as a scalpel is to surgery. Client meetings without thoughtful questions can produce a kind of scar tissue, formed from the estrangement that occurs in the absence of collaboration. Collaboration between customers and sales professionals grows – sometimes exponentially – when questions reveal needs and illuminate workable solutions.

Setting and achieving clear goals is another unmistakable marker of people who have the desire to create *excellence* in their lives. A basic commitment to set and achieve goals is so essential that it seems impossible to create any measure of sustained *excellence* without it.

So much has been and will be said in this book about goal-setting because of the integral role it plays in our achieving personal and professional potential. Goals are intermediate benchmarks that establish a natural progression to the realization of potential.

There are few certainties in life, but here are two of them. Every sales professional I have worked with in thirty years who seeks a sustained measure of *excellence* does so by setting goals and working passionately to achieve them. On the contrary, virtually all of the underperforming sales professionals I have known share a common trait: a lack of consistency in setting and achieving personal goals. This is not coincidental. Those who really desire *excellence* distinguish themselves by setting and achieving goals.

Desire for Excellence

Score 1 - 10 (1 = Strongly Disagree   10 = Strongly Agree)

	YOUR SCORE
1. I am teachable.	
2. I am committed to territory objectives.	
3. I face challenges expecting positive outcomes.	
4. I am a good listener.	
5. I ask good questions.	
6. I am always on time.	
7. I am well prepared for every meeting.	
8. I work with a sense of urgency.	
9. I am willing to perform difficult tasks.	
10. I work to exceed expectations.	
TOTAL POINTS	

Being on time to business appointments may seem trivial and unrelated to high-level performance, but I beg to differ. Arriving on time – or early – for meetings with customers may not be a panacea, but it is one of the most reliable indicators of wellmanaged territories. Sales professionals who are punctual have better-managed territories and above-average customer satisfaction. They meet revenue goals more consistently, and they excel in product comprehension.

A meeting scheduled with a customer is a commitment. Honoring commitments with exactness is essential to building trust. Sales professionals who are complacent about commitments of any kind, especially those that impact clients' work schedules, will rarely be taken seriously. Being late to appointments with clients is rude and reveals an insensitivity that interferes with collaboration. Being late to an appointment, especially without calling in advance to warn the customer, is simply unacceptable.

For most customers the product and the product representative are inextricably connected. In nearly all new relationships, customers assess the sales professional's competence and capabilities with the same intense scrutiny they direct to the product. Sales professionals who arrive late for meetings therefore calls *the product's* performance into question, not just their own. At its worst, tardiness carries the odor of arrogance. At best it implies a casual attitude toward about important details. Neither condition fosters the development of trust.

Outstanding sales professionals know that when it comes to building strong relationships with clients, there are no small or insignificant matters. As Benjamin Franklin liked to say, "Even a small leak will sink a big ship." Selling in complex environments is a demanding voyage through stormy seas. There will be waves enough crashing over the side of the ship. The last thing you need is to spend extra time and effort bailing water that rushes in through cracks you cause in the hull by failing to honor your commitments.

Sales professionals who arrive on time show respect for their customers, their products, companies they represent, and themselves. Promptness is the norm; while there may be demerits for being late, don't expect dividends for arriving early. Dividends are paid only when you exceed expectations.

Principle C. Improved Competency Improves the Prospect of Creating Excellence

Character is, for the most part, who you are as a person and as a sales professional. Competency is about your proficiency in the critical areas of selling. While the dictionary definition describes competency as "requisite or adequate ability or qualities," the leaders quoted to the right seem to push the threshold above the baseline of simple adequacy. J. Paul Getty reminds us that success in business (or selling) requires us to know "all it is possible to know." The former NFL great Joe Namath explains proficiency in quarterbacking as preparing in such a way that "I know I can do what I have to do." Competency in selling is both knowing and doing.

What is Competency?

Webster's Ninth Collegiate Dictionary 1 :
Having requisite or adequate ability or qualities
2 : Having the capacity to function or develop
in a particular way

J. Paul Getty – To succeed in business, to
reach the top, an individual must know all it is
possible to know about that business.

Charles E. Wilson – There is no royal road;
you've got to work a good deal harder than
most people want to work.

Alexander Graham Bell – A man, as a general
rule, owes very little to what he is born with. A
man is what he makes of himself.

Benjamin Franklin – There are three things
extremely hard: steel, a diamond and to know
one's self.

Andrew Carnegie – As I grow older, I pay less
attention to what men say. I just watch what
they do.

Joe Namath – What I do is prepare myself until
I know I can do what I have to do.

In this section about competency it is not my intent to give you a simple definition, but rather to show how you can identify levels of competency in your professional life. As you work through the section, "Character Traits of Competent Sales Professionals," try to make a mental note of the many and varied ways that competency is demonstrated in selling. At the end of the section you should be able to identify at least eight different ways in which competency is demonstrated in how you work.

Just remember, most sales environments are dynamic, with rapid change and wellpositioned competitors. Multiple product options and aggressive pricing permit the customer to select features and benefits that best align with product selection criteria. With the proliferation of information on every topic imaginable, it may seem that customers can research and select products at their leisure, without the help – or interference – of product representatives. This may be true when shopping for durable goods from big box retailers, but it is rarely true in transactions involving sales professionals. The technical skill and competency of the sales professional remains a significant influence in most final product selection and purchasing decisions.

Sales professionals who listen effectively, understand the customer's needs, have a clear view of the product selection criteria, have a good working knowledge of the competitive alternatives and are sensitive to the reality of budget constraints can become the primary resource customers use to differentiate products. This collaborative relationship is the by-product of sales professionals who consistently display exceptional technical skill and competency.

Practice 4: Work to Improve Your Sales Ability and Add Value to Your Customers

Sales professionals who value competency as an essential component of product differentiation develop a passionate obsession with learning. They are constantly reading relevant material about the industry, market trends, competitor changes, economic forecasts, and customers. They become skillful users of their own product and understand all of the relevant technical nuances. Their mastery of the product enables them to address a wide range of questions without turning to the technical support team. They incorporate continuous learning into their regular routine to the point that study is as commonplace for them as exercise is for a person who is passionate about health and fitness.

Sales professionals who are passionate learners generally come to sales training meetings with good questions and leave with pages of notes. They ask questions to understand, not to score political points with their peers. They can dine at the training table without ever getting full. Their appetite for knowledge is exceptional and insatiable. They have learned to recapture down time by listening to educational programs while traveling in a car or reviewing notes and technical material while traveling on a plane. Their feet are constantly moving in the direction of expanding their capability to be effective resources to their customers in a wide range of issues related to their product.

Sales professionals of great competency, who are passionate learners, understand that the responsibility for expanding their knowledge ultimately rests on them, not on corporate training programs. They distinguish themselves by their intimate knowledge of competitors, which equals their understanding of their own product. More significantly, passionate learners know their customers' environment. They know the industry, its regulations, its technology, the intricacies of testing and approvals, the complexities of budget constraints and the overall ambitions which drive product selection. They have developed the ability to see the buying decision from the customer's perspective – an ability which comes only from a longstanding commitment to learn from all available resources.

Highly competent sales professionals are familiar with all the subtle nuances of the territory in which they operate. They are well-versed in industry trends and maintain current, reliable forecasting data. They understand that their own ability to be reliable technical resources and dependable consultants to their customers plays a significant role in the buying decision.

Any serious effort to *create excellence* will require diligent study and an ongoing commitment to be as knowledgeable about competitors products as you are about your own. We live in an age where information is readily accessible via the Internet. In many instances even the most proprietary information can be accessed in a matter of moments. Consequently, there is no excuse for sales professionals not being current on market trends, changes in regulation, economic forecasts, and new product iterations from competitors, which may impact customers' buying decisions. Those who remain indifferent to this information compromise their ability to become effective and reliable resources to their customers. Over time, the result will be an ever-diminishing market share.

Customers are sophisticated, discriminating buyers, whose loyalty to products and companies shifts continually with the emergence of new ideas, new technology, new product features, and new competitors. The sales professional's presumption that previous buying preferences portend the future is dangerous folly. Highperformance sales professionals who are programmed to *create excellence* exert a sense of consistent leadership in their relations with their customers. They are obsessed with improvement. Those who improve technically add value to their product offering and can reasonably claim a continuance of business. Those who don't improve forfeit opportunities for future business.

The effort that was sufficient to produce a result even a few years ago will likely not be enough today. Nowhere is this more apparent than in the world of athletic competition. Gold medal performances from previous Olympiads may not be sufficient to advance an athlete to the finals four years later. The constant pressure from competitors to raise the bar of competitive *excellence* requires all participants to improve their skills. Only when skills are constantly refined and improved will there be recognition on the awards podium at the conclusion of the event.

The same is true in professional selling. Providing your customers today with the same level of technical support as you did two years ago will not produce the same result. The bar is raised daily, and customers' expectations rise with it. The process of re-earning business from your customers requires constant attention; you must continually improve your ability to help them answer their ever-changing needs.

Sales professionals need to know their competitors almost as well as they know their own products. Evaluating competing products can be a daunting task for the customer. Where high-trust relationships exist, knowledgeable sales professionals can be an invaluable resource, helping customers to make sense of the chaos. Sales professionals who can explain differences without derision and benefits without belittling are the customer's indispensable allies in the decision-making process.

Sales professionals who are skilled in *Personal Leadership* exercise good judgment and restrain their urges to make unfavorable comments about competitors. They are able to provide credible information while refraining from unsubstantiated, self-serving, purposely demeaning gossip. High-performance sales professionals use their expert knowledge of competitors to serve customers, not to advance their own agenda. Intelligent customers can tell the difference

Becoming a skillful product technician is an important demonstration of competency in selling. A sales professional who is a skillful product technician is not simply a person who can regurgitate the technical details of the product. That exercise requires the head, but it is the effective deployment of the heart that distinguishes the skillful product technician from traditional product representatives. Involving the heart is a *Personal Leadership* skill. A sales professional who feels a sense of compassion for the customer can position the product clearly in terms that address that customer's unique problems and needs.

Sales professionals routinely give customers technical product "dumps." In doing so, they subtly abdicate their responsibility to think creatively within the context of the customer's needs. This type of presentation suggests, "Here is what my product can do; I will let you do the intellectual heavy lifting and find a place that makes the most sense."

It has been said that a gentleman is "a person who knows how to play the accordion and doesn't." In selling we might say, "A professional is a person who could explain every technical nuance of the product and doesn't." An excellent sales professional may be a skillful product technician, but consistently exercises restraint. Despite having a commanding knowledge of the product's benefits and superlative features, the professional consciously selects only relevant material that will benefit the customer.

A skillful product technician is a sort of editor, constantly deleting lines from the presentation, if they are not in the overall interest of the customer. It is a boorish display of arrogance for a sales professional to waste the customer's time dumping heaps of non-essential product data. The skillful product technician has mastered the ability to select from a large inventory of information only the few items that will be of most benefit to the customer making a buying decision.

Sales professionals of distinction work to build trust with all stakeholders in the enterprise. Both the long-term strategy and the tactical map of the territory represent the collaborative thinking of senior sales leaders, the technical team at the corporate office, customers, and fellow associates on the sales team. Those who seek short cuts in the execution of a long-term plan wade in a pool of their own arrogance, their boots filled with thin promises and unsupportable claims about product performance.

Sales professionals who seek a high level of performance through their commitment to *creating excellence* work within the parameters and practices established by the organization. Contravening these practices is duplicitous and disloyal; it is not the action of a sales professional of character and competency. Some sales professionals style themselves "mavericks" and routinely violate established policy "to serve better the interest of their clients." In truth, these are charlatans, masquerading as customer advocates while they promote their own self-interest.

Competent sales professionals and thoughtful customers recognize that it is impossible to belittle the organization while extolling the virtues of its product. Where deficiencies exist in organizational practices and policies, high-performance sales professionals leverage the collateral of high-trust relationships to make needed corrections. They become the sort of catalyst for change within their organizations that they seek to become in the buying habits of their customers.

In dynamic sales environments competency is demonstrated by compliance with standard organizational practices, not by wanton disregard or disrespect. Sales professionals who disrespect the companies they work for are more likely to violate other commitments; this propensity will not go unnoticed by customers. It is also true that any organization that seeks to control and manipulate associates by capricious policy changes, failure to honor compensation agreements, or unwillingness to respect corporate commitments forfeits any reasonable expectation of generating a culture that fosters high performance. The ecology of these organizations is toxic; the sales professional in such an organization should find another employer.

Compliance with standard practices is not an excuse for static thinking. Creativity and innovation are life-sustaining commodities in any organization and rely upon the imagination of the sales team for sustenance. Even the most dynamic organizations, where change is fueled by constantly evolving market conditions, require the sense of order fostered by compliance with standard practices. Compliance with standard practices is what allows a great aircraft to take flight. Likewise, competent sales professionals work with, not against, standard practice and in so doing soar to new heights.

One of the mistakes I made early in my career was tolerating members of the sales team who were consistently noncompliant with organizational practices, but were producing respectable sales revenue. Justification seemed simple enough, when I looked at the monthly revenue totals, but my overlooking their abuses was little more than an organizational sell-out. Rogue members of a sales team invariably take hostages, and for all practical purposes I was bound and gagged.

My voice was muted because I tolerated unacceptable practices. The result was a type of organizational mediocrity. Sales leaders who ignore behavior that consistently violates standard practices for any reason, including revenue production, have lost control of the organization. They allow their own convenience to obscure the *vision* leaders should have, which could save them from the pitfalls of organizational permissiveness.

Practice 5: Understand Customer Needs and Communicate Clearly

Much of the discussion about competency in selling revolves around a clear focus on customers and an ability to communicate effectively. Sales professionals who exhibit great competency present their product in a context that is directly aligned with the customer's needs. Selling solutions in this manner is a key *Personal Leadership* imperative that requires considerable skill and technical competency.

Product representatives often discuss how their product solves various problems for customers. But it is one thing for a product representative to define the solutions based on product features and benefits; it is quite another for sales professionals to define solutions based on their comprehensive knowledge of client needs. The phrase "solution-oriented selling" is an engaging topic for sales meetings; it suggests that the sales professional knows which solutions are relevant to the customer.

Selling solutions based on client needs depends on knowledge that cannot be manufactured in a marketing think-tank. The most reliable method for gathering this type of intelligence is listening to customers. This requires a willingness to listen with the intent to understand, not with the intent to influence outcomes. Only a person of character will set aside self-interest long enough to understand completely and genuinely the needs of someone else, with no direct concern for personal gain. In the final analysis, the only legitimate solutions are those defined by the customer. Any claims to the contrary are little more than the sound of wind rustling through the trees. And the longer the wind blows, the more barren the branches will become.

The single most distinguishing aspect of competent sales professionals is developing the capacity to work consistently to understand customers' needs. Sales professionals who possess this skill clearly differentiate themselves from their competitors. While this is a difficult skill to acquire and implement effectively, it is easy to identify. This singular ability lends a conspicuous professionalism to the interactions with customers.

Customers' willingness to collaborate with sales professionals largely depends upon this aspect of the relationship. When the client truly believes that the sales professional understands all aspects of the buying decision from the customer's perspective, collaboration can begin. While many sales transactions occur every day without significant collaboration, it is in the atmosphere of collaboration that the best potential solutions can be discovered. These discoveries, in turn, produce satisfied customers and contribute to long-term relationships.

Simple questions may not be enough to clarify customer needs. In the beginning customers may not fully understand their own needs. For example, an architect designing a building in a large metropolitan area may be unaware of recently adopted seismic requirements that may impact product selection decisions. A health care professional in a rural community may not have current information about new federal guidelines regarding the disposal of certain medical equipment. A couple planning for retirement may not know of tax law changes that may permit more aggressive investing in tax-deferred annuities.

A customer's lack of clarity about a need does not diminish its reality. If there is a relationship of trust, the customer will be willing to accept information from the sales professional that may influence buying decisions. Sales professionals who respect their customers, who understand their objectives, empathize with their concerns, identify with their reservations, and constantly seek to understand the full context of the buying decision will be welcome collaborators in the decision-making process. Then their teaching about technical aspects of the buying decision will be effective.

Sales professionals who seek to understand customer needs are not content with standard surveys and conventional methods of need analysis. They know that canned questions are far less important than their determination to understand the customer's needs. Those who are passionately determined to understand customer needs recognize that the buying decision ultimately must be in the customer's best interest, not the salesperson's. In most instances, if we treated our customers as our best friends, there would be no need to rehearse standard questions to be asked during an initial interview.

During much of the past three decades, I have asked this question during interviews with prospective members of our sales team: "During your first meeting with a client, the meeting is cut short and you have only five minutes. What would you want to accomplish during those five minutes?" The response is almost always something like this: "I would provide a brief product summary and ask for a return appointment." I fear that is precisely what happens too much of the time.

Skillful, competent sales professionals begin initial meetings gathering information, not dispensing it. Only when the customer's needs are clearly established should the product be introduced as the solution to pressing problems or to provide some other benefit to the customer. In initial interviews with customers, less is more – less talking about your product, less chattering about potential benefits, and less insistence about shifting buying practices.

Customers need sales professionals to be more willing to listen and ask intelligent questions, and less eager to make flashy presentations and spectacular promises. In the final analysis, in most buying transactions it is the performance of the sales professional, not the product, that counts. That performance is immeasurably enhanced if the sales professional is willing to set the product aside and concentrate fully on understanding every aspect of the customer. On that understanding a longterm relationship can be built that will transcend even price differences.

Over the past three decades I have listened to countless sales presentations by product representatives who have been well trained to explain how their superlative product would fundamentally change the complexion of our business. They skillfully integrate technology into their presentations and support all conclusions with sophisticated research data, field studies, and customer satisfaction surveys. It is always quite interesting; and on occasion it is even relevant.

As a general rule, however, I am disappointed by the lack of preparation these sales professionals consistently demonstrate. There seems to be an epidemic of product representatives and organizations operating on the basic belief that selling is nothing more than persuasion, and assuming that the buying decision in most transactions is driven by emotion. It is not surprising that their presentations are designed to create a certain level of emotional intensity. The product representative measures the crescendo of emotion in the meeting, and at precisely the right moment moves to close the sale by asking a series of questions which lead the customer towards a buying decision.

Sales professionals who exhibit traits of both character and competency understand that techniques work well for managing contact files in a large database or for planning purposes, to execute the annual sales plan. They also recognize that techniques are not designed to change or control the behavior of people. Outstanding sales professionals have learned that the process of selling is something that is done *with* another person and not *to* another person. Selling at the professional level seeks the customer's consent to effect a transaction that has clearly-defined benefits. The responsibility of making a persuasive argument for how a product solves problems and adds benefit and value rests squarely on the sales professional.

These are two contrasting views of selling. One diminishes the customer with strategies designed to manipulate and ultimately control behavior. The other operates from the basic assumption that customers are intelligent people who are capable of processing relevant data to make informed buying decisions. Which view sales professionals choose in large measure reflects their own beliefs about themselves.

Competent sales professionals naturally respect and value customers. They refuse to act out of self-interest; instead they are vigilant in protecting their customers' interest. They recognize that the trust they have earned through character and competency must never be compromised. Selling that relies on manipulation techniques is easy to learn and equally easy to deliver. Selling that is rooted in character and competency is difficult to learn and can take years to execute fully. One validates and affirms the customers' competency to make informed decisions. The other marginalizes the customer by assuming that a clever appeal to selfinterest, coupled with leading questions, will produce mutual benefit.

Developing the skill to present your product in a professional manner is an essential selling competency. A formal presentation to customers is a critical moment for two reasons. First, it is an opportunity to present the product and to explain how the product meets a need or solves a problem for the customer. The second reason is equally important. It is an opportunity for the sales professional to demonstrate proficiency with the product, to acknowledge industry trends or the impact of new technology on the market, and to demonstrate comprehension of the customer's needs.

Professional presenters understand their audience. They refrain from esoteric and confusing techno-babble. They are driven by a need to communicate with clarity, and the tone of their presentation reflects compassion for the listener. Their material is relevant to the customer, and they exercise restraint in the volume of information they present.

Outstanding sales professionals understand that the formal product presentation will ultimately say as much about them as it says about the product. Customers listening to the presentation will be influenced by the technical merits of the product as well as the technical skill of the presenter. Both are essential to moving the sales process forward to a final buying decision.

Professional presenters display spontaneity. They abhor repetitious phrases or canned one-liners. Each presentation is unique, even if it technically similar to others. While standing in close proximity to their audience, sales professionals can sense the mood of the room and adapt the pace of the presentation to different levels of understanding, or even move in a completely different direction, as needed. They have the skill to speak with their mouths and listen with their eyes simultaneously.

Sales professionals who are expert presenters innately know that the quality of their presentation will be judged ultimately not by whether they covered all the relevant topics on their agenda, but whether the group understood some basic elements that will help them in future product selection decisions. Effective presenters know that presenting is not about them, but rather about those who have come to listen. Presenting is not performing; it is ultimately about the effective two-way transfer of information.

Professional presenters respect time commitments. They use technology, samples, and graphic material appropriately to enhance the learning process, but they never abdicate to electronic media their responsibility to teach effectively. They recognize that the presentation is a measure of their skill and competency as sales professionals, and they seek opportunities to differentiate their abilities from those of their competitors.

Sales professionals who are competent presenters work within themselves. Their presentation is a distinct and genuine reflection of who they are, not of who they think their audience would like them to be. Effective presenting does not have to consist of high-energy histrionics or wellorchestrated humorous anecdotes. Your presentation needs to be clear, reasoned, well timed, and comfortably placed in the context of customer needs. Any effort to do something else will compromise your credibility and promote a sense of incredulity in your listeners. Customers who like and trust you but remain skeptical about the product are still likely to make favorable buying decisions. Customers who like your product and trust its ability to perform but are skeptical about you are likely to make unfavorable buying decisions.

In addition to making good presentations, you also need to have proven competency in teaching. Teaching and presenting are two entirely different skill sets. A competent sales professional has acquired both. Presenting is typically done before larger groups; there is little intimacy with the audience. It is generally the one-way flow of information, from the presenter to the audience. It is more formal and less personal. While there is a frequent need to adapt, without ongoing feedback from the audience it is rarely necessary to change the substance of the presentation.

Where presenting is formal, teaching is informal. Presenting often lacks the sense of intimacy with the audience that effective teaching demands. Presenting typically follows a well-defined course determined in advance by the presenter. Teaching may begin with a well-defined course, but it constantly adapts itself to the students. As a general rule presenting is an easier skill to acquire because it is more structured, less flexible, and uncomplicated by constant interaction with the audience. Presenting asks the group to follow you to a previously-established destination. Teaching asks the group – within the limits of the material – "What is your desired destination?"

As a practical matter, most sales professionals I have known are above-average presenters and below-average teachers. Effective teaching is a skill that all competent sales professionals should aspire to attain. In fact, if most sales professionals would openly talk about their role with clients as *teaching* rather than *presenting*, the quality of communication would dramatically improve.

Competency

Score 1 - 10 (1 = Strongly Disagree 10 = Strongly Agree)

	YOUR SCORE
1. I am passionate about learning.	
2. I am a skillful product technician.	
3. I work to sell solutions.	
4. I am compliant to organizational practices & policies.	
5. I am a professional presenter.	
6. I am an effective teacher.	
7. I know my industry.	
8. I know my competitors.	
9. I seek collaboration with my customers.	
10. My customers trust me.	
TOTAL POINTS	

Teaching can be a risky proposition for most members of the sales team. It seems to surrender control over outcomes. But effective teaching should not mean allowing the students to define the curriculum; it should invite them to assume a higher level of personal ownership. The sales professionals I know who are competent and skillful teachers are inundated with questions. The quality of questions is generally in proportion to the quality of the teaching. Questions from participants are usually an excellent barometer, showing bhow well participants are working with and understanding the material.

Effective teachers create an environment that fosters learning. They pace the information to the level of the participants, review critical concepts, ask questions to measure comprehension levels and implement the use of an accountability tool. This tool can be as simple as a short handout with summary questions that participants are asked to complete on their own.

Effective teachers create an expectation of learning, while presenters often assume a sense of tacit toleration from the audience. There is an enormous difference between the two. If your product demands a deep level of understanding by your customers, you may need to shift from presenting to teaching.

Teachers measure their effectiveness by their students' comprehension and retention of the material. All too often, presenters measure their effectiveness by their own proficiency in presenting technical concepts. Sales professionals who are leaders seeking to work "at the end of the bar" recognize that the best way to have product information sink deep into the minds of customers is found in skillful teaching.

Principle D. People of Character Naturally Build Collaborative Relationships

What is character in professional selling? Can you describe one or two traits that demonstrate the behavior of high-character people in selling? Take a minute and review the information at the right, and then let's determine if we can provide a working definition of character in your work as a sales professional.

What is Character?

Webster's Ninth Collegiate Dictionary 1 : One of the attributes or features that make up and distinguish the individual **2** : The complex mental and ethical traits marking often individualizing a person, group or nation **3** : A person marked by notable or conspicuous traits.

Sophocles – Rather fail with honor than succeed by fraud.

Horace Greeley – The darkest hour of any man's life is when he sits down to plan how to get money without earning it.

Mark Twain – It is better to deserve honors and not have them than to have them and not deserve them.

Robert Louis Stevenson – Sooner or later everyone sits down to a banquet of consequences.

Shakespeare – He is not great who is not greatly good.

Ralph Waldo Emerson – The essence of greatness is the perception that virtue is enough.

Euripides – Wealth stays with us a little moment if at all; only our characters are steadfast, not our gold.

Malcolm S. Forbes – To measure the man measure his heart.

The dictionary definition is interesting but neutral, since the character traits of a sociopath could meet this description. Shakespeare and Emerson speak to a sense of virtue or goodness grounded in the concept of social decency, equity and propriety. Horace Greeley warns against sedition fueled by greed while Mark Twain derides a capitulation to vanity over honor. Let me give you a short summary of six distinguishing traits of sales professionals who exhibit character in the way they work and sell. These traits should be included in any definition of character in the profession of selling:

◆ Extends trusts/Assumes the best in others

- ◆ Subordinates personal interest to personal values

- ◆ Honors commitments

- ◆ Loyal to customers and associates

- ◆ Not a complainer

- ◆ Possesses a service mindset

My hope is that, after you review this section and consider the two practices, you will have more information to formulate your own working definition of character. As with the other two sections in this chapter, please take some time to complete the selfassessment exercise before moving on to the next chapter.

Practice 6: Think of the Sales Transaction in Terms of Customer Benefit

Sales professionals of character consider a commitment to be a promise. Because they understand that the foundation of all customer interactions is trust, their commitments – promises – are the object of constant vigilance. This clarity about trust provides a reference point in all conversations, sales calls, product presentations, and follow-up phone calls.

Honoring commitments starts with exercising the self-discipline to say "no." The complexities of operating in a competitive market on a daily basis can lead to a tendency to succumb to pressure, most often to pressure exerted by customers. Sales professionals of high character make informed decisions about product availability and intended use and aggressively pursue new opportunities. They are willing to take risks, but not when it involves compromising a relationship with a client. Few things speak more loudly to a client about a sales professional's desire to subordinate personal gain to customer interest than having the courage to say no.

Sometimes saying no sounds like, "That is not a good fit for my product," or "The required delivery schedule is not compatible with our current production," or "The color and style you have selected are not available," or – hold your breath – "There is a less expensive way for you to solve this problem without using my product."

Honoring commitments starts with telling the truth. Sales professionals who overpromise and under-deliver always find themselves on the short side of the trust curve. For sales professionals who take a long-term view of developing high-trust, collaborative customer relationships, finding the self-discipline to say "no" is a matter of protecting the customer, even when it means protecting the customer from mistaken ideas about products and performance.

Many interactions with new customers struggle under the accumulated weight of negative assumptions based on years of experience with sales professionals. These assumptions grow out of a litany of examples of previous sales representatives exploiting a relationship for personal gain. The resulting distrust is a barrier to the selling process, but be patient. Never use a hand grenade when a ladder will do. Even the sturdiest barriers will admit welcome guests.

Character is a personality trait that benefits from periodic personal introspection and assessment. Sales professionals of high character who subordinate personal benefit to the interests of the customer will be discovered over time. So will sales professionals who don't. Even one misguided decision, if it can be construed as self-serving or exploitative, can produce a pungent odor that lasts for decades.

During my first year in sales I was responsible for preparing a bid on a large project in a Midwestern city. Within a week after we tendered our proposal, the customer notified us that a contract would be forthcoming. This news arrived at about the same time that I learned of some serious errors and omissions in our bid. I immediately contacted the customer to discuss the problems and withdraw our proposal. The exchange was not pleasant. In the aftermath, legal salvos were exchanged. In the end, the customer was left to pay the difference between our price and the next lowest bid. Mistakes or even incompetence might have been understood and tolerated, but a lack of character was indefensible.

For more than ten years I carried with me a sense of uneasiness about this experience. It was a disturbing episode, where I had to face the ugliness of making a choice to save myself rather than to honor a commitment to a customer. It took me a decade to muster the courage to make a phone call and schedule a meeting with that company's president. I thought that the passage of time might have dulled the pain of his financial loss, but his memory of the debacle was still vividly intact. I offered a belated apology coupled with a good faith gesture at restitution. He accepted graciously and without a hint of condescension or ridicule, though either might have been appropriate. He was a man of magnanimous character; retribution was beneath him.

For the next fifteen or twenty years, we regularly exchanged cards and greetings during the holiday season. There was no discussion of doing business together again. We both seemed to understand that the consequences of poor decisions can last a lifetime.

While we can't change the consequences, we can change the thought processes that produce those consequences. While I still carry the regret, I am thankful that it happened during an early season of my career, so that I could learn from the bitter taste of having lacked the self-discipline to put the interests of customers above my own.

Sales professionals who possess great personal character share a common orientation toward service. They nearly always view their work as serving their customers. They view the selling process as a service they willing provide to customers, without the presumption of quid pro quo. They know that subtly inferring an obligation on the customer's part is manipulative.

Service-oriented sales professionals abhor coercion and manipulation. They are engaged in a highly-collaborative process of solving problems and providing solutions, and of understanding the customer's needs in such a way that there is a sense of shared ownership in the outcome. They always subordinate their personal interest to the overall interest of the customer. They know that their contribution   to the process is entirely predicated upon trust. They instinctively understand that pursuing self-interest destroys credibility and trust.

A service-oriented sales professional is a person whose meaningful contribution exceeds expectations. This contribution is largely determined by how well the sales professional knows the customer's needs and locates the product in a strongly solution-oriented context. Service-oriented sales professionals possess broad-based industry knowledge, are conversant with emerging trends, and can skillfully discuss all technical requirements associated with the buying decision. This service mindset helps the customer differentiate between products with similar market price points and benefits. Sales professionals understand that a genuine commitment to serve customers elevates the perceived value of their products.

Some sales professionals try to build relationships with clients at the expense of their relationship with their own company. They may shift blame to the corporate office to avoid accepting responsibility for inaccurate or incomplete information. They may suggest to the customer that part of their role is to protect the customer from the capricious behavior of the corporate office. In these and other ways, they unwittingly make it impossible for the customer to trust them.

One of the most common mistakes in the selling profession is undermining the reputation of part of one's company, such as the technical support teams at the corporate office, in order to elevate one's status with a customer. This practice is duplicitous and demonstrates a serious character deficiency. Customers are bright people who are interested in making informed decisions. Sales professionals who demonstrate consistent disloyalty to the company or companies they represent are more likely to use customers as a shield later, to hide their own shortcomings from the corporate office. It is unwise to assume that your customers will fail to make this connection, when it is obvious to everyone else.

Outstanding sales professionals are effective bridge builders. They construct a platform across which there can be free interchange between the customer and seller, including resources at the corporate office when needed. Narcissists who value loyalty only between the customer and the product representative fail to build the necessary bridges of loyalty between customers and products, customers and brands, and customers and companies.

The interaction with the customer that is intended to lead to a purchase must focus almost entirely on the needs, interests, goals, budgets, time constraints, and project objectives of the customer. When it becomes more about the sales professional than the solutions offered by the product, the purchasing process will be frustrated. The competency and skill of the sales professional is essential and may ultimately be the determining factor in the business transaction; however, the intimation that the sales professional can be trusted while the company or product cannot is a notion that will collapse under even modest attempt at critical thinking. It may win short-term sales, but not long-term customers.

Customers will rightfully assume that solid, competent sales professionals of character will represent products and services of similar quality. Generally speaking, the more credible the product or service, the more credible the sales professional. The reverse is also true. This customer inference is sometimes referred to as the "halo effect." A customer who has succeeded with one product or service from a company will extend the resulting good will initially to a new line extension offered by the same company. This also applies to members of the sales team. Any effort to acquire the halo by removing it from the product or company you represent will undermine trust. Conversely, when professionals of high character build high-trust relationships with customers, that trust extends to products, services, and companies.

Practice 7: Build Strong Relationships

One way to assess the overall quality of your work is by the level to which you extend trust to people around you. People of character distinguish themselves by the way they extend trust. People who yearn to be trusted and to work and ultimately thrive in high-trust cultures understand what is required to build relationships of trust. After carefully assessing all relevant factors, their basic predisposition is to trust. They sense that the extension of trust, even in situations where it may not be fully warranted, is the most effective way to empower people.

People of character generally operate with the assumption that the world in which they live and function is more similar than dissimilar to themselves. They naturally assume the best in others. Consequently, they speak of others without cynicism. Skeptics may judge this accepting and trusting nature to be either naïve or gullible, we tend to see the world as a reflection our own attitudes. To a certain extent both trusting and suspicious world views become self-fulfilling prophecies.

Sales professionals of character do not extend trust indiscriminately. They carefully assess the character and competency of people and, based upon that judgment, willingly extend trust. They know that, to be trusted, they also need to trust. They understand that being trusted is a shared emotional need and that few things can lift, motivate, and inspire others more than the simple and mature extension of trust. They know that their efforts to *create excellence* in their lives are greatly benefited when they assist others on the same journey. Few motivators in life will lead to the conquest of tall summits more effectively than appropriately extended trust.

Sales professionals of exceptional character possess the ability to solve problems in an environment complicated by divergent opinions and attitudes among stakeholders. People of solid character have a strong sense of who they are and act consistently with their own deeply held values. This sense of self allows them to accept and value other opinions. The pride that can compromise the search for solutions that will ultimately produce mutual benefit is conspicuously absent.

People of strong character respect and value others; consequently, they are skillful listeners. They understand that listening is not an opportunity to formulate a retaliatory response to defend a position, but rather an opportunity to be influenced by another perspective that will lead to the best possible outcome. Their compassion leads them to listen intently and empathetically. The effort to understand another person's perspective engages all the senses in the listening process. The entire experience of communicating is significantly enhanced, which contributes to more effective problem-solving.

Good character naturally inspires trust, which is fertile ground for collaboration. It is in collaboration, not compromise, that the best solutions are found. A person of character is forward-thinking and solution-oriented. This mindset removes obstacles from the past that may compromise effective problem-solving. The forward-looking focus on solutions overcomes the tendency to be reactive and propels discussion toward realistic and achievable outcomes.

Sometimes a commitment to do your best work can be demonstrated in how willing you are to help someone else around you improve. It takes a person of character to reach out to someone else and provide helpful mentoring. Mentoring is rarely convenient but desperately needed. It is a way to leave something of great worth on the trail, to alert other hikers to the proper routes and help them find safe passage to the distant summit. It is about giving something of value, and valuing something else. Sales professionals of character seek out opportunities to mentor, encourage, coach and teach other sales professionals. It takes a person of character to celebrate the accomplishments of others and not feel diminished in the process.

Outstanding sales professionals seek opportunities to mentor, because they provide meaning to their experience and enlarge their contribution to the organization and the industry. Great mentors are great leaders. They understand how to inspire others to have confidence in their own abilities, to perform hard tasks, and to learn difficult new skills. Their authenticity allows them to talk candidly about failures and weaknesses and to make even difficult ascents seem possible. They understand that mentoring is lifting someone else without self-aggrandizement, but rather with a desire to help. They become skillful at providing second opinions and asking probative questions that contribute to the process of self-discovery. A mentor is a teacher, and a teacher who is passionate about the material and who genuinely cares about the students' progress and development gives a gift that will last for generations.

Some of the best sales professionals I have worked with cannot readily identify important mentors in their careers, yet they themselves are committed mentors. The call for mentoring does not come from the leaders of sales teams; it comes from the hearts of experienced and successful sales professionals who realize that success in any life endeavor depends on the contributions of many other people. Mentoring is a expression of gratitude. It is an acknowledgement that reaching the summit required the help of many people. Great mentors are effective leaders and people of great character.

Doing your best work will require you to eliminate the tendency to complain and blame others. Outstanding sales professionals seem to operate from a common belief system. A core belief is that, of all the variables in the sales success equation, none is as important as their commitment to produce *excellent* results. Competitors may lure away customers with deep discounts. Economic reversals may erode a growing market share. Technological advancements may threaten current product positioning. However, none of these is as essential to long-term success as the sales professional's acceptance of full responsibility for results in the territory.

Sales professionals who are engineered to *create excellence* don't complain. Complaining is a pernicious act; it is being duplicitous with oneself. Members of the sales team who are incessant complainers have learned a subtle way to justify a diminished position. They offload responsibility to other people, organizations, competitors, customers, or even unforeseen, random "acts of God." High-character sales professionals understand that complaining and criticizing marginalize only the person who is speaking, not the targeted of the attacks.

Some members of the sales team may interpret this unwillingness to launch an allout frontal verbal attack, when evidence supports their position, as weakness or as capitulation to organizational politics. Some may even attempt to occupy what is sometimes construed as the "moral high ground," by suggesting that those who refuse to toss daggers deserve a similar fate or worse. Sales professionals of high character recognize that there is a difference between gratuitous criticism and seeking solutions to complex problems. One seeks to build and lift, while the other seeks to degrade and destroy.

The historic visit of Egyptian President Anwar Sadat to Israel culminated in the 1978 Camp David Accords, which included mutual recognition of both countries and a cessation of hostilities that had continued since 1948. His initial visit and the subsequent signing of the treaty largely alienated Egypt from much of the Arab world. It would have been easier for Sadat to join the Arab chorus criticizing and condemning Israel. Courage and character were needed. He possessed a vision of peace and the character to understand that any legitimate step forward would only be made in an atmosphere devoid of criticism, where even small seeds of trust could take root.

Anwar Sadat was a man of character who made a conscious effort to ease and lift tensions in a troubled region of the world. His refusal to attack Israel verbally earned him not only the Nobel Peace Prize, but also the respect and admiration of people around the world.

Reckless criticism and wanton complaining are not the same as seeking solutions; sales professionals of high character, who are leaders, understand the difference. One who carefully and intently seeks solutions without criticism or complaint will be revered for great inner strength. From this inner strength trust will flow in abundance. This is true in the world of international politics, and it is equally true in the world of professional selling.

Integrity drives the commitment to work towards your personal potential. Integrity is always about character. The choice to pursue your potential is a choice to be completely honest with yourself. When all the information has been gathered, it is the sales professional who has the clearest understanding of what revenue numbers can be achieved in the territory. That same professional conducts a personal inventory of assets and talents and determines what limits, if any, to impose on the pursuit of *excellence*.

Sales professionals of character set their own goals, work to their own clock, hear their own voice, and create their own symphonies. They welcome support and encouragement from team members and sales leaders, but ultimately they are the only ones who truly know whether or not they are working in a manner consistent with their own and the territory's potential. It takes a person of character to acknowledge when the bar has been set too low, to risk raising the standard for performance. *Creating excellence* is a risk that all sales professionals of character are willing to take.

High-character sales professionals, who practice the skills of leadership, are low-maintenance and high-performance people. They require the least amount of management and leadership, and consistently provide the best results. Sales professionals with character who possess the competency and desire to pursue *excellence* seem to believe that nothing is out of reach. They work to their own ability regardless of circumstances, because they know that the ultimate measure of their success will be found in raising their performance to their potential.

Character

Score 1 - 10 (1 = Strongly Disagree   10 = Strongly Agree)

	YOUR SCORE
1. I am an effective problem solver.	
2. I extend trust to other people.	
3. I subordinate personal interest to personal values.	
4. I work with a service mindset.	
5. I assume the best in other people.	
6. I work to mentor other people.	
7. I am not a complainer.	
8. I honor commitments.	
9. I am loyal to customers and associates.	
10. I consistently work to my own potential.	
TOTAL POINTS	

Creating Excellence, and the Eight Symptoms of Sales Paralysis

It might be helpful to use the term "yield rate" as it relates to the overall impact of the individual selling skill on the Eight Symptoms of Sales Paralysis. Now, keep in mind that these assessments are subjective in nature, but when you consider the impact of the skill of *creating excellence* on the symptoms of Sales Paralysis it should become clear time spent in this area will have profound impact on your work as a sales professional. Borrowing time from other tasks to improve this skill makes practical sense. The results will eventually be noticeable on the monthly sales report.

Creating excellence is a *character*-driven skill that also includes technical competency and your overall desire to produce outstanding results. Take some time to review the impact of this skill on areas of your professional life that may be keeping you from working more consistently to your own potential.

Symptom	Impact	Comments
The Passion is gone	MEDIUM	Producing excellent work creates its own level of energy.
Inattentive listening	HIGH	Character powers the process of listening to understand.
Winging it	HIGH	Working to your own potential eliminates faulty preparation.
Lack of a sense of urgency	HIGH	People of character recognize the need to respond urgently.
Contemplation of a job change	MEDIUM	Working to your potential is challenging and demanding work.
Feelings of frustration	HIGH	Strong character allows you to take control of tough situations.
Blaming others	HIGH	Sales professionals of character accept responsibility for outcomes.
Low energy for problem solving	HIGH	The combination of character and competency increases energy levels.

The Skill of Creating Excellence: A Way to Leave Marks on the Trail

Some time ago my wife Michele and I traveled with some close friends to western Wyoming in search of remnants of the historic Emigrants' Trail. This was the common east-to-west passage used for westward migration from 1846 until the completion of the transcontinental railroad in 1856. During those few short years, over 500,000 people, mostly in wagon trains, left the edge of the frontier in Iowa City and began the trek west. Most were traveling to California or the Pacific Northwest.

Even after 160 years, the trail is still visible, particularly in parts of western Wyoming. To the north and east of Farson, Wyoming, in a barren stretch of wasteland, where a plateau rises above the Sweetwater River, is a place called Rocky Ridge. There the trail's elevation rises about 1000 feet in 3.5 miles, but it is the rocks embedded in the trail that presented the most formidable obstacle, particularly to wagons being pulled by teams of oxen.

From a short distance the protruding rock formations appear as battlements, sharp projections three to four feet high, and lined up like columns of soldiers. Even now it is difficult to believe that the trail over Rocky Ridge was the best available option for weary westward emigrants. It seems impassable today; one can only imagine how it must have appeared to emigrants with tired feet, empty stomachs, tattered clothes, and exhausted livestock, and with hundreds of miles of trail already behind them.

There is one sight on Rocky Ridge that I still recall with absolute clarity. It is of rugged rock worn smooth by the passage of emigrants, with their caravans of wagons and cattle. Even today evidence remains on the trail of their passage, subtle trail markings which are a living testament to their courage, fortitude, and determination to press forward against insurmountable odds. They did not remove the rock or seek an alternate passage. They pressed forward, and in the process they altered the terrain to the point where markings in stone still remind us of the perseverance of another age.

In your professional life, what trail markers are you leaving as evidence of your passage through a career in professional selling? Are you working in such a way that some rough stones are wearing smooth, insuring an easier passage for those who follow? Are there signs of your work that will inspire others years from now? More importantly, can we find durable evidence that you are on a path leading to personal and professional *excellence*?

As you reflect on the material in this chapter I hope you will try to identify trail markers in your professional life that would indicate you are exhibiting the various shapes and forms of *excellence*. This chapter contains a lot of information about trail markers; it is designed to help you recognize the role of character and competency, and a desire for *excellence* in your work as a sales professional. We have just reviewed thirty different practices to help you understand what the pursuit of *excellence* will demand from you in your territory. There were three self-evaluation exercises in this chapter to help you assess your performance and understand key practices   that will lead you to developing and and practicing the skill of *creating excellence* in your professional life.

I would suggest that you complete these exercises at least annually and track changes from year to year. More specifically, I would suggest that you write a list of important changes you will make to help you improve in areas that might reveal some potential deficiencies. Professional lives built upon the skill of *creating excellence* will leave indelible imprints that will provide evidence to others for years to come of your contribution to building a trail worthy of the emulation of others.

The Relationship of Principles and Practices in Developing the Skill *("Learned Power")* **of Creating Excellence**

Principle A. Excellent work produces excellent results.
> Supporting Practices:
>> 1. Work to develop collaborative relationships
>> 2. Work with the expectation of positive results
>> 3. Produce consistent quality
>> 4. Work to improve your sales ability/add value to customers

Principle B. Creating excellence begins with a strong desire to produce outstanding work.
> Supporting Practices:
>> 1. Work with the expectation of positive results
>> 2. Produce consistent quality

Principle C. Improved competency improves the prospect of creating excellence.
> Supporting Practices:
>> 1. Work to improve your sales ability and add value to customers
>> 2. Understand customer needs and communicate clearly

Principle D. People of character naturally build collaborative relationships.
> Supporting Practices:
>> 1. Think of the sales transaction in terms of customer benefit
>> 2. Consistently do your best work

CHAPTER 6

Execute

Constancy Amid Change

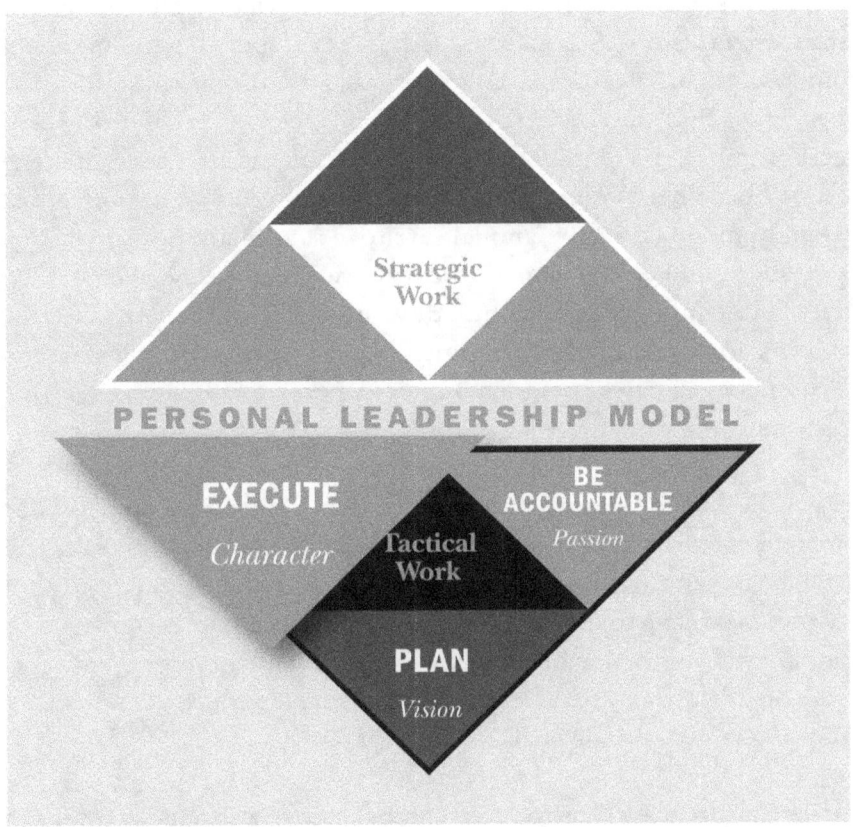

Figure 6-1 Execute: The *Character* Component of Tactical Work

EFFECTIVE SELLING is really about displaying key *Personal Leadership* traits. If you are convinced of nothing else in this book, I hope you will embrace the notion that selling and *Personal Leadership* work in harmony to create the symphony of your career. Spending time improving basic skills in essential areas of selling is a recommended practice. However, unless that improvement takes place in the larger context of *Personal Leadership*, it will rarely yield the desired results. Selling is not simply a matter of identifying prospects, presenting a product, and asking for the order. It is infinitely more complex and involves a multiplicity of recurring decisions. Sales professionals who are consistently successful understand that the *Defining Skill* that leads to high levels of revenue production is *Personal Leadership*.

At the very basic level, *Personal Leadership* in professional selling is about constructing a clear territory *vision*, creating a viable plan, and consistently *executing* a well-conceived strategy. Each of these components comprises many decisions. Leaders understand that these decisions must be made in the context of specific objectives, and that nearly every decision should be filtered through the overall *vision* of what the territory can become. Without a clear *vision*, conceived by assessing potential and embodied in the annual territory sales plan, decisions about asset and resource allocation will be reactive in nature and will be driven more by the immediacy of competitive influences in the market rather than by a long-term strategy designed to lead to optimum revenue production. The reactive approach is merely incremental; the *vision*-driven approach is exponential.

It is at the level of *execution* that the *Defining Skill* will become most apparent in your work. When the time comes for you to *execute* the sales plan, it will be imperative that you summon everything you have learned about *Personal Leadership* to deploy available assets and resources so as to move you closer to your vision of the territory. Squandering these valuable tools will jeopardize your effectiveness as a leader and reduce your chance of achieving target revenue goals for the year.

Earlier in this book I introduced the concept that leaders work at the end of the bar. That statement is a *Personal Leadership* imperative. It suggests that the more time spent on high-leverage work, the higher will be the level of results produced. *Execution* is about finding time every day to move towards the end of the bar. The skill you demonstrate in allocating scarce resources and assets is a way for you to find the much-needed leverage in your daily work, which over time will enable you to lift some mighty large rocks.

Principles and Practices in Developing the Skill to Execute

The two primary principles, laws or assumptions which support the skill of *execution* are the simple notions that the consistent *execution* of good plans has the power to produce great results, and that *execution* is defined by the overall quality of your daily work in the territory.

Your work on a comprehensive market assessment has given you a different look at your territory, customers, competitors and possibly market changes, and has provided a glimpse of some new opportunities. This new *vision* of the territory and of your ability as a sales professional has helped you develop the skill to craft a workable plan that will bring the newfound opportunities into reality over the course of the coming months or years. Now it is time to go to work.

The *vision* of your territory that is recorded in your plan describes what you can produce. How effectively you implement that plan today will determine whether or not those interesting possibilities can be converted to solid revenue numbers. Staying in the moment and executing the plan require self-discipline. Your work on developing the skill of creating excellence in the previous chapter will put *execution* well within your grasp.

The real work of this chapter will be presented in two sections that address managing the scarce resources of time and money, and then the allocation of various assets at your disposal. You will also be given an opportunity to complete three self-assessment exercises. Please remember that these short exercises are a way to review key practices that lead to skill development. As I have stated repeatedly, it is the development of the skills that provides the "learned power" for you to transform your territory. Before that discussion, please consider a few other topics related to *execution*.

The objective of this chapter is to provide you with some tools or practices which will assist you in implementing your sales plan. The topics are presented in order, beginning with today's task and continuing through the final section about contract closing. This chapter will also conclude with some short summary comments about the role of *Personal Leadership* and the *execution* of the sales plan.

Everything we have discussed thus far is this book has prepared you to become more committed to *execute* the sales plan. It is in the skill of *execution* that that your dreams for your territory and your professional life take the form of phone calls, product presentations, follow up, prospecting, weekly planning sessions, and yes, actual contracts.

Execution is a Character Statement

Constancy of *character* is required to *execute* the sales plan. People of *character* who consistently *execute* the plan nearly always produce quality results that are recognizable.

I grew up in the late 1950s and early 1960s, when the polio vaccine was still relatively new. Doug Yates was a few years older than me. He contracted polio, which left him partially paralyzed from the waist down. During all the years that we were growing up, he walked with crutches, as he still does today. Doug had the remarkable character to convince all of us that he was not diminished by the disease. He was never a victim, and none of his close friends ever felt sorry for him.

Even after four decades I vividly remember playing on his little league baseball team and standing behind the home plate umpire to be Doug's pinch runner. What is even more amazing is that I watched him pitch, inning after inning, from a sitting position on the pitcher's mound, and I never really thought it was unusual.

Later in life, Doug had a successful career in financial planning and made frequent trips to Africa to pursue his passion for big game hunting. He did just about everything a person could possibly imagine in life, with a sense of dignity and grace that made it seem effortless. It took me years to begin to understand how much effort that really required.

It is that same apparent effortlessness that I have watched time and time again in the company of outstanding professionals who have worked to develop exceptional virtuosity in various aspects of selling. What seems easy for them, even effortless, almost always is the result of tedious practice, careful planning, frequent study and consistent execution. They may not have been throwing fastballs from the sitting position, but the skill they exhibited seemed as just as effortless.

Doug Yates made no excuses. He never complained, and he worked twice as hard as anyone I knew to perfect the simple motion of throwing a baseball or swinging   a bat or golf club with one arm. As a young man I admired his courage, determination and competitiveness. In my later years it is his towering character that I find most appealing. Doug's character led him to accept the reality of his own limitations, but also to refuse to allow his limitations to limit his pursuit of his own potential. The projection of our limitations on Doug was something he consistently ignored. He knew his potential, even when it was hidden from the rest of us. Can the same be said about your life?

Each one of us has a unique set of limitations and challenges. They may not be as obvious as Doug's, but we all know what things hold us back from achieving our potential. You don't have to be the best presenter, the most skilled prospector, or the most relentlessly organized person on the sales team to *execute* your annual territory sales plan and create excellence in your professional life. You just have to be the best you can. If you can do that day after day, month after month, and year after year, these ordinary tasks, done with extraordinary consistency, will produce remarkable results. A person of *character* produces quality work consistent with individual potential.

Execution also requires a commitment to *Personal Leadership*. Leaders make conscious choices that bring their best effort forward through the consistent *execution* of the territory sales plan.

As we move through the material in this chapter keep the image in your mind of Doug Yates sitting on the pitcher's mound, as a reminder of the commitment and courage required to *execute* life plans successfully. Great plans have little value without the personal resolve to implement your best critical thinking. *Execution* is about making those tough throws from the sitting position or swinging the bat with one arm. It may not seem natural, and it may not be easy, but, if your plan is solid, your revenue numbers will be home run quality.

Principle A. Execution – Use Good Plans to Produce Great Results

Planning is what you could do. *Execution* is what you are doing. Planning is creative, non-confrontational, and can be done over an extended period of time. *Execution* is exhausting, can be filled with grueling hours spent satisfying challenging customers, and nearly always needs to be done quickly. Planning can be done with your shoes off or your feet on the desk. *Executing* the plan requires your shoes to be on and your feet to be on the ground. *Planning* can be mentally demanding. *Executing* the plan can be physically demanding. Goal statements take form on paper as part of the annual sales plan; they come to life in the constant *execution* of the plan.

Executing any plan requires moving your feet. Great achievements in life are conceived in the mind but are accomplished by the feverish moving of your feet. Even the best plans fail when voices remain silent, hands hang down, and feet are stuck in clay.

Execution is determined principally by what you do today, not by your plans from yesterday or your good intentions for tomorrow. *Execution* is about right now, today. Ask yourself the simple question, "What is the most productive use of my time today to achieve my goals?" The answer will set you on a course where even the most impossible dreams become possible.

Planning is purposeful and inspiring. It helps you describe on paper things that only your mind can see. *Executing* the plan requires a determined sense of purpose, commitment, and an understanding that the work you produce will be available for everyone to see. Planning engages the mind in creative thinking to produce a document that ultimately appears on paper. *Executing* the plan engages the heart in inspiring work that ultimately appears on pavement. Planning projects an air of importance. *Execution* projects an air of urgency. Planning describes who you can become. *Execution* shows who you are.

The world's best planner could also be a consistent under-achiever, and the hardest worker in your organization could produce mediocre results. *Execution* is not simply about longer hours and more disciplined work. It is about working the right number of hours on the right things at the right time. The confluence of careful planning and consistent *execution* leads to constant engagement in high-leverage activities. Where daily work schedules are filled with highly productive activities, the inevitable result will be highly desirable revenue numbers.

Effective planning requires *vision*. Consistently *executing* a plan requires *character*. *Vision* involves broad knowledge about market conditions and shifting economic trends which may impact consumer demand. *Character* involves knowledge of pressing issues, commitments, responsibilities and activities that require immediate action to insure continued customer loyalty to your product brand. *Vision* subordinates your current view of the market to new possibilities based upon a market assessment. *Character* subordinates your desire to pursue less productive, trivial, and time-wasting activities to the new reality in which you honor commitments to yourself, which you made as part of your complete personal assessment.

How well and how consistently you *execute* the plan for your sales territory will be the most definitive statement you can make about yourself as a sales professional. Self-discipline will be required to *execute* tasks that are outside the comfortable range of your skill set. Patience will be required to foster relationships that can ultimately become collaborative in nature. Fortitude will be required to continue moving forward in the face of discouragement. Humility will be required to understand the need to change and improve. Courage will be required to pursue a course where others have failed. Ultimately, *character* will triumph in the pursuit of any lofty endeavor that is supported by a strong *vision* and propelled by inspiring sources of motivation. High-character sales professionals stay in the moment and defend their time as a priceless possession. This is because, when it comes to achieving sales goals, their time really is priceless. So, for today, keep your feet moving in the direction of your goal. Tomorrow will come soon enough.

Practice 1: Execution Requires Working Your Plan – Today!

The three elements of Tactical Work describe particular moments in time. Your territory plan describes what you *will do*, while being accountable involves what you *have done*. Writing the territory *plan* is an exercise that looks forward, while accountability looks backward. *Execution*, on the other hand, is in the present. It is the clearest indicator of who you are. As a consequence it is a reliable predictor of who you will become as a sales professional.

Execution is that pivotal moment in time that will show your capabilities as a leader.

All leaders at some point will be faced with critical choices and must ultimately make decisions about the allocation of available resources, based upon priorities. These priorities are determined by the leader's *vision* and are *executed* principally by the leader's *character*. In other words, by assessing potential and planning, you have described to yourself what your territory can become. The unanswered question is, will you demonstrate the *character* required to move yourself and your territory across the difficult terrain, toward the realization of your *vision* ?

Because of that simple question, *Personal Leadership* is the *Defining Skill* in professional selling. Most sales professionals fail not because they lack clarity about market opportunities, but rather because they are unwilling in the moment to perform the difficult tasks that lead to success. Most sales professionals spend the bulk of their time away from company associates. They are generally alone in making decisions about allocating time and resources. *Character* is what fortifies a person's resolve to do the hard things and to ask the difficult questions even when alone. *Character* is the primary inoculation against the natural tendency to avoid risk and, with it, the humiliation of rejection. *Character* is the most reliable assessment of who you are as a person and the greatest single determinant of your overall effectiveness as a leader.

If you refuse to perform the difficult tasks required of successful sales professionals, you have, in large measure, abdicated your claim on your own personal potential. In essence you have appeased the yearnings of the worst part of your nature, which pleads for you to take a break from the arduous tasks that remain undone and justifies your breaking commitments to yourself about weekly prospecting hours or the number of follow-up contacts with customers. It begs you to under-perform and tries to persuade you to believe that there are shortcuts in the road ahead. Appeasing this part of your nature is selling out. *Character* is about selling up. Appeasement is capitulating to your worst self. *Character* invites you to accept nothing less than your best self.

Some of the most naturally gifted sales professionals with whom I have worked over the years have been seduced by the voice of appeasement. These are intelligent people with excellent communication skills and a solid work ethic. They relate well with customers and company associates. In many respects they are sales and marketing anomalies. Outwardly they seem to possess all the key characteristics for success in selling, but over time I have learned that the outward skills are not the problem. It is the inward shortcomings that eventually sabotage their success. Their work habits are dominated by appeasement.

Some sales organizations adopt strategies to combat the numbing effects of appeasement by implementing greater systems of accountability. These organizational accountability systems usually create environments of low trust and a culture that inhibits personal empowerment. If there is a way to inoculate the sales team from the growing proclivity toward appeasement, it will be found in high-trust environments. Members of the sales team need to accept more responsibility for their lives and their territories, not less. Weekly call reports might sound like a good idea, but too often they spring from organizational arrogance. They imply that the team at the corporate office knows more about the territory's needs than the frontline sales professionals.

By contrast, high-trust cultures foster personal empowerment. As a rule, it is only when the organization's culture is saturated with trust that members of the sales team are willing to take the risks that lead toward personal and territory revenue potential. I have never seen a single instance where high-control, low-trust sales cultures produced an environment conducive to achieving optimum revenue potential. To extend trust is to endow with power. Where trust is responsibly extended to people of character, the result nearly always shatters expectations.

A constant throughout my career has been the compelling relationship between organizations of trust and people of character. This combination is like a rocket fuel that propels the territory into a higher orbit.

High-character people will do well in any organization, regardless of the culture, but low-trust cultures tend to lower the ceiling of revenue potential by diminishing the sales professional's capacity to work at optimum levels. In such cultures outcomes may be good, but they will rarely be great. Greatness requires the added motivation that only a high-trust culture inspires.

Because *execution* happens in the present, your commitment today to the *execution* of the sales plan is what validates your conviction of your own potential. Every time you refuse to engage in less productive and potentially time-wasting activities, which rob you of valuable time engaging with customers, you affirm your deepest belief about yourself: "I can achieve my greatest potential." Your constancy in working the plan with precision will not only get easier over time, but will increase your effectiveness in the more challenging and less desirable tasks in your territory.

The personal affirmation, "I am," describes what you are doing right now, not what you hope to do, plan to do, might do, should do, want to do, or wish to do. "I am" is a statement of personal conviction about yourself. When this statement is uttered by a person with strong character, who desires to produce quality work consistently, personal revenue potential is not far away. If you have worked on developing the skill of creating excellence, it will need to be evident as you consistently work to *execute* your annual sales plan. Here are a few ways to evaluate how well you are doing right now. How true are these statements of you right now?

- ◆ I am aware of my annual goals and program them daily into my work schedule.

- ◆ I am reviewing my schedule daily to insure that my time is allocated to the most highly productive activities.

- ◆ I am integrating new information about my territory, customers and competitors into my plan and constantly updating my goals and implementation strategy.

- I am working everyday to improve my ability as a sales professional.

- I am not procrastinating difficult tasks.

- I am working hard to stay motivated.

- I am aware of the potential of my market.

- I am aware of my potential as a sales professional.

- I am completing essential tasks today that will lead me to my annual revenue goal.

Booker T. Washington, the American educator and reformer, said, "The world cares very little about what a man or woman knows; it is what the man or woman is able to do that counts." That simple phrase describes most of the world of professional selling. Planning is about knowing, but it is of little importance without the "doing" of *execution*.

Principle B. Execution Is about Quality

Quality in professional selling requires a sense of personal vigilance about producing your best work in every customer interaction, every piece of correspondence, every proposal, and every technical analysis of potential product use. *Execution* is not simply about the number of trips to the batter's box. It is about the quality of swings that should ultimately put you in a position to score runs. You may think the "end game" in selling is all about quantity. But the quantity of revenue you desire will only be realized through the quality of your daily work.

In an earlier chapter on creating excellence, I identified thirty characteristics that were key to constantly demonstrating the character that will enable you to produce excellence in your life. If you are struggling with consistent *execution* , I suggest you review that chapter and make a personal assessment of your performance relative to each of the character traits listed.

Strategic Work creates an environment that allows you to flourish in all aspects of Tactical Work. As I have said already, most sales professionals live in the world of Tactical Work and spend little or no meaningful time on the three skills of Strategic Work. Your best effort in Tactical Work will never deliver the results that a serious and thoughtful investment in all three skills of Strategic Work can produce. Breakthrough revenue production takes form in Strategic Work.

What this means for you is that *creating excellence* and *execution* are inseparably joined together, and it takes *character* to make both fully operational. The same is true of the other skills in the *Personal Leadership Model*. For example, if you are an effective planner, you also most likely do well in the long-term thinking required to assess potential, since both require a sense of *vision*. *Vision* is about producing the map; *execution* is about taking the hike. Looking back over your sales career, if you can identify a weakness that has contributed to performance that is less than your potential, you are taking the first step toward realizing your goal. My experience suggests that the weakness you identify is most likely to be in one of the three *Personal Leadership Drivers*, and from there manifests itself in a corresponding skill, in either Strategic or Tactical Work.

Consistent *execution* of your sales plan is nearly always a definitive statement about your *character* as a sales professional. *Character* is the *Personal Leadership Driver* that powers both creating excellence and *execution*. Both these components of the *Personal Leadership Model* are in large measure defined by careful attention to quality.

In other words, if you are struggling with consistency in *execution*, the problem is most likely *character*-related, so reviewing the material on creating excellence will prove beneficial over time. The more you become aware of the need to create excellence, the more the quality of your daily work will improve and your commitment to consistent *execution* will increase. Just remember that creating excellence is not a relative term; it does not measure the quality of your work against others within the organization. It is an absolute imperative that forces you to assess your current output relative to your own ability. You are the ultimate judge. *Character* inevitably produces a sense of equity in your assessment. In the final analysis, you know what you are capable of producing. Make that assessment the most important one in your life.

The daily *execution* must be a qualitative endeavor, in order for the territory to move forward. Every action by the sales professional must share a common thread: a commitment to produce consistently excellent work. This excellence is seen in the timeliness of follow-up calls, care in preparing all correspondence, consistency in regular prospecting activities, preparation for all customer meetings and presentations, commitment to continuing education and self-development, and attention to every other detail of professional selling. Consistency in daily *execution* and an unwavering commitment to all goals and objectives for the territory require constancy of *character*.

To *execute* you must be consistently engaged in the diverse activities of professional selling, while also keeping a careful watch over resource and asset allocation, managing scarce resources, and conducting regular planning sessions to adjust the plan according to changing market conditions. Outstanding Strategic Work will mean little if the sales professional is pulled away from consistent *execution* by seemingly pressing matters which take hostages in the form of valuable time and resources.

Executing consistently is hard work. For sales professionals who are programmed to react to the events of the day, which arrive in their office via e-mail or voice mail, *execution* can initially seem stifling, confining, and restrictive. Some may describe it as controlling. While a certain level of spontaneity has its merits, significant achievement in selling will require the sacrifice of undisciplined schedules. It will require that you perform difficult tasks like prospecting for the agreed-upon number of hours on the specified number of days, consistently throughout the year. This is what leaders do.

For the most part, sales professionals who are top performers in your industry share your aversion to certain aspects of selling. For example, they don't naturally enjoy rejection any more than you do. They simply have mastered the ability to subordinate their own lack of interest or proficiency in one area to the understanding that personal and territory revenue potential will be attained only through consistent *execution* of the sales plan.

If you have planned well, trust yourself. Trust the plan. Trust your judgment that this map of your territory will lead you to your revenue goals for this year.

My experience suggests that, even with a clear *vision* of the territory firmly in place, sales professionals' motivation to stay committed to the plan wanes over time. We tend to relapse into old patterns of behavior that are safe, comfortable, and unproductive. The emergence of *Personal Leadership* as the driving force behind effective selling will require the sales professional to perform the hard tasks and difficult jobs, even when the almost overwhelming desire is to be grinding out reports, responding to e-mail, or reviewing a new competitor's Web site back at the office. Successful *execution* will require all three of the *Personal Leadership Drivers* to be fully operational.

Practice 2: Understand How to Manage the Scarce Resource of Time

From a selling perspective it will not matter significantly whether you have more or less of the assets and resources outlined in this section than your competitors. What will matter is how effectively you use the tools available to you to implement the strategies of your sales plan and to achieve your annual revenue goal. Don't spend a lot of time worrying about what you don't have. That is a needless expenditure of valuable energy. Just stay focused on the assets and resources in your sales stockpile and concentrate using them judiciously, leveraging their value by achieving important strategic objectives for this sales year.

In this section on managing the resource of time I will present material on ten different topics related to effective time management in professional selling. You may want to try to identify each one as you read through the paragraphs that follow. There will be a short self-assessment exercise at the end of the section as a brief review. Please keep in mind that the line between planning and *executing* is often blurred, as will become evident in this section. It is less important to understand to which skill the task is assigned and more important simply to complete the task.

Time is a scarce resource. While the amount of time available to achieve our annual goal is the same for all of us, how it is used differs widely among sales professionals. Leaders understand the nature of this invaluable resource and apportion it so as to move the territory closer to the realization of important goals and strategic objectives. Most sales professionals don't need more time to be successful; they simply need to concentrate the available time on highly productive activities. They need to be more attentive to the difference between working hard and working effectively. All sales activities are not the same, and an effective leader has the discernment to sort out the parasitic events that feed on key time windows during the day.

I have seen significant territory reversals over the years. In most of these instances the greatest single factor behind vast differences in revenue production has been the wise appropriation of time. It was rarely the sales professional's technical skill and competency, market changes or new developments in product technology. Those factors generally exert a long-term influence over the territory. Daily decisions to focus on high-leverage activities, made by a sales professional who understands time, influence both shortand long-term revenue production.

Personal Leadership requires judgment. *Personal Leadership* in selling requires it almost on a non-stop basis. Without a clearly defined *vision* and a fully developed plan, the sales professional reacts to changing conditions daily. This is a defensive posture, in which tactical decisions about the territory are remade weekly or even daily. Without a fully developed map, the route is unclear, and it is easy to get lost on unmarked roads, some of which dead-end at barren fields. A comprehensive plan is an offensive tool designed to be used preemptively, to eliminate time-wasting dead ends. A well-conceived *vision* is like a GPS system, directing you away from barren fields and toward the more fertile parts of your territory. The combination of a viable plan and the *execution* of high-leverage activities on a daily basis insures that the best use is made of the invaluable resource of time.

Sales professionals are well aware of available planning tools. Most often, these are used to schedule appointments and record follow-up notes. But a planning tool really needs to be more than a daily diary of events, where you record your whereabouts as you move from place to place. It should your primary repository of contacts, sales goals and follow-up notes, and a place to incorporate specific elements of your sales plan for the year. It also must be portable. It should always be nearby, whether you are in the car or meeting with a client.

If you use your planning tool only to schedule meetings with clients, you will find its contribution to your sales effort to be minimal. You may be indifferent to the specific nature of the tool itself. A planning tool to a sales professional is like a putter to a professional golfer. It needs to feel well-suited to your style and comfortable in your hands. A good putter has rescued many a golfer from errant shots. Over time, as clubs are upgraded and bags are changed, the putter remains. It is an ally, an old friend and a confidant. Planning tools serve a similar purpose.

Sales goals and strategies change from year to year. Clients come and go, and key contacts at the corporate office change regularly. Your planning tool should be a constant and dependable resource, allowing you to make those four-foot putts even under extreme pressure. It should be familiar terrain, a single-source reference guide for everything essential in your life. Used properly, it helps you manage one of your most important resources: your time.

Here are a few keys to consider in selecting your planning tool. First, it must be easy for you to use. Remember that famous gunfight scene in your favorite spaghetti western? You and another member of the sales team are standing on the dusty street. At the count of three, you will "draw" to find a client's phone number and your dry cleaner's address. How will you do? The information needs to be easily accessible.

Second, your planning tool must be relatively dynamic, allowing for changes in both information and the volume of material being stored. Finally, it has to be able to travel with you in the car and to your meetings with clients. No exceptions!

While most planning tools can integrate all aspects of your life into one place, far too many people fail to exploit this power. They compartmentalize their personal and professional lives. If you are to leverage this scarce resource, your time, to your full advantage, you must program all facets of your life in a single location.

Most sales professionals have full lives outside of work. Frequently, personal commitments and schedules overlap with professional responsibilities. They all should be considered as you plan your work week. This is most likely and most efficient when you use a single, easily accessible planning tool.

Early in my career, work commitments often required extensive travel. I will never forget being at an airport in Canada after a few days of meetings and realizing that it was my youngest son's birthday. I frantically tried to make arrangements to get home earlier than planned, but without any success. By the time I arrived home, my five year old was sound asleep. Some might think missing important family gatherings is a normal occupational hazard, but in this instance it was simply the result of poor planning. Meetings can be rescheduled; birthdays can't. Sales professionals generally work at their highest level when there is an appropriate balance between their personal and professional lives. A fully integrated planning tool facilitates that balance.

Weekly planning sessions are the catalyst that moves the sales strategy into the dayto-day operation of the territory. This meeting is one of the more obvious examples of high-leverage work. It is in the weekly planning session that you can spend an hour reviewing the week, assessing critical components of the sales plan that need attention, planning for important activities that need further preparation, and in   the process saving yourself three or four hours of wasted time. Sales professionals who conduct this meeting consistently always get better value from their time.

Weekly planning sessions are principally an offensive weapon. They require you to think ahead, to plan, to anticipate, to adjust and to adapt. This is where you can apportion your time, before other activities start clamoring for visibility. Working your schedule in advance, a week or possibly two weeks, allows you to say yes to critical sales functions that will advance your agenda for the territory, and simultaneously say no to other, less-important activities that may deserve attention, but have a lower yield rate in return for your time.

Planning ahead is the great equalizer. It allows you to think clearly about important strategic goals and objectives, and to schedule your time accordingly. Without a regular meeting to plan and schedule your time, you will always seem to be driving on the freeway behind a dump truck loaded with gravel, dodging and weaving to avoid the inevitable cracked windshield without bumping into motorists in the adjacent lanes. With your eyes fixated on the tumbling rocks in front of you, you are more likely to miss your exit. The ability to see miles ahead insures that you will make the right turns and arrive safely at your desired destination. Weekly planning meetings are a great way to avoid those nasty cracks in the glass.

Once the plan is fully assembled, with well-conceived implementation strategies in place, how does all this planning migrate into your daily work? Too many times it doesn't. It simply remains on the shelf, collecting dust, while work in the territory continues as usual. Transferring the plan from paper to practice allows you to mobilize your best critical thinking about territory needs, as you choose daily activities to answer them.

This one aspect of selling can make all the difference between a solid year and an exceptional one. The sales professional's ability to program the sales plan into daily and weekly activities is a significant way to leverage the resource of time.

There must be a process that allows the goals and strategies in your plan to find their way into your daily work. The more effectively you do this, the more you will spend your time on activities specifically designed to move your territory toward its long-term potential.

If one of your goals this year is to prospect for five hours a week, and your implementation strategy calls for one hour of prospecting every morning, how does this activity get plugged into your work week? First, review the sales plan every week, so it is firmly fixed in your mind. Next, be sure to allocate time in your planning tool for daily prospecting; you can do this during the weekly planning meeting.

Not all of the goals and strategies in your sales plan involve activities, like daily prospecting, for which time can be set aside on a weekly basis. For example, one of the key elements of your plan this year might be making presentations to ten of the largest accounts in your territory that are not currently buying your product. At the beginning of the year, utilize your planning tool to schedule this work. You may program the initial contact with one account to be made in early February, then schedule contacts with the others over the next eight to ten weeks. Write the account name and the contact person in your planning tool and identify the day and hour when you will make this initial call. Every other aspect of your sales plan needs to be programmed into your planning tool in a similar way.

Your planning should control most daily tasks and appointments in your territory, but, without a transfer method to move goals and strategies into your daily planning tool, much of your planning will be marginalized. Your planning tool should become a sort of command and control center for all the operational elements of your territory. Rely on it to give you relevant information about your schedule, and consult it concerning the availability of discretionary time. The planning tool must integrate the key elements of your sales plan in order for your sales strategies to gain any momentum. When it does, you will leverage the resource of time.

The third skill in Tactical Work is *being accountable*. The next chapter will focus on this important aspect of professional selling. Accountability plays an important role in leveraging the resource of time in the lives of sales professionals. The greater the level of accountability, the greater the probability that time will be expended on activities that are aligned with the important strategic objectives. If there is no accountability, there will generally be no forward movement in the territory. It is that simple.

The combination of a weekly planning session and a planning tool provides the sales professional with some built-in safeguards to insure that work performed during the week is consistent with established goals. Programming a system of accountability into the management of your territory is like purchasing insurance for your automobile. The greater the accountability becomes, the more assurance you have that the territory will be "dent free" at the end of the year. Insurance is about peace of mind. A well-developed system of accountability provides the same type of comfort.

It is impossible to have a serious discussion about maximizing time without also having a serious discussion about accountability methods. Accountability is a bulwark to insure the proper and timely implementation of the sales plan. Sales professionals who eschew accountability in any form, even when it is of their own design, are destined to a career of watching others pass by on their way to the podium at the annual awards banquet.

Accountability is a principle designed to increase lift in the territory. Choosing to ignore it will result in a lot of grounded flights. Much of the lift that comes from even simple accountability tools is rooted in the effective use of the scarce resource of time.

Execution in Tactical Work requires constancy amid change. The sales plan should have deep foundations of meticulous research that consumes large amounts of data. Once the foundations have been poured, they should only be reconsidered in the face of a large amount of compelling information. In most cases, it will not be the foundations of the plan, but rather some of the "framing," or strategic elements, which need revision or modification. Accommodating change is an important way to preserve the rich resource of time. Inflexibility is a stubborn fool that will impose greater costs even for minor revisions, once the building is in place.

Developing the flexibility to adapt the plan to changing market conditions is an important asset in your territory. Just be careful about tinkering with the foundations. Trust your judgment in assessing potential, and be willing to move forward with well-conceived strategies even when difficulties arise. Just because the road is steep is not sufficient reason to attempt a different route. The route should only change because of new information about road conditions, weather reports, traffic delays, or other information relevant to your selected course. Continue to process carefully new information about your territory, customers, and competitors. Adjust and modify as necessary, and allow yourself the flexibility to pursue new opportunities that were unseen a few months ago. Even the best maps need periodic revision. Having a current map of the territory is perhaps the best way to insure that time is always used effectively.

Practice 3: Leverage Budgets to Improve Revenue Production

This section on budgets will be much like the preceding section on time. There will be ten specific topics presented, and at the conclusion of the section a short selfassessment exercise will help you to evaluate your own progress in managing the scare resource of money.

In most organizations and with most sales professionals, the funding available to support sales programs is scarce. There are always more legitimate opportunities to spend money than there are available dollars. As with time, the challenge with this resource is insuring that whatever dollar amounts are allocated to your sales plan are spent to fund programs and activities with the highest yield rate. Understanding the differences between yield rates is an important aspect of leadership in selling.

I have been surprised over the years that some elements of selling seem to be institutionalized in the minds of sales professionals and, consequently, they seldom stand back far enough to ask whether an activity provides the best opportunity to move closer to the year's revenue goal. In the industry where I have worked, I have found that trade shows typically offer low yield rates in terms of generating viable customer leads. They have a relatively high front-end cost, so in the final analysis the cost per lead can be staggering. Yet because these shows are a sort of rite of passage, large amounts of money continue to be allocated year after year, and sales professionals are anxious to spend long hours on the trade show floor in search of potential new customers.

Because money is scarce, the decisions about its effective use need to be made in the larger context of the goals and strategies for the territory this year. Trade shows might be a good way to meet new customers; the pressing question is whether or not there is a better alternative. That a sales activity is *good* is not sufficient justification to allocate scarce dollars to it from the sales budget. You should always be in search of something *better*, seeking ultimately to spend funds on the *best* available option. The following are general guidelines that will help you stay focused on finding the best ways to expend this scarce resource, money.

The interconnectedness of Strategic and Tactical Work is seen almost daily in decisions that need to be made about your territory. When you conduct the market assessment portion of assessing potential, it may seem like that exercise is principally designed to quantify the market revenue potential for your territory. It has other implications as you move further along in planning and budget allocation.

Clarity about the market is paramount in designing a long-term strategy. This clarity is also useful when deploying resources and assets during the sales year. For example, if the market assessment reveals low brand awareness among one narrowly defined group of potential buyers, then funding a sales effort that would specifically address this deficiency may be an important sales priority in the current sales year. The market assessment is designed to reveal market needs; the strategy flows naturally from it to address those needs. The greater the perceived market need *and* opportunity, the higher the potential yield rate.

Work done on a comprehensive market assessment casts a long shadow over the sales professional's work in the territory throughout the year. That one exercise in understanding and forecasting trends, competitors, regulatory factors, the impact of new technology, and buying habits among key customer groups provides the broader context for strategic decisions and for some of the day-to-day tactical decisions in the territory.

Like time, money is generally allocated best when it is allocated well in advance. Your budget for the sales year should be allocated in concert with your final work on the goals and strategies portion of your annual sales plan. Otherwise you run the risk of funding programs and activities that may have value, but which are not completely aligned with your long-term strategy to address pressing market needs. Key market initiatives for the sales year should be developed with one eye on the market assessment and the other on available dollars for your territory. If your goals and strategies for this year are not supported by the necessary financial resources, you are conducting little more than an exercise in wishful thinking. All operational plans for the current sales year need to be firmly grounded in the reality of your funding.

Allocating your annual budget in advance and in alignment with major sales initiatives is another leadership imperative. *Personal Leadership* is driven by a *vision* of new possibilities and steadied by the discipline of *character.* You will need *character* to say no to some legitimate expenses this month so that you can say yes to activities that allow you fully to *execute* your plan. You need a leader's self-discipline to spend your sales budget only on activities identified through advanced planning.

If you will develop a cohesive strategy for your market, then carefully set aside resources well in advance to fund your complete program, you can lay claim to the realization of your own potential. You might be able to visualize clearly what your market can produce, but you will never reap the harvest if you lack the self-discipline to fund in advance the key strategic initiatives for the current sales year.

Consistently generating revenue that is at or above established goals provides a dividend to the sales professional in the form of commission payments, bonuses or perhaps even a measure of job security. Consistent operation within established budgets provides a dividend to the company, insuring that the proper balance exists between revenue and the cost of sales. Sales professionals who assume that exceeding revenue goals justifies exceeding budget numbers marginalize their own contribution by exaggerating their own relative worth. There are no entitlements in professional selling. Sales professionals who are effective leaders understand that they have a fiduciary responsibility both to drive business for the company they represent, by producing revenue, and to keep costs in line by operating within established budgets for their territory. Ignoring either of these realities is reckless at best.

Without exception, the finest sales professionals I have known are obsessive about revenue numbers and are borderline compulsive about managing budgets. They manage budget allocations as if they were their own money, and they refuse to spend budget dollars simply because they can. They generally know months in advance if their year-end expenses will exceed the established budget. When this happens, they nearly always either engage the corporate team in a discussion about making provisions for additional funding, or they respond with a willingness to bring expenses back in line with year-end targets. Outstanding sales professionals are equally committed to generating revenue and controlling costs. *Character* is the *Personal Leadership Driver* that supports *execution;* this is seldom more apparent than in managing budgets. *Character* is about acting with propriety in any stewardship, and few responsibilities are more important than controlling costs through the proper management of your budget.

There are many different metrics for assessing the overall effectiveness of sales team members. I happen to believe that very few, if any, are as relevant in evaluating sales effectiveness as the cost of sales ratio. This is a very simple calculation that measures total expenses in the territory as a percentage of gross revenue. Every sales plan should establish year-end targets for this number. Periodic monitoring of this number throughout the year will provide you some useful feedback on your overall performance in both generating revenue and controlling costs.

No specific ratio is applicable to all industries and all products. However, within your organization right now you should be able to find some historical data that tracks the top revenue producers and their corresponding territory expenses. If you have been selling in the industry for some time, you should be able to review your own numbers and determine a reasonable maximum sales total and a corresponding baseline (budget) for required expenses to support that level of performance.

Cost of Sales Ratio

$$\frac{\text{Total Sales Cost/Budget/Salary/Commissions, etc.}}{\text{Total Revenue Produced in the Territory}} = \text{Cost of Sales \%}$$

Periodically monitoring the cost of sales ratio is like monitoring your heart rate during a workout. It is an important vital sign that indicates the overall fitness level of the territory, and it is almost as easy to check as your pulse. Where sales professionals are conscious of this important ratio, it has an impact on decisions about expenditures throughout the year. If you will monitor this ratio periodically, even every other month, it will give you a reference point for balancing the important relationship between producing revenue and controlling costs. The higher the number, the greater the possible need to initiate some type of corrective action. This is just one way to confirm what you most likely already know about the relative health of your territory.

Much of what I have already said about properly managing your budget and monitoring your cost of sales ratio also relates to the notion of viewing your territory as an individual profit center for the company. This has as much to do with how you think as it does with how you work. There is a tendency for some sales professionals who work away from the regional or corporate office to feel somewhat disconnected from direct responsibility to contribute to the company's overall financial well-being. Thinking of your territory as an individual profit center is one way to reestablish that connection.

The concept of an individual profit center moves past budget control and the cost of sales ratio. From the most fundamental perspective this concept, like much of what we have already discussed in this chapter about character, is directly related to quality. As a rule you can almost always be assured that, when the discussion involves character, quality is not too far away. In the context of understanding your responsibility to be an individual profit center, the discussion of quality is directed related to price.

Not all sales organizations have wide latitude in establishing product pricing. If you control or significantly influence pricing, you also have an implicit responsibility to insure the relative quality of the price as it relates to gross margin objectives for the company. Perhaps the single most common problem I have experienced among members of a sales team is the tendency to be overly zealous about contracting work at a price point that puts the company in an unfavorable position. I worry about the technical capability of a member of the sales team whose only leverage in securing an order is lowering the price. Price-driven sales strategies make sense for big box retailers, but if price becomes the sole determinant in product selection decisions, the role of the sales professional is marginalized.

Sales professionals have a responsibility to establish in the minds of customers a baseline standard for expectations about overall product performance and the associated service that will be provided. Skilled practitioners of selling position their product squarely in terms of well-defined customer needs. When a transaction is conducted by a seasoned professional, the customer understands clearly the value of the product benefits and in most instances differentiates one product from another not only in terms of perceived benefit, but also by the relative skill and competency of the product representative. As a rule, the more competent the sales professional, the greater the latitude in establishing product price points. The inverse of that is also true. If your mindset is entirely driven by offering a lower price, you are *selling out*, not *selling up*.

A sales professional's ambivalence or even mild inattentiveness to the relationship of product pricing to the overall financial health of the company often causes a loss of credibility within the organization. Members of the sales team can seem narcissistic, interested only in the payment of commissions and not in generating quality sales that benefit the entire organization. Most sales organizations have sales team members with the reputation of being willing to go to bat for the customer by going to war with the company. Such careers tend to be short-lived.

Product representatives who are outstanding professionals understand that revenue production is not simply a matter of quantity; it is also about quality, or consistency in generating *profitable* revenue. Profitability is almost always about price. Members of the sales team who can produce revenue while maintaining profitable margins understand what it means to operate as an individual profit center for the company.

If you rely on the corporate marketing team to provide up-to-date information about competitor pricing, you may be disappointed. Sales professionals fully engaged in the work of selling will themselves be, almost without exception, the best monitors of market price points. It is critical that you keep a log of project pricing in your territory, broken down by product type, competitor, and location. You should be the resident authority on product pricing in your territory.

The collection of market price point data is invaluable to you, as you assess your current sales strategy. How effectively you process this data will determine the efficacy of your strategy in response. Do the products your customers are selecting at a lower price provide the same overall value? Are they choosing these products because they do not fully understand the overall value your products provide? Do the product benefits you have described to your customers satisfy their specific needs? What do you need to do to reshape your message to have greater influence on their final buying decision?

Monitoring market price points and your overall *closing ratio* tells you how well you are matching product benefits with customer needs. Later in this chapter I will discuss the difference between a selling philosophy based on compassion versus one based on contempt. If you are convinced that, despite your best efforts, customers are stupid and will never fully "get it," you sell from a position of contempt. You can mask it with charm and pleasantries, but over time they will discover your contempt. The mask will slip off.

Budgets
Score 1 - 10 (1 = Strongly Disagree 10 = Strongly Agree)

		YOUR SCORE
1.	I conduct a complete assessment of the needs of my territory.	
2.	I carefully plan the allocation of my budget based upon territory needs.	
3.	The bulk of budget dollars are allocated at the beginning of every sales year.	
4.	I allocate dollars based up perceived "value" or opportunity.	
5.	I am constantly aware of my "cost of sales ratio".	
6.	I consistently operate my territory within established budgets.	
7.	I clearly explain the price of my product relative to the value it provides in satisfying customer needs.	
8.	I recognize my responsibility to be a profit center for the company.	
9.	I never simply spend my budget because "I can".	
10.	I am aware of the market price point for my product.	
	TOTAL POINTS	

More often than not, the mask simply allows you to hide from your own unwillingness to accept your responsibility to understand your customer completely and to offer solutions based on clearly identified needs. Contempt for customers is born of arrogance; careers in selling usually die of such arrogance. On the other hand, compassion assumes that customers are intelligent and will make informed buying decisions based upon a thorough review of the information. Contempt will lead you to try to *manipulate* outcomes. Compassion will empower you to *influence* outcomes.

Practice 4: Learn How to Allocate All Available Sales Support Material

I am always surprised when seemingly capable sales professionals lack a clear understanding of the assets and resources that are at their disposal. If they were merchants operating a small business, they would likely have a firm grasp on their inventory. Assets and resources are not always tangible items neatly stored on shelves, but they should be properly accounted for and identified in a way that allows easy retrieval.

Somewhere in your office, preferably in the appendix portion of your annual sales plan, you should have an inventory of assets and resources for your territory. If the company you represent doesn't provide a formal list, it will be easy to assemble. Like the scarce resources of time and money, the wise and timely deployment of these other resources can very often make the difference between winning and losing an order. I have provided a sample list in **Figure 6-2** to help you get started. Once you start thinking in terms of developing a comprehensive asset and resource inventory, you may find many other items for your list.

What assets or resources do you have that will support your claims about product performance? These could be studies from independent agencies, quality and reliability test reports, approval letters from various regulatory bodies, or perhaps a litany of customer testimonials. Corporate data is good. Data collected from independent bodies is better. A legacy of satisfied customers is best. Document your claims about product performance and fill your inventory with every possible piece of information that will help your customers come to a similar conclusion.

I would guess that most members of our sales team become familiar with and actually use less than half of the printed and electronic marketing and sales support information that we make available from the corporate office. (It is not always the same half.) Take some time to become familiar with every available piece of printed or electronic sales support currently available. Not only will it be useful at some point during the year, it may also help you learn something new about potential solutions which you are not currently discussing with your customers.

Most organizations have a wide range of product presentation material on various media. Even outdated material can contain useful morsels of information, particular about the product's history. Much of this older material can be edited and converted to usable formats for use by sales professionals.

1. Marketing brochures and mailers

2. Social networking accounts/links to relevant websites

3. Customer testimonials

4. Copies of outdated trade ads & promotional campaigns

5. Projects lists/Clients served

6. Trade articles

7. Product samples

8. Oral histories about the company, officers, etc. Need the story of the origin of the product and the company!

9. Detailed description of unique solutions provided by the product

10. Competitor analysis

11. Test reports/Listings/Governmental acceptance, etc.

12. Success stories of members of the sales team. Why were they successful?

Figure 6-2 Sample inventory of assets and resources for your territory.

Many sales professionals seem to think presentation material comes packaged with an expiration date. It's true that, depending on the industry, much of it can have a relatively short shelf life. But making a complete inventory of all material, regardless of expiration date, is a good way to catalog potential resources to assist customers in making buying decisions. If you will review all available company resources in various media formats, you will likely find a few splendid nuggets that can strengthen your message to your customers.

Sometimes the most beneficial part of a sales meeting is learning who in the organization is the keeper of company treasures. These treasures can include oral histories of the company's origins, back stories about the development of new products, and interesting sidebars about factors that have influenced long-standing relationships with key clients. You can also gain new understanding about who are the key resources within the company to help you address pressing product questions or provide new insight about effective marketing methods. This collection of resources includes not only the support team at the corporate office, but also fellow members of the sales team. Identifying who can be a resource on what specific topics is an important addition to your growing inventory.

Despite the call for a measure of uniformity in product presentations, these differ according to sales professionals' individual preferences. One of the most valuable items you can have in your asset and resource inventory is a copy of the basic presentation material used by top performers on your sales team. Understanding how proven professionals present the product will help you retool your own presentation and perhaps reveal some hidden weaknesses that have been holding you back.

I would also suggest that you collect some valuable metrics or "key indicators" about your performance in key areas, relative to the top company performers. Having this information in an easily accessible format will help you make adjustments to your sales activities during the year. You might include:

◆ Weekly prospecting hours.

◆ Weekly hours with clients.

- Monthly dollar volume of total bids.

- The weekly number of new product presentations to clients.

- The annual cost of sales ratio.

- The annual contract closing ratio (contracts as a percentage of bids).

Sales Assets

Score 1 - 10 (1 = Strongly Disagree 10 = Strongly Agree)

	YOUR SCORE
1. I regularly exchange information with other members of the sales team about the company and our products.	
2. I am seeking to master all technical aspects of my sales responsibility.	
3. I am very familiar with all company marketing support material and use it effectively.	
4. My presentations are professional, well conceived, interesting and clearly presented.	
5. I am an effective teacher.	
6. I have a broad knowledge of my industry.	
7. I add value to projects through my professional expertise.	
8. I measure my performance in key areas relative to other members of the sales team.	
9. I have conducted a complete inventory of available sales assets.	
10. I am constantly learning.	
TOTAL POINTS	

Tracking your performance according to these key indicators is a excellent way to monitor your relative progress within the organization. But remember that the ultimate objective of the *Sales Leadership Model* is not to measure your performance relative to your peers on the sales team. It is to hold you accountable for your performance relative to your own potential. Having a key indicator list in your resource inventory is just another tool to help measure your progress.

The resources of time, money and sales support material are critical to the success of every sales territory. The skill of a capable leader is needed to deploy these tools to maximum advantage. The deployment strategy is conceived by the annual market assessment and takes final form in the annual territory sales plan. Utilizing these assets and resources to accomplish the goals and strategies of the marketing plan requires the virtuosity of an accomplished conductor of a symphonic orchestra. When the brass, wind and percussion sections play the right notes at precisely the right time, the results can be breathtaking. The same is true in professional selling, when the leader of the territory uses to maximum efficiency the available instruments, which when *executed* in perfect harmony, can produce results that nearly always result in a thunderous applause.

Practice 5: Execution Is about Contract Closing

I hesitate to provide information about contract closing at the end of the chapter on *execution*. It is neither a footnote nor an afterthought. In the world of professional selling it is the culminating experience, by which our peers, associates and the senior sales leadership team measure us. After all the assessing, planning and character development work, if you can't consistently finish by closing orders, your time on the sales team will be brief.

While contract closing is the destination we seek, the process itself should be more of a byproduct of how we work than a particular moment in time. Failing to see the contract closing part of selling as a natural extension of consistently executing the six key selling skills is like refusing to see how arriving at your next appointment will be impacted by the proper care and maintenance of your car, the selection of an appropriate route, adequate fuel levels or changing weather conditions. Contract closing will naturally occur when you exercise your responsibility as a leader and implement the skills of Strategic and Tactical Work. It is a journey you take with your customers, not something you do to them.

Before I take you through a brief description of the contract closing process, let's consider what that process is *not*. This has been written about extensively, and my views are probably a minority opinion on this topic. It is not:

- ◆ A technique to manipulate behavior.

- ◆ A process of coercion.

- ◆ A memorized set of phrases leading a client to say "yes."

- Behavior that is threatening or bullying.

- About how much time and effort you spent developing this project.

- About you.

Your basic philosophy about contract closing should not be simply about asking the client to make a buying decision. It begins with how you view your customer.

Sales professionals who are practiced in the skill of *Personal Leadership* understand that their role includes identifying client needs and presenting workable solutions to problems which are sometimes quite complicated. They are trained to sell products, but they instinctively respect the customer's interest in the buying transaction. Sales professionals who are leaders know that in the discipline of selling there is no room for customer contempt.

Paradoxically, I find customer contempt pervasive in the profession of selling. It is seldom overt, yet the lingering nuance of veiled derision for customers is surprisingly commonplace. If you are to become an effective leader and move your territory to greater heights of revenue production, you will need first to answer this question: "Do I view my customers with compassion or contempt?" It is easy to ask, but the answers are frequently complex.

The term *compassion* in the context of selling has two specific components. First, are you willing to view the buying transaction from the perspective of the customer? In other words, are you fully prepared to subordinate your interest to that of your client? Second, do you assume that your customer is an intelligent, competent person who can process technical information, conduct a fair comparative analysis, and make an informed buying decision?

There are two primary ways in which sales professionals commonly demonstrate contempt for their customers. The first is a basic belief or attitude. The second is a practice, more or less. These two can be equally troubling in building relationships of trust with clients.

Let's take a closer look at the two faces of contempt in selling.

My experience suggests that far too many professionals view their customers with contempt and disdain. They speak about them with derision and to them with condescension. They like the revenue the customer provides; they just don't like the customer. In most instances this attitude is born of arrogance and nourished by self-interest. Many in the selling profession assume that they are sufficiently clever to mask their contempt with patronage and humor, but inevitably they are found out. Over time their narcissism is revealed, and they are relegated to the fringes, their careers marginalized by their own grossly inflated egos.

You most likely will not hear a group of sales professionals talk openly about their disdain for customers. Their language is generally a bit guarded, but if you listen long enough you can hear the echoes of contempt. It is stitched carefully into phrases which make it clear that the customer lacks the basic intelligence to reach an informed buying decision. It is as if to say, "If that customer had only half a brain he would be able to understand that my product performs twice as well as my competitor's and is half the price!"

Right, we all understand: Your customer is an idiot. After hearing your presentation, how could any reasonable person buy anything other than your product? (That's a bit melodramatic, but you get the picture.)

Selling is the process of *influencing* buying decisions. You will forfeit your ability to influence outcomes if you speak down to customers. Speaking down, reacting, complaining, whining and becoming argumentative are all symptoms of contempt. Given enough interactions with the customer, your attitude will become apparent. It is not enough simply to learn to say the right things; you must change your basic attitude about your client. If you can't change that, you had better hope that you are selling a product that a customer only buys once in your lifetime.

Sales professionals who are outstanding leaders recognize the importance of customers. They value not only their business, but also their opinions. They respect the customer's ability to make informed buying decisions. They recognize that the customer's selection of other, competing products

– which may legitimately be inferior – reflects more on the salesperson's ability to explain key differences than the customer's inability to process complex data.

Let me be blunt. If you cannot fully eradicate contempt for customers from your thinking, you will never reach your potential as a sales professional, and nothing in the rest of this book will change that.

Sales professionals who are effective leaders listen to their customers, work hard to build collaborative relationships and recognize that trust is an essential ingredient in any buying transaction. If you feign regard for a client while being consumed with contempt, you are being duplicitous. I have worked with hundreds of sales professionals over the past thirty years. In most instances a person who has a duplicitous character, particularly someone who has obvious disregard for customers, is easier to spot than a dolphin in a public swimming pool. Maybe the reason you are not getting the business you expect from that customer is because he or she is a much smarter than you think.

When our oldest son was in his second year of law school he invited my wife, Michele, and me to participate in a mock court that was conducted in a federal courthouse. The judge for the proceeding was a federal prosecutor, and the jury box was filled with senior undergraduate students who were completing their degrees in sociology. My wife and I were both sworn in as witnesses in a murder trial argued by a small contingent of law students.

It was an interesting case, purposely filled with complex legal issues that needed attention from the young prosecution and defense teams. The trial lasted about two hours, and at the conclusion of closing arguments the judge asked that the members of the jury to deliberate in the courtroom, so that the attorneys could benefit from their discussion of the evidence.

Each member of the jury was asked to comment on the proceeding. Not surprisingly, they all had a slightly different opinion of the case. However, at the conclusion, the jury verdict was unanimous. The defendant was acquitted.

Once the verdict had been rendered, the judge then thanked the members of the jury for their service and politely excused them from the courtroom. When the last member of the jury had left the room, the judge left his seat on the bench, walked over to the young law students, and rested himself on one of the tables in front of the defense team. The first words out of his mouth drew thunderous laughter from everyone in the courtroom, especially the young law students. Remember, this is a federal prosecutor who makes his living by influencing juries. He simply folded his arms and observed philosophically, "The first thing you have to remember is that all juries are stupid."

I found myself laughing, but not at the comment. It was something you might suspect a prosecutor might think, but reason would suggest that they would never utter those words of contempt in a public setting. But there they were, reverberating off the hallowed walls of a federal courthouse. It was as if he was taking the gloves off and saying, "Now listen, I may humor the jury when they are in the courtroom, but you need to understand that every jury at every trial is a bunch of idiots. The sooner you understand that basic concept, the easier your life will be at trial."

I don't know anything about that federal prosecutor. He may have had a distinguished career, and his work may be a credit to his profession. But his attitude toward the people he is seeking to influence is offensive. He came across as an intelligent and bright attorney who was smug and arrogant. The jury box that evening was filled with bright young minds that were more than capable of understanding the arguments of the case and coming to an informed verdict. His contempt, prejudice and seething disdain would have unavoidably spilt into the courtroom in a relatively short time. I find that it is nearly impossible to favorably influence people for whom you have little respect.

My fear is that many sales professionals harbor similar sentiments. If you view your customers as that prosecutor views juries, it will be only a relatively short time before your contempt seeps into the client's office. The less willing you are to view the buying transaction from the perspective of the customer, the more vulnerable you are to breeding a sense of contempt. The more you blame decisions to reject your product on the client's diminished capacity, the less likely you will be to accept responsibility for your own inability to favorably influence a buying decision. The more inclined you are to believe that the problem is with your customer and not with you, the more paralyzed you will be in trying to move your territory forward.

On the other hand, the more you respect your clients and see them as smart people who are more than capable of reaching a favorable verdict about your product, the better chance you will have to participate in a collaborative experience that will inevitably produce a steady revenue stream.

You may have been breathing easy during this discussion about the first form of contempt, since you hold your customers in high regard and consistently treat them with respect. I hope you fare as well during the next part of this discussion.

The second aspect of contempt is undoubtedly more obvious and more prevalent, since its purveyors have virtually built an industry on it. Contempt can be found not only in your attitude towards customers, but also in how you practice various aspects of selling. What appears to be just a selling practice on the surface can in principle be a manifestation of the low regard you hold for your customers.

Let me be a bit more specific. If your approach to selling is based in any way on a philosophy designed to manipulate buying decisions, your behavior is contemptuous. For example, if your standard practice in closing deals includes any subtle form of coercion or cleverly designed techniques or strategies – such as "trial" or "power closes" – implemented for the specific purpose of getting the customer to say yes, you are practicing contempt for your customer.

You are thinking, "But these techniques work!" So does a loaded gun, but no rational salesperson tries to close sales with one.

Techniques should never be used to coax a buying decision out of a customer. Again, sales professionals who are leaders subordinate their own interest in the transaction to that of the customer. The instant you cross the line and start trying to manipulate a customer's behavior, you have damaged your own credibility and discarded any rightful claim to that customer's business.

You simply cannot have it both ways. If you value trust, you can't practice techniquebased selling. If you seek collaboration, you can't do anything that would even hint of coercion.

Any way you look at it, methods designed to manipulate outcomes are veiled forms of contempt. You know when people are doing this to you. Your customers are bright enough to figure out when you are doing it to them.

If you view the contract closing in terms of methods or techniques, you are deeply invested in what I have already described as customer contempt. Any effort to manipulate behavior is contemptuous. While it may work for single transactions, in environments that require significant collaboration and where product repurchases are a common occurrence, manipulation strategies destroy trust and compromise the sales professional's ability to make a meaningful contribution to future buying decisions.

Contract closing is a process, not a single event. It begins with the first customer interaction and continues well after the order is placed. If you understand this, your success rate in securing contracts will increase dramatically over time. The process begins with a clear sense of respect and compassion for the customer. Again, in the context of professional selling compassion is your willingness to view the transaction from the customer's perspective and your understanding that the sole purpose for your involvement is to determine how you and your product can add value to the customer. It is selling with a service mindset. Let me give you two contrasting examples of contract closings.

Example 1. A few months ago my wife, Michele, had arranged for a company to visit our home and provide us a design option for replacing the countertops in our kitchen. The sales representative from the company calculated the sizes and then presented the prices for the different types of stone surfaces. He had a neatly prepared offer sheet which summarized the quantity of material to be ordered, the possible color choices along with available installation dates. After he reviewed the offer sheet he told us that he could only guarantee the prices while he was with us.

When Michele explained that she would like to visit the showroom the next day to look at some larger samples, so that she could resolve questions about color and also see how the joints in the stone were sealed, the sales representative first hesitated, and then escalated the pitch to move us closer to making a buying decision on the spot.

Michele emphasized again that she liked the product and was ready to buy, but there were just a few technical issues that need resolution. His response was, "We don't do business that way. I am authorized to offer this price, but when I leave the price is no longer valid." Michele was trying to turn him around and offered a compromise saying, "How about if I spoke to your manager and explained the situation, would that help?" He answered by saying, "If you make that call, it will most likely just get me fired."

We liked the product and the price was reasonable, but the terms of the offer were unacceptable. It felt that we were taken hostage by a sales representative and the policies of his company that prevented a reasonable resolution of our concerns about product selection. The terms of the offer were positioned in such a way that they felt, at least to us, a bit coercive. The added element of possible termination only added more distaste to a situation that was rapidly becoming intolerable. Needless to say, we chose another supplier for our countertops.

Example 2. A few years ago I met with a local technology company about incorporating computer animation as a way to demonstrate various different applications for our products. The type of animation we needed was different from what this company was doing, but after discussing the concept with the local sales representative he was willing to discuss it with his technical support team and to prepare a proposal.

A couple of weeks later at a follow-up meeting he came prepared not only to review the offer with me, but to show me a short computer-generated segment of how the finished product would look, if we chose to contract for his company's services. He had done his homework in setting our product in the context of a viable solution.

He suggested that I take some time to discuss it with other members of our leadership team and said that he would call me next week to discuss our decision.

The positioning of the offer was rooted in a solution-oriented environment that allowed me to experience in advance the benefit of product selection. The skill of this professional to frame the offer in the context of a clearly identifiable benefit accelerated the buying decision. It also eliminated the need for considering other proposals from competitive companies.

Most of us can easily recognize when we are working with a skilled sales professional. The buying transaction is always in the context of the needs of the customer, not the job security of the product representative. The process of contract closing is the natural result of needs that are clarified, benefits that address pressing customer concerns, and prices that reflect the realistic budgetary constraints of the buyer. Skilled professionals understand that the process of contract closing begins with the first interaction with the customer and remains an integral part of every subsequent communication. You will close contracts successfully in direct proportion to your ability to understand the needs of your customer and clearly explain how your product solves a viable need.

Sales professionals who have compassion for customers look up. They speak with language that builds trust and inspires confidence. Those who sell with contempt talk down. Their language, no matter how practiced it may be, is littered with condescension which ultimately destroys trust.

This is not difficult to understand. How do you like to be treated, when you are making an important buying decision? Behave that way with your customers. Forget what you have heard and read about power closes and accept that your customers are intelligent people who are capable of making informed buying decisions. You want that type of respect, and your customers deserve it.

In the paragraphs that follow I will introduce you to three phases of contract closing. These do not necessarily occur in a clean, linear timeline.

For some projects with short sales cycles, these phases might overlap, and in some instances, where projects have long sales cycles, the time between phases could be several months. It is not important to commit to memory the standard practices of each   of these phases. It is important to recognize that the process of influencing buying decisions begins with the very first customer interaction. The more you understand the customer's needs and solve problems in a collaborative way, the closer you move toward an actual buying transaction.

Discovery. For some reason this aspect of professional selling is consistently the weakest link for most members of the sales team. Most sales training programs are designed around products, not people. Accordingly, there seems to be an overwhelming urge to talk about products, benefits and features rather than doing the tedious work of discovery.

The discovery portion of contract closing generally begins in the very first meeting with the client. This is where you ask questions, learn the client's business and become familiar with how buying decisions are made, develop a feel for how the organization values your type of product, and familiarize yourself with the company's past purchases of competitive products. This is a meeting where you ask questions, take notes and listen attentively.

Discovery has two components. The first is assessing whether or not this customer is a good fit for your product. It may turn out that your customer has some interest, but you don't, for a variety of possible reasons. You are exploring the possibility of doing business together and obtaining as much information as you can, so you can reach a definitive conclusion. The second component is identifying possible solutions that your product can uniquely provide to the client. The discovery process rarely takes place during product presentations. It is generally more productive either one-on-one or with a small group.

As a rule, discovery is not a single event. It takes place over an extended period of time and may involve multiple meetings. The more information you have about your customer, the better prepared you will be to participate in collaborative problem solving.

Collaboration. For most clients products are interesting, but ideas are irresistible. When ideas are bundled as viable solutions to pressing problems or as a means to accelerate strategic initiatives, the sales professional is in a position to form an important alliance in which collaboration can begin. It is a rare occurrence for a sales professional to collaborate in problem solving or possibility thinking without having dedicated serious time to meaningful discovery. Selling is more about listening and learning than it is about speaking and teaching. All the product knowledge in the world is of little value, if you don't understand the subtle nuances of your customer's business.

Collaboration is what ultimately differentiates sales professionals from product representatives. Collaboration depends on an extension of trust, which the sales representative earns through willingness to subordinate self-interest to the client or the project. Where self-interest is projected, trust soon evaporates. In collaboration the sales professional assumes the role of a confidant and consultant and can provide ideas and solutions that are in the customer's best interest. Where collaboration regularly occurs, buying decisions ultimately follow.

Offer and Acceptance. The sales professional's responsibility to overcome objections on any topic, from pricing to product performance, is not its own phase of contract closing. It is embedded in every aspect of the selling process. Objections may be raised in the first meeting with a customer, during a formal product presentation, or after an initial offer is tendered. Selling is fundamentally about influencing buying decisions. If you lack the skill and competency to respond appropriately to difficult questions or to address serious objections about possible product selection, your customer will seek answers elsewhere.

Part of your preparation for every client meeting must be anticipating every conceivable question or objection. New members of the sales team are often given some latitude by customers on complex technical questions, but most customers assume that few questions about your product are entirely original. Almost all possible questions have been asked and answered previously. Navigating the rolling waves of objections is a unique opportunity for the sales professional to demonstrate confidence and competency under pressure. Where the waves are breaking, the shore – here, the order – is usually not far away.

Skilled sales professionals relish thoughtful questions and even entrenched objections. They signal customer involvement and the possibility of an eventual buying decision. Questions and objections naturally result from critical thinking; without them you can generally assume that neither you nor your product is being taken seriously. Tough questions also accelerate discovery, moving you closer to collaboration, and therefore closer to a final decision about your product.

The sooner you can discuss price and address all questions related to budget considerations, the sooner you can concentrate on shaping the overall value message of your product for your customer. Don't put off talking about price. It is on everyone's mind, and it should be on the tip of your tongue. Unless you take the offensive and resolve this question, it will grow into a mammoth objection that blocks serious discussion about product benefits, and in the process marginalizes your credibility as a collaborative partner.

A discussion of price is obviously not a formal offer. It is simply a matter that needs to be addressed. If your product price position is noticeably higher than the competition, address this matter squarely up front. Don't let the customer be the first to bring it up. You must lead with this, or you will appear either out of touch or duplicitous. Acknowledge the difference in price, then demonstrate that the overall value of your product to the customer will more than offset any price differences. Be sure you can deliver on that promise.

The offer, when it occurs, must be clear. Ambiguity will be viewed as either careless or self-serving; neither leads to final acceptance. Up to this point you will have been careful and consistent in subordinating your interest to the client's. Sloppy proposals can sabotage your good work in developing high-trust relationships.

While the offer is not the finish line, you should treat it like one. Save some of your best work for this part of the selling process. Where possible, review the offer with the customer and address any questions about its content or special circumstances. If you can learn to present an offer with the same level of professionalism that you present your product, you will position your territory for sustained revenue growth.

Presenting the offer is your chance to make your own closing argument, before your customer decides whether you have made your case and earned the right to do business. Summarize the benefits. Review the overall value of the product to the customer. As much as possible, position the offer in terms of solving a pressing problem for the client. This summation shouldn't contain any new information. It is simply a re-statement of the position you have articulated since the conclusion of initial discovery. If your product presentation is well positioned through thoughtful discovery and you were allowed to collaborate with the client on solutions to important problems, much about the offer and acceptance phase of contract closing will be a formality. I am not suggesting that this process is easier than what you may have previously learned about contract closings. In fact, it is more complex and more difficult to *execute* effectively. But it is the only viable approach to successfully negotiating contracts within the framework of high-trust relationships.

Execution and the Symptoms of Sales Paralysis

Execution has high impact on "Winging it" and "Low energy for problem solving." One aspect of the Eight Symptoms of Sales Paralysis that we have not discussed is the obvious fact that some are more prevalent than others, and some have a more debilitating effect on revenue production than others. In my opinion, "winging it" is both very prevalent and extremely debilitating. Consequently, while *execution*'s overall impact may not be as broad as that of the three skills of Strategic Work, it still offers noteworthy gains the level of work in the territory.

Symptom	Impact	Comments
Winging it	HIGH	Consistent execution of the *Plan* eliminates costly detours.
Lack of a sense of urgency	LOW	Executing the *Plan* allows for different levels of response.
Contemplation of a job change	MEDIUM	Working your *Plan* creates a new level of confidence in the future.
Feelings of frustration	LOW	Following the *Plan* moves you past the pitfalls that bring you down.
Blaming others	MEDIUM	No time to pass blame when your head is down working your *Plan*.
Low energy for problem solving	HIGH	The process of executing generates control. Control bumps energy.

As we continue our discussion on the skill to *Be Accountable*, it will become apparent that these three selling skills, despite their importance to the long-term success of the territory, will have less impact on the nagging symptoms of Sales Paralysis than the three skills of Strategic Work. However, even small gains in offsetting Sales Paralysis will result in important gains in overall revenue production in the territory.

Execution: A Quality Statement

Execution is what you are doing today. The more closely your *execution* is aligned with the annual territory sales *plan*, the more likely it is that revenue will move closer to the market's overall potential. Understanding and implementing the skill of *execution* requires the discipline of an effective leader. Judiciously allocating key discretionary assets and resources in a way that advances the territory in accordance the sales plan is a *Personal Leadership* imperative. It requires keeping your head up while your feet are moving fast.

Rarely will you find any meaningful shortcuts in the *execution* of the sales plan. Rarely do people of *character* seek shortcuts up the mountain. Shortcuts are suckerpunches. They feign a path of relative ease, while hiding the dismal reality of a steep climb beyond the next turn. The way to accelerate up the mountain is not by searching for a shortcut, but by taking on more fuel by understanding completely why you want to climb higher than you have previously been. That topic will be discussed in the next chapter. There simply is no other way to arrive at the summit of your own greatest professional achievement.

Doug Yates has accomplished more in his life than most of us dream about. He began his journey with serious limitations and persevered by learning to adjust and adapt to a new and ever changing set of realities. He isn't distinguished by his great plans, but rather by his great *execution*. He allowed himself to think big, while requiring himself to work hard. *Executing* is all about work.

PART I

Passion

THE FINAL *Personal Leadership Driver* that powers the selling process is *Passion*. Don't underestimate the role of *passion* in producing enviable sales totals. I have worked closely with members of the sales team who developed a sense of *vision* and were people of solid *character*, but who found themselves almost constantly in the bottom third of the annual sales report. All three *Personal Leadership Drivers* must be fully operational to sustain the effort required to produce the type of revenue that is consistent with your ability and the potential of your territory.

Passion in professional selling most often takes up residence in the skills of *identifying motivators* and learning to *be accountable* – two fundamentally different skills connected by the same *Personal Leadership Driver*. In the next two chapters you will come to understand how *passion* can be a compensatory leadership trait. In many respects, people with *passion* can still produce enviable revenue numbers, even though they have underdeveloped skills in *Vision* and *Character*. However, it is only when *Vision, Character, Passion* and the six associated skills are fully operational in your life that will you start to experience what it means to work at a level consistent with your own potential. This singular objective is what makes the *Personal Leadership Model* unique in the world of professional selling.

From the first two skills in Strategic Work we have learned more about what needs to be done to align our performance with our potential, and how this work needs to be done to insure that our customers benefit from the highest quality of work available. The third and final skill in Strategic Work forces us to look inward to answer the basic question, "Why should I pursue my potential and create excellence in every aspect of my professional life?"

Understanding why reveals the level of *passion* we have for lofty goals. Without *passion* even our grandest designs for our sales territories will have a very short shelf life.

The entire *Personal Leadership Model* would collapse under its own weight, if there were not a clear mechanism in place to insure the development and sustaining of the highest possible levels of personal motivation. In most sales organizations a significant difference between moderate-level performers and the consistent high achievers can be measured in terms of sustained levels of motivation, passion, and desire to achieve goals and produce outstanding work. The selling skills involved in both Strategic and Tactical Work quite literally depend upon the fuel of motivation to produce effective execution and final completion. Working to sustain personal motivation is an important aspect of *Personal Leadership* in selling.

If you cannot sustain the passion to achieve for long periods of time and through stretches of adversity, it is unlikely that you will ever realize your professional potential. To be complacent about your own motivation makes no more sense than to ignore your physical health. Most of us are programmed to spend countless hours understanding the technical aspects of our products and becoming collaborative resources to our customers in solving problems. All of these functions are vital to long-term success in selling, but, without a clear understanding of what motivates you to improve and achieve goals that inspire your best effort, you will grow weary over time, and your fatigue will compromise your ability to sustain an optimal level of performance. It will diminish your effectiveness as a skillful collaborator.

Sales professionals who are considered truly outstanding by their peers, customers, and company associates maintain a level of excellence for a long period of time. We have all seen a member of the sales team catch the proverbial lightning in a bottle one year and disappear from the radar screen the next year. Short bursts of motivation are elusive and can leave us feeling uncertain about future outcomes. Likewise, short-term success can promote feelings of insecurity, and over time we can become dismissive of legitimate, hard-earned accomplishments in our past. To become truly outstanding as a sales professional requires consistent success over long periods of time. This requires consistency in the achievement of lofty goals, which, in turn, require our best effort and our constant attention to the factors that drive us to improve and excel every year. *Identifying the motivators* is our only inoculation against relapses into mediocrity.

Passion is what moves you to do hard things; to make one more phone call or to prospect another tedious hour. It is what drives you to hold yourself accountable for goals and strategies even when no one else seems interested. *Passion* is generated by looking inward; the outward results will quite often surprise you.

CHAPTER 7

Identify Motivators

Finding a Renewable Source of Energy

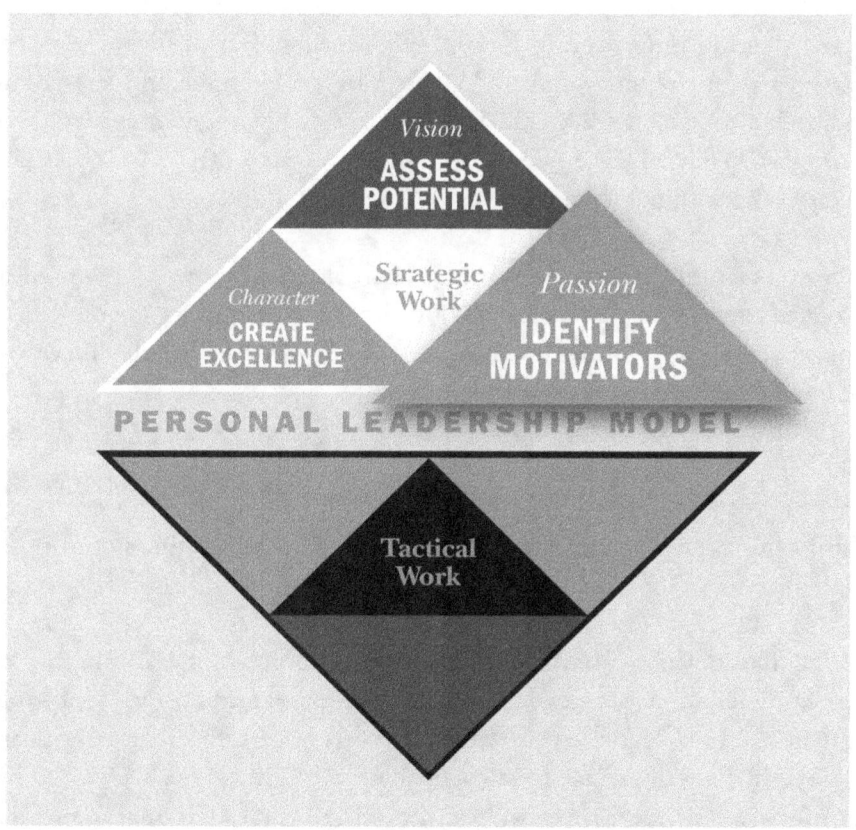

Figure 7-1 Identify Motivators: The *Passion* Component of Strategic Work

MOTIVATION moves us. It propels us towards our dreams and moves us within reach of extraordinary feats found in the stratosphere of human performance. It can nudge us out of our natural solitude and into new places, hidden places, where learning abounds, potential is achieved, and the realization of our greatest hopes becomes common-place. Motivation can also propel us to take risks.

When our oldest grandson, Wiley, reached his fourth birthday, he received a morning phone call from his grandmother. I listened as she explained to him that she had birthday presents for him and that she was anxiously looking forward to his visit later in the day. The phone call was not noticeably different from calls in previous years. Wiley's father had recently finished college, and the family had moved to a new location about a mile from our home.

Later that morning, around 10:30, I was working in my office when I received a frantic phone call from Wiley's mother. I immediately sensed the fear in her tone. Her voice crackled with pain as she urgently pleaded, "We have lost Wiley, and we need help." I ran from my office. I was outside their home within a few minutes.

This typical mid-February morning was cold and damp. As I parked in front of their house, I was greeted by a team of neighbors assembled for the search effort. Rolling down my car window, I asked Wiley's mother, "How long has he been gone?"

She said, "About fifteen minutes."

I told her that I would widen the search, while the others continued the effort door-to-door in the neighborhood.

Wiley had never before attempted to walk to our home alone, nor, to my knowledge, had he ever accompanied his parents on the one-mile journey across several well-traveled roads and unfamiliar neighborhoods. It made no sense to suspect that he might be on his way to his grandparents' home, except for the simple fact that birthday gifts awaited him there. He knew the general direction, and that alone may have been enough to propel this blond-haired, blue-eyed, energetic young boy into the cold on an ill-advised journey.

About five blocks from his home, in the general direction of our house, I spotted Wiley. He was sitting with his legs crossed and his arms folded on the grass in the front yard of a home. The owner was standing a few yards away. She was a kind, elderly woman, who obviously had determined that Wiley was lost. She was trying to obtain the information needed to locate his concerned parents.

Wiley sprang to his feet, when he saw me, and I hugged him tightly in my arms. Apparently, that embrace was sufficient to convince the kind neighbor that she could release Wiley into my custody without further investigation. I called Wiley's mother, and for a few moments things in the world were right again.

Even Wiley's four-year-old mind could grasp a clear image of birthday gifts from his grandmother long enough to increase his sense of yearning. With his conscious mind completely absorbed in the vision of highly desirable rewards, his subconscious mind provided some ideas about how he could obtain these gifts. Unfortunately, his rational, four-year-old conscious mind abdicated its responsibility to convince him that walking across town in the middle of the winter, crossing several busy intersections, was a very bad idea. Still, there is a useful pattern here.

Controlled, sustained thinking about realistic and achievable outcomes which are firmly grounded in critical thinking and analysis can motivate us out the door to face cold, harsh winters and the uncertainty of difficult journeys. Sustained thinking about desired outcomes, set in the context of personal benefit, increases our personal motivation. The personal energy provided by positive thoughts and emotions, when preceded by an effort to assess potential and an underlying commitment to create excellence, can propel us across the busy intersections of life, where peril lurks, and onto a course that, when properly planned and consistently traveled, will lead us to gifts that would make our grandmothers proud.

Principles and Practices in the Development of the Skill of Identifying Motivators

I have repeated several times already that this book and the *Personal Leadership Model* in particular are primarily about skill development. Principles point us in the proper direction and provide us with the philosophical answers to pressing questions about why certain things need to get done at certain times and in certain ways. But the upward lift that will propel you to new heights in revenue production will only be found in the "learned power" created by skill development. Principles lead us to practices. Practices lead to the inculcation of skills in the routines of our professional lives. So try to understand the principles, but be diligent in working on the practices. The transformative power you seek to achieve your potential as a sales professional will be found in the consistent application of the *six key selling skills*.

It is in the *six key selling skills*, powered by the three *Personal Leadership Drivers*, that your hands will be repositioned at the end of the bar. The longer your hands remain in that position, the more likely your sales totals will be to experience significant growth, and the more clarity you will have about a workable plan to see your territory sales potential become a reality.

The organization of this chapter will be somewhat different from that of the previous four skill chapters, in that the three principles will be presented separately at the beginning of the chapter. The three practices will follow. You will find that a repetition of the practices will help you realize the overall objective of each of the individual principles, laws or assumptions about the role of motivation in the selling process.

Principle A. Sustaining Motivation for the Long Term Fuels All Great Achievements

We live in an age of energy shortages. Renewable energy seems like only the shadow of a distant dream. Offshore drilling is finding political favor, fossil fuels markets are becoming increasingly competitive, and innovative alternative sources of energy are becoming more commonplace. The diverse world economy and the ability to sustain life on this planet depend upon the development of new, long-term, presumably renewable energy sources. Fuel is a life-sustaining commodity.

Fuels mined from deep within the earth have a short shelf life. Energy found deep within oneself has no expiration date.

Hydroelectric power is energy produced by water turning large turbines below manmade dams; a single dam can produce enough electricity to power a large city. Personal motivation is energy mined from thoughts, turning the hearts and minds of people, sometimes subconsciously. From this single source of energy will come solutions to the most complex problems of our time. Disease will be eradicated, the scourge of poverty abolished, great mountains climbed, records broken, relationships healed, and personal potential realized.

Energy is a commodity we take for granted almost daily. It provides the power to move us to inspiring destinations and important life celebrations. It allows us to read thoughtful words from previous generations. Energy powers the vehicle we use to travel to our dreams, and to arrive at places never before thought possible.

Motivation is the energy of the heart and the fuel source for all great human achievement. It is mined from the *passion* of life, stored in the deep recesses of the mind. The arrival at any personal destination depends upon it. Goals evaporate without it. Records remain unbroken in its absence, and the human spirit is muted when motivation ceases to exit. Motivation is the buoyancy in life that makes the impossible seem possible, hardships seem manageable, fears seem marginal, and perseverance seem doable.

The energy that powers the world is produced with a well-conceived plan, consistent execution, and a disciplined will to push past failures and setbacks. The energy that powers the human spirit is no different. The energy of personal motivation is intensified by planning, fortified by self-discipline, and magnified by the desire to overcome adversity. Personal motivation is a renewable source of energy that costs nothing to produce and pays enormous dividends.

Solving the world's long-term energy problems is a formidable task that will require vision and unparalleled creative innovation. And whether future generations are powered by corn harvested in Cedar Rapids, recycled garbage from Duluth, or windmills from Mobile, one thing is certain: new sources of cost-effective and renewable energy will be developed. In a critical sense they will be developed from the same sources as in the past, from deep within the minds of people who are fueled by the desire to succeed and driven by inspiring mental images that propel them to greatness.

Human motivation is the fuel source behind every invention, every piece of art and every scientific discovery in the history of the world. Motivation is the fuel mined from dominant thoughts. Your ability to create stimulating mental images of high-performance outcomes provides ready access to this renewable energy source.

At this moment your life is the sum total of your thoughts. Your future will be no different. You can change your life and your future by changing your thoughts. Thoughts are the energy of the soul. What are you thinking about?

Principle B. Motivation Sustains Commitment through Long Sales Cycles

Learning to *identify motivators* is a key to effective *Personal Leadership* at any level, and it is particularly relevant to the world of professional selling. Few things can have greater impact on your pursuit of your potential as a sales professional than the concepts outlined in this chapter. I have lived them myself, and I can say without equivocation that these basic principles have changed my life.

Controlled thinking and visualization were shockingly new to me 25 years ago. I remember the place, the time and the person speaking, when I was first introduced to them. They made complete sense at the time, and they continue to do so. I ascribe any measure of success in my professional life to the information in this chapter, more than to any other skill in the *Personal Leadership Model.* Here is one example.

For much of what might be described as the "middle portion" of my career, I spent about thirty percent of my time working as a lobbyist. The regulation we were attempting to have passed would have considerable impact on the selling environment for our products. It was analogous to developing a design alternative to seat belts. The enforcement officials who were caretakers of the existing regulation were content with things as they were. Our job, by analogy, was to persuade them that a new technology would improve safety for the general public.

The process itself was excruciatingly complex, and the challenge of educating hundreds of decision makers about the virtue of new technology seemed, at times, overwhelming. It officially started in February 1986 and was eventually completed in 2000. The new national regulation legitimized our emerging technology.

We were successful, and our impact on product acceptance exceeded our expectations. The details of committee work, annual membership votes, revised submittals, and overcoming floor objections are not important to this discussion. What is important here is that, over time, I learned how to experience the adrenaline rush of the hearings so vividly in advance that I could hear the objections, work through a response strategy with a team of consultants, and maintain a strong offensive stance with key committee members.

I repeated this process over and over in my mind. This allowed me to feel in advance the exultant joy of the final floor vote in favor of the proposed changes. To a large extent, the image of that single moment breathed life into a project that could have died after the first few years of failure. Bringing about an important legislative initiative took sixteen years. Nothing contributed more to our success in this prolonged effort than creating compelling mental images of desired outcomes, as outlined in this chapter.

The mental image of our desire outcome had become so real to me, that I distinctly remember arriving at the airport after the final vote, walking into the boarding area, and laughing silently to myself that the experience looked and felt just as I had imagined it, with the one exception. There were no signs and no roaring applause from company associates at the airport, as I had envisioned. I had seen the "movie" so many times that I knew the ending. Those brief images provided enough fuel to keep the process alive through sixteen years of rejection and frustration. It will work for you, too, as you endure what I hope will be much shorter sales cycles in your territory.

Principle C. Motivation Comes from Understanding Yourself

What motivates you? Do you know? Can you positively describe the two or three most significant motivators in your life? Personal motivation is the fuel source that will sustain both your long-term commitment to producing excellence and your achievement of your greatest potential. It is crucial to understand where that motivation comes from, in order to cultivate and protect it. If the supply of motivation fails, the result can be the institutionalization of mediocrity.

We may be able to sense that we are under-performing. Perhaps, in those lucid moments when we think deeply about the territory, we may glimpse the rudiments of a vision that increase our understanding of what might be possible in our sales careers. Crafting a clear *vision* for our work and committing ourselves fully to creating excellence through the achievement of our own potential are crucial, but we will never fulfill the *vision* or the commitment without sustained motivation.

Those of us who ride the diet and weight loss roller coaster understand the importance of drilling deep into our source of personal motivation. We see the vision of a healthier body and embrace the principle of becoming our best, but somehow the constant grind of the treadmill wears us down, and we begin to believe that our personal goals are far beyond our reach. At first we resist mediocrity, but over time, without proper motivation, we gradually accept a reality that falls far short of our ability and potential.

Increasing our sales numbers is like decreasing our body fat. Both require us to identify clearly why we are attempting to scale this summit. If you don't know your three most important reasons for wanting to succeed in your career and cannot discuss them with considerable specificity, your lofty revenue goals will likely fade faster than your attendance at the local fitness center. Unless you fully tap into the sources of your personal motivation, the other components of Strategic Work will be impotent to move you toward your own potential. The more clearly you can see desired outcomes in your mind, the more your *passion* for them begins to grow. For example, money is often cited as a primary source of motivation for sales professionals; it is probably the most common response. But why is there such disparity in motivation levels among professionals who embrace the same motivator?

It is critical that we plumb regions of our heart and mind to understand why we want to succeed. This subject of identifying and enhancing personal motivation has been carefully examined by very qualified authors for most of the latter part of the twentieth century. What began, at least to some extent, with the work of Napoleon Hill, and was expanded by Maxwell Maltz and others, has come to be widely embraced and reformulated in the contemporary success literature. Here I will provide a brief summary of some points from that literature which relate to personal motivation in the context of professional selling.

Many of us are programmed to believe that, since life offers no viable shortcuts to successful careers, we should marginalize methods that seem too simple. We applaud difficult climbs and dismiss paths which do not require long hours of arduous toil. Consequently, we may be inclined to discard the suggestion that a task so seemingly menial as controlling our thoughts may have the power to shape our professional destiny. Its apparently simplicity may seem to trivialize a serious undertaking.

Nothing could be further from the truth. Controlling our thoughts is not simple, and the outcomes are never trivial. Thoughts produce emotions; even random thoughts can influence behavior. Well-conceived thoughts, sustained over long periods of time and saturated with clear, rich images of desired outcomes, can push us forward at an accelerating rate.

The subconscious mind lacks the ability to differentiate fully between fact and fiction. Consider the strength of emotions generated by watching the images embedded in celluloid play out on a silver screen in a movie theater. The impact of the experience largely depends upon the audience's willingness to suspend disbelief and process the story as if it were real events playing out in real time before their eyes. In certain kinds of movies, people scream with the same shrill pitch and authentic emotional intensity we might expect in real life. The same is true of tears, which flow naturally, as if we were actually living the experience.

What we are watching is not happening in real time, and usually it is fiction. Yet our experience of it is real, including the physiological and psychological responses within our bodies and minds. If we can tap into that power to create feelings and emotions within ourselves, we can access the fuel source that will sustain our longterm motivation towards outstanding achievement.

Several years ago my wife and I were driving in separate cars to a destination about fifty miles away. Most of the drive was on interstate highways, and the total time from start to finish was approximately one hour. When we arrived at our destination, the restaurant where we were having lunch, I was stunned when she stepped out of the car. Her face was red, her eyes were swollen and puffy, and even her speech was a bit halting. Clearly, she had been crying for much of the past hour. My heart raced as I anxiously awaited some explanation for the dramatic change in her appearance and mood in a relatively short period of time.

We both had worried for some time about one of our children. She told me that she had been ruminating over a lot of different concerns. For some reason, when she started the drive, she began to imagine a funeral service for one of her children. Essentially, she attended it while she drove. She heard the speakers, smelled the flowers, listened to the music, touched the casket, and stood at the graveside. Of course it wasn't real, but to her subconscious mind it was as if she were actually living the experience. By the time she arrived at the restaurant, she was physically and emotionally drained. The funeral was imaginary, but its emotional and physical effects were quite real.

This solitary drive, filled with clear and sustained thoughts about a single subject, illustrates how thoughts can produce powerful physical and emotional responses. Bear in mind that these responses occur without the conscious mind intervening to judge whether the thoughts involve material facts or just some whimsical fantasy. She willingly suspended her disbelief and allowed her subconscious mind to accept her thinking as reality.

It is important to note that the thinking was sustained and that the images were clear and appealed to her senses. She could smell the flowers and hear the speakers. These are important clues to the type of subconscious visual images that will create a vivid emotional response and move us toward our goals.

Controlled, clear, concise thinking drives our motivation. This thinking is not about outcomes, but rather about personal benefit. We must be able to describe clearly to our subconscious mind why we are choosing to take risks, make sacrifices, work long hours, learn new skills, perform unsatisfying tasks, and even forgo short term gains.

My experience suggests that goal setting alone lacks the innate power to move people forward. A clearly defined revenue number for a territory is important, and it settles in well to the rational, conscious mind. But a sterile number alone usually lacks the power to move us on an emotional level. Until we are moved consistently, our *passion* remains dormant, and we follow a course that will likely lead us to mediocre, rather than meteoric, performance.

The serious question to be answered in seeking the level of personal motivation required to produce optimum performance is, Why? Or, in the parlance of professional marketers, What's is in it for me? This may seem to contradict my earlier insistence on the importance of seeking the customer's interest ahead of one's own, but arguing that self-interest should come second is not the same as arguing that it should not exist. Sales professionals must at least know what they want from the profession before they can uncover the great personal fuel repository they need to achieve their personal and professional potential.

Many sales goals can be reached without drilling deep into the inner fuel reserves. But reaching the summit of success will require much more than self-discipline. It will require that you identify and understand your own inner fuel source. Personal motivation is the ultimate renewable energy. We just need to find out how to tap it in our lives. This is a learned process that involves at least three key elements.

Practice 1: Simulate Outcomes and Stimulate Emotions

If I could teach members of our sales team or even my children one key to understanding how the subconscious mind drives outcomes in our lives, it would be this apparently rather benign concept of creating a productive life by first seeing our desired actions clearly in our minds. Thoughts are precursors to actions.

Who we are at this very moment is the collective representation of our past thoughts. If you can embrace this concept, then it is easier to accept that, by changing our thoughts, we can change our lives and our professional careers. This type of thinking does not consist of casual reflection throughout the day on our lives or our greatest ambitions. Such casual thoughts can create a sense of light and understanding in us about pressing life issues, but they are a 60-watt bulb. Lifetransforming thought requires a powerful laser.

The successful sales professional who operates with a 60-watt mentality sets a sales goal, reviews it regularly, establishes some short-term and intermediate goals, and holds periodic accountability sessions. This person seems driven to succeed, is fiercely competitive, and displays a dogged determination and self-discipline.

Nothing comes easily; at the end of the year there are always scratches and scrapes from the usual battles with competitors, and from seeking to understand the everchanging preferences of customers.

By year's end the numeric goal is achieved. Awards are presented, and applause is graciously accepted. However, even before the dessert is served at the awards banquet, a familiar feeling resumes gnawing in the stomach. Within a few hours it progresses to a full-fledged bout of anxiety.

It happens at the same time every year. The year-end meeting is intended to celebrate outstanding sales achievement, but far too many sales professionals hear another message echoing almost imperceptibly beneath the congratulatory speeches: "Tomorrow is the start of a new sales year. Your sales totals are rolled back to zero, and your new goal is 15 percent higher than your record-breaking year. Get to work!" The carrot cake goes to waste. Many in attendance find that their appetites have disappeared as quickly as the pianist who played classic show tunes during dinner.

The sales professional who has developed a capacity to think consistently with laserlike precision still fights the same battles, struggles with the same pressing market issues, and is subject to the bumps and bruises commonly associated with a career in professional selling. The difference is not only in how satisfying the dessert tastes at the annual meeting, but in the relative ease with which new sales years and correspondingly higher sales goals come and go.

The sales professional who has disciplined the mind to think with laser-like clarity anticipates challenges, expects positive outcomes, refuses to be paralyzed by price increases, and has already personally assigned a higher revenue number for the next year. This professional's internal power source is noticeably different. It burns a higher-octane fuel drilled from the deep caverns of the mind. This person can sustain the highest levels of motivation for the longest periods of time. The reason is simple: this sales professional has clearly identified the personal benefits associated with outstanding achievement and is living them internally well in advance of the new sales year. This is not a dreamer, but simply a salesperson who understands that, when it comes to high levels of motivation, thoughts reign supreme.

This clear, concise, and concentrated thinking must be conducted with a precise purpose in mind. The purpose is to portray in your mind, in rich visual images,   the primary benefits of achieving a desired goal. Once you have clearly identified those benefits, you have the material you need to produce in your mind some short, live-action mental footage – in a sense, your personal movie trailer. It is important that you are specific about physical and emotional details, including taste, smell, the tone and tenor of voices, comments from family members and friends, and even your own private sense of satisfaction in accomplishing an important objective.

When the post-production work is complete, label it and mentally put in on a shelf where it will be easy to retrieve. Depending on what you are trying to achieve, your mental video archive could consist of several short productions that will become as real to your subconscious as movies at the local theater. Each of these short mental pictures should be distinctly different but evoke the same emotional response. For this to be effective, you have to believe in advance in what you are creating in your mind.

Most of these short mental movie trailers will need to be edited and revised over time. If you do your best work in creatively designing them and re-viewing them consistently, every day, you will experience at least two no-ticeable changes in your professional life. First, your *passion* to achieve lofty goals will increase. In fact, the more you rehearse these mental trailers in your mind, the greater will be the sense of urgency you feel about your work, your determination to realize the future you envision, and your con-fidence in your own ability. If these short productions are rich with sensory images and clearly-defined benefits, your mind and body will produce the emotions necessary to push you toward your goal.

The second noticeable benefit you will see is the flood of new ideas that will come pouring into your mind. The more you think in a concentrated and sustained way about realizing your goal, the more your mind will use your professional experience to provide you with new ideas and insights that will move you closer to your goal. Even one new thought about solving customer problems, more effectively communicating product benefits, improving product presentations, or finding new ways to prospect for clients may ultimately make the difference between moderate and high achievement. The more you can implement the practice of sustained thinking about a specific subject, the more you can expect a flood of interesting ideas to start bubbling up from your subconscious mind.

Exercise 1. What I would like you to do for the next few minutes is to set the book down and practice *Step 1: Simulate Outcomes*. Take a sheet of paper and write down the three or four benefits that would come to you personally from achieving a particular goal. Once that is complete, you will be ready to do the creative work of visualizing your own short movie trailer. Here are a few things to keep in mind as you complete this exercise:

1. Focus on outcomes or the specific benefit to you of achieving a particular goal. Plumb the regions of your mind to understand why you are prepared to make whatever sacrifice is reasonably needed to accomplish this objective.

2. Review the image in your mind. Experience in advance what it would feel like to you to accomplish your goal. Remember, the images must be real to slip past your conscious mind.

3. Become familiar enough with the image so that you can replay it later today, tomorrow, etc.

Take whatever time you need to complete this exercise. Now begin.

When you are finished with the first exercise, take some time to answer the following questions:

1. Were you able to clearly identify and visualize at least three specific benefits from achieving this goal?

2. Did the mental image which you created show you experiencing the desired benefits of achieving your goal?

It is not likely during a short exercise like this that you will experience the flood of new ideas or the surging of strong emotions, but it will happen as you are able to sustain a level of controlled thinking about desired outcomes over an extended period of time on a repeated basis. This is not difficult work, but it is still important. There is powerful fuel below the surface of your mind. Your job is to find it.

Practice 2: The Images in Your Mind Must Move You

The images you create in your mind must move you at a deep emotional level. Please keep in mind that this discussion is only about identifying and understanding sources of your own motivation and tapping into the power of the subconscious mind to drive you to sustain peak performance levels for extended time periods. This is not about creating a territory sales plan or implementing a well-conceived strategy. The ideas that come to you from sustained levels of concentrated thinking may be viable additions to your plan, but the primary benefit of this exercise is to stimulate the type of emotions that will propel you to perform at peak levels.

Step one is to write a script for that mental movie trailer. Step two is saturating the final production with powerful mental images that speak to you of the personal benefit associated with achieving lofty goals. There are no script consultants to assist you in this portion of the exercise. You are completely on your own. If you are unable to identify clearly and then visualize the personal benefits of climbing the mountain, you will find yourself confined to a solitary life at the mid-mountain base camp.

Step two is creative and demands both detail and clarity. It is one thing to portray a congratulatory exchange between you and your company CEO at the annual meeting; it is quite another to feel the handshake, to hear the tone of his voice expressing kind words of support, to visualize the room filled with associates and friends, and then to experience all of the smells, sounds, music, decorations, food and excitement of the occasion.

To tap into your internal power source, black-and-white images will not do. You will need resplendent colors displayed in high definition and projected on your mind with a three-dimensional quality. The clearer and more emotionally vibrant the images are, the more real the experience becomes. The more real it becomes, the more abundantly your subconscious mind will produce the emotions that will push you up the mountain.

Earlier in this chapter I described my wife's mental attendance at the funeral service of one of our children. The images in her mind felt real, and her sustained level of concentration allowed her to navigate past the scrutiny of her conscious mind and deep into her subconscious. This is not an exercise in self-hypnosis or some type of transcendental state. It is not frivolous daydreaming or childish selfdeception. Sustained thinking about clear images that empower the subconscious mind is a normal part of daily life and is regularly engaged when critical problemsolving is required. For most of us this is an underutilized resource, but it has the potential to reshape our ability to generate and sustain the required motivation to move closer to our own personal and professional potential.

Deliberately engaging in clear and sustained visualization may seem a bit awkward at first. But this is not a corporate Karaoke party where, sometime before the end of the night, the rest of the sales team will hear your impersonation of Neil Diamond. You have already used this technique hundreds of time in your life. You likely have used some form of visualization before an important presentation with customers, or the night before a high school basketball game, or in the early morning hours, ruminating over a vexing problem at work. Nothing about this experience should seem new or awkward. It should be as easy as watching your favorite television program and as natural as idly daydreaming in your car on the way home from work. Your subconscious may seem like a benign river; however, with the proper tools, even a slow-moving stream can produce enough energy to power a great city.

The power of your subconscious to produce strong emotions will largely be influenced by two factors. The first is the clarity of the visual images you create in your mind. The second is how effective you are in selecting personal benefits to move you on a deep emotional level. When you can see the images in your mind and at the same time feel something inside of you, you will have drilled into a live well that will produce a lot of energy over time.

This process of writing and producing what amounts to short, up-tempo, and inspiring mental movie trailers is an acquired skill. The more emotional effort you exert, the deeper the drill goes in search of fuel. The difference between finding your own source of energy and prospecting for fossil fuels is that you know where the mother lode is buried.

Your stockpile of potential energy is as unique to you as your finger-prints. Find the reasons that you want to succeed as a sales professional, then begin to write the script. Just don't forget the details.

Exercise 2. This exercise will be similar to the one you completed in the previous section, but with more detail. The images in step one may have been in black and white with a smattering of color and mostly still images. The purpose of step two is to create powerful visual images, moving, authentic, genuine and true-to-life images that have the capability to move you on a very deep emotional level. Step one was an introduction to visualization. Step two is the more advanced course.

It will be helpful for this exercise if you can set the book down and find a quiet place to relax and close your eyes. The elimination of ambient sounds will help you to slip past the gatekeeper, your conscious mind. The purpose of the exercise is simply to help you learn a new skill that will enable you to tap into powerful forms of motivation. For this exercise it is not necessary that the visualization experience be related to selling. It just needs absolute clarity in its images, sounds, the tonal quality of voices, facial expressions, lighting, background noises, room decorations, weather conditions, time of day and every other detail of the experience.

During this short exercise you will mentally step inside an image created in your mind and live the experience in advance. I suggest that you select one of the topics below, which may be described as rich sensory life experiences. Once you learn the skill, it can easily be adapted to specific areas of your professional life. Here are a few choices:

1. It is your youngest daughter's wedding. She is dressed in a beautiful gown, the guests have arrived, the music is playing, and you have three minutes alone with her. Visualize every emotional detail of that experience.

2. Your are in a single engine airplane flying 2000 feet above the ground with a parachute on your back. You have completed the instruction, the door is open and you can see tiny objects below. The wind is whipping your sleeves as you tighten your goggles and your instructor gives you the sign to jump. Visualize every emotional detail of the dive from the time you leave the plane until your friends greet you on the ground.

3. You are attending a memorial service for a close high school friend who passed away unexpectedly. Only minutes before the service starts a family member asks you to give a two-minute eulogy. There are two hundred people in attendance, and the organ is playing. Visualize every emotional detail from the time you agree to speak until you sit down.

When you have selected the subject for your visualization exercise, please set down the book and take whatever time you need to complete this step. Remember, the images in your mind must move you. Begin now.

When you have completed the exercise, answer the following questions before moving on to the next section.

1. What emotions did you feel?

2. Did your subconscious mind believe that the images you were creating were real? How do you know for sure?

3. Were the images you created saturated with visual clarity?

4. Did the experience you created seem real to you?

The key to mining the caverns of the subconscious mind where motivation is stored in rich abundance is to slip past the conscious mind with believable images that you create but also believe are real. Once you are past the conscious mind, your subconscious will ask no questions. It will only supply you the emotion, ideas and motivation to make the images you have created real.

Practice 3: Refuel on a Regular Basis

Refueling regularly is vital. For many of us, producing short mental movie trailers replete with sensory rich images may be the easiest part of tapping into the hidden reserves of our personal fuel source. Cleverly crafted mental images which inspire and move us will have little value, if they remain neatly stored in the chambers of our mind. Creativity, imagination and self-evaluation provide the inspiration that breathes life into them. Self-discipline will determine whether or not they will have the power to change our lives.

One of the beauties of these well-conceived mental images is that you won't need a DVD player or an iPod to connect to your mental video library. These images are completely portable. They are available anytime, anywhere. However, I would suggest a few considerations.

There is a reason that Hollywood movie producers like audiences to see their new releases in the relative solitude of a darkened theater. This environment minimizes the distractions. Distractions arouse your conscious mind and compromise your ability to accept the events portrayed on the screen as real. To leverage fully the effect of this experience, you must similarly control your environment, to minimize, if not altogether eliminate, potential distractions.

The best visualization experience generally occurs when your body is at rest. It also helps to be in a quiet place or to put on some music that will help you to feel completely relaxed.

It will help substantially if your inner environment is similarly calm. You can purchase a seat at the opening of a new Steven Spielberg adventure, but if you're thinking about problems at the office or traffic frustrations or your enthusiasm about tomorrow's golf outing, the film will have little power to move you on an emotional level. The same considerations apply when you prepare for an exercise of visualization.

Unless you can find a way to work around your conscious mind, any effort you make at serious visualization will amount to little more than daydreaming.

Daydreaming is the emotional equivalent of fool's gold. It may seem real, but it lacks the power to engage your subconscious mind completely, so it will never be a legitimate source of fuel. Your conscious mind is the keeper of the gate, judging what is real and what is not. Slipping past the gatekeeper is not difficult, but you must control both the internal and external environments and be ready to give yourself completely to the images on the mental screen in the theater of your mind.

With your mental movie trailer in finished form and both external and internal environments suitable for reflection, you are ready to begin engaging your subconscious mind in generating the emotions which will move you towards your goal. The obvious question to be asked is, how frequently you should do this? The answer is different for every situation and for every person. How much fuel will it take for you to mount a serious assault on the summit in your mind? The more consistently you reflect deeply on your mental images depicting the personal benefits of achieving your goal, the more your subconscious mind will drive you in that direction.

My experience with this process of visualization and deep, controlled, reflective thinking suggests that, for significant undertakings requiring weeks or months of planning and preparation, I need to refill my tank on a daily basis. The more fully my subconscious mind accepts ownership in the project, the more connected I feel with viable methods to achieve the desired goal. I find that, if I have done an adequate job of "selling" my subconscious on the desired outcomes, it continues to work, providing me with potential solutions, while my conscious mind works on other matters. My subconscious typically delivers its information when my conscious mind is not engaged in problem solving. Most often this is in the early morning or at night. Sometimes it happens when I am driving, if I am relaxed. As you become fully engaged in this process, you will learn in a relatively short period of time how and when your subconscious mind will implement its own information delivery system.

Designing powerful mental images and replaying them frequently in your mind is taking the offensive in the struggle to control your subconscious mind. While this offensive maneuvering is vital to producing the emotions that fuel your motivation, please don't dismiss the need to protect your subconscious mind with a well-orchestrated defensive strategy. There are few things in life over which you have complete control, but you can control your thoughts. Most of us have developed patterns of thinking which resemble an emotional roller coaster. We move higher, both emotionally and intellectually, when we dictate the texture, quality, and fundamental nature of the mental inputs we send to our subconscious mind. Ideas and images that lift and inspire us move us to a higher level.

On the contrary, images which demean or debase life or people, or attempt to challenge our best intentions, can accelerate a downward emotional spiral. Sustained negative thinking destroys our confidence in our own competency and our ability to create things of value in our lives. It generates its own source of destructive fuel. The more this fuel contaminates your tank, the more unlikely the achievement of your goals becomes. You can choose to reject the influence of negative stimuli in your life and completely control which images are delivered to your subconscious mind. The achievement of lofty goals will require your best work in developing and implementing effective offensive and defensive strategies.

Identifying Motivators and the Symptoms of Sales Paralysis

As I first introduced the *Personal Leadership Model*, I emphasized the need to reallocate time spent performing the activities in tactical work to the more personal performance-based skills found in Strategic Work. The summary shown below provides some insight about how this key selling skill dramatically impacts every one of the Eight Symptoms of Sales Paralysis.

It is important to remember that in most instances the substantial revenue increases you are looking for can be achieved by modest gains in personal performance. As I have already explained, a ten percent improvement in your productivity could produce a corresponding gain in revenue production that is double or triple that amount. In many instances the bump in revenue can be significantly more.

The key to effective *Personal Leadership* in selling is making good judgments about the allocation of your time and available resources. Sales professionals who are effective leaders feed off their own well-defined sources of motivation. They frequently drill new wells, and they never cap old ones that have consistently produced. Even small gains in your ability to tap into your personal fuel reserves can push those numbers on the monthly sales report higher and higher.

The pernicious symptoms of Sales Paralysis destroy careers, disrupt organizations and disenfranchise customers. Learning to identify the motivators in your life won't solve all of the problems in your territory, but it will give you the much-needed energy to fix just about every other aspect of your career that is wallowing in mediocrity.

Symptom	Impact	Comments
The Passion is gone	MEDIUM	Producing excellent work creates its own level of energy.
Inattentive listening	HIGH	Character powers the process of listening to understand.
Winging it	HIGH	Working to your own potential eliminates faulty preparation.
Lack of a sense of urgency	HIGH	People of character recognize the need to respond urgently.
Contemplation of a job change	MEDIUM	Working to your potential is challenging and demanding work.
Feelings of frustration	HIGH	Strong character allows you to take control of tough situations.
Blaming others	HIGH	Sales professionals of character accept responsibility for outcomes.
Low energy for problem solving	HIGH	The combination of character and competency increases energy levels.

In some respects motivation in the selling process can be viewed as a legacy skill, because it impacts virtually every aspect of professional selling. It is one of only two skills in the *Personal Leadership Model* that exert decisive influence over all Eight Symptoms of Sales Paralysis. Only creating excellence can boast a similar impact on the development of highly productive sales professionals.

Identify Motivators: A High-Performance Skill

When some sales professionals see the word *skills*, they think of things like presenting, prospecting, closing, planning, and perhaps even following up with clients. Motivation is not frequently thought of as a skill; it often appears to be innate rather than acquired. But this chapter on identifying motivators is entirely about teaching a basic skill that can be learned and should be practiced daily.

Motivation drives high-level performance. Running hard without replenishing their fuel, sales professionals with above-average ability can develop fatigue. Over time this fatigue can give way to a sense of complacency about the territory. In a matter of a few short months a once-vibrant territory needs resuscitation.

This book is about understanding how the practice of key *Personal Leadership* skills in the selling process can propel you toward your potential as a sales professional. Part of that propulsion comes from your ability to identify key sources of personal motivation. Motivation provides the energy to sustain the emotional stamina required to pursue lofty goals and implement well-conceived plans. Understanding what motivates you is part of *Personal Leadership*.

My young grandson Wiley was motivated by the image of presents to undertake a perilous journey. He may have lacked the wisdom and judgment to face the hazards that stood between him and the excitement of opening birthday gifts, but he didn't lack motivation. The incorporation of *Personal Leadership* skills into professional selling provides you with a context to assess both risk and opportunity. When the opportunities have been clarified, it provides an almost unlimited source of fuel for your journey. Tapping into your own motivational source begins for you, as it did with Wiley, by visualizing desired outcomes (for him, the presents). Just remember to look both ways when you cross those busy intersections.

The Relationship of Principles and Practices in Developing the Skill *("Learned Power")* to Identify Motivators

Principle A. Sustaining motivation for the long term fuels all great achievement.
    Supporting Practices:
        1. Simulate desired outcomes
        2. Create moving mental images
        3. Re-fuel regularly

Principle B. Motivation sustains commitment through long sales cycles.
    Supporting Practices:
        1. Simulate desired outcomes
        2. Create moving mental images
        3. Re-fuel regularly

Principle C. Motivation comes from understanding yourself.
    Supporting Practices:
        1. Simulate desired outcomes
        2. Create moving mental images
        3. Re-fuel regularly

CHAPTER 8

Be Accountable

Developing a Metric-Based Reality

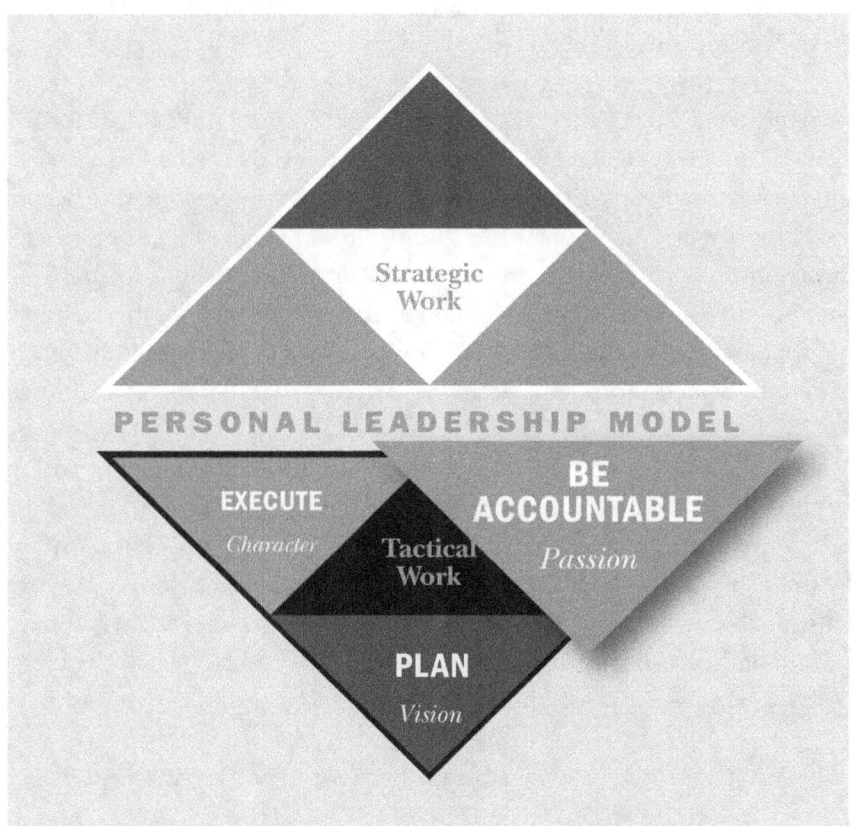

Figure 8-1 Be Accountable: The *Passion* Component of Tactical Work

LEARNING TO *be accountable* for our choices can be difficult. It can also be expensive. A few years ago my wife and I were in Beijing, China, where we took a tour of some interesting sights in the region. The final stop of the day was a large factory where jade was being crafted by skilled technicians into an assortment of shapes and forms commonly associated with the history and culture of China. We were impressed but rather reluctant buyers. After some persistence we decided to purchase small bookends in the form of lions.

In Chinese culture lions are most often represented in pairs and are referred to as Fu Lions, or guardian lions. They are commonly seen protecting the entrances to Imperial palaces, the tombs of emperors, temples, and in some instances the homes of important government officials. It is believed that these lions have powerful mythic protective powers. As it turns out, during our trip to China these lions failed to protect us from our own complacency in currency conversion.

We negotiated a price that was past the upper limit of our budget for souvenirs. Somehow we managed to justify the expense based upon either the expert craftsmanship or the fact that these pieces might one day become family heirlooms. As it turns out I think we were right at least on the second assumption. When the credit card bill arrived it became apparent that when we did the currency conversion at the jade factory we miscalculated the price by one decimal place. What was pricey before suddenly became exorbitant when multiplied by ten. We had cars that didn't cost that much.

When I looked at the credit card statement, my heart stopped and my hands went cold. I put up a good fight for nearly a year in an effort to return the merchandise, but in the end we were left alone to confront the unsavory reality of accepting the consequences of a poorly executed math problem. Ultimately I was *accountable* for what went wrong, and those jade lions in our home have become a symbol of what it means to *be accountable* for poor choices. They remind me that I should have:

- Asked for a signed written statement of the transaction in U.S. dollars.

- Asked for a written copy of the return policy.

- Studied enough basic information to have been able to do some rudimentary currency conversion.

- Known enough about the value of jade to determine if the contracted amount represented a fair market value.

That purchase was an expensive lesson in *accountability*. I hope you have never made a mistake like that, but I have watched far too many sales professionals marginalize their careers by failing to become fully *accountable* for their territories. In many instances the resultant financial losses would have purchased a bevy of jade lions. In some cases commissions were forfeited. In other instances jobs were lost and careers disrupted, and financial turmoil ensued. Every decision I have made about the termination of a sales associate was far more costly to that person than the price I paid for bookends in Beijing.

Principles and Practices in Developing the Skill to Be Accountable

This chapter focuses on two primary principles, laws or assumptions. The first is the idea that *accountability* improves performance. More will be said of this. However, I think it is a principle which most of us find self-evident. The second principle is understanding the role of *passion* in the *accountability* process. This is where the *Personal Leadership* component comes into play. You need *passion* as a leader to suffer the setbacks and disappointments that inevitably come in the pursuit of any worthwhile endeavor. Professional selling is fraught with challenges; they come almost daily. *Passion* that is affixed in your new skill of identifying motivators will provide you the resolve to finish the work, to execute your plan, to achieve your goals and to realize your potential.

Principles, Skills & Practices

Principles *(laws or assumptions)*: A. Accountability improves performance. B. Passion drives accountability.

Skill *(learned power)*: Be Accountable

Practices *(repeated exercises for proficiency)*: 1) Regularly assess your "accountability quotient." 2) Practice the "five steps" to improve personal accountability.

While I have only listed three primary practices for your work in this chapter, you will note that, as you read through this material, there will be at least fourteen specific exercises or practices for your consideration as you work to develop this skill in your life. Your new *vision* of the territory will require your best effort. *Accountability* will provide a system of checks and balances to continuously monitor your performance.

Being accountable is about sustaining your effort. It is about keeping your hopes and dreams alive, when the similar aspirations of those around you have faded. It is about keeping your head up and your feet moving, when the enticement to compromise principles is lurking all about. It is about not giving up or giving in, even though your performance may already meet your associates' expectations. It is about not capitulating to something you know is less than your best effort. Most dreams die because they are underfunded, in terms of allocated energy reserves. People who learn to be *accountable* stockpile fuel by tapping into their own deeplyheld images of their best work.

The skill of *accountability* requires you to learn to measure and report on your progress in executing the annual sales plan. But it goes beyond the goals and strategy section of the sales plan. In its highest form learning to *be accountable* is a willingness to accept responsibility for the potential of your territory and for your overall performance as a sales professional. The system you develop to measure performance (metrics) is a clear indication of how well this skill is executed in your life as a sales professional.

If you have learned *accountability* practices by exercising greater self-control, it may be time to learn a new skill that engages your heart to provide the personal motivation needed to push you through the normal tough patches of disappointment and discouragement that occur in every sales year. Learning to *be accountable* involves various components that should be standard practices in each sales territory. Some of these are weekly or even daily practices, but you will need more than standard practices to sustain you. Most likely you have already learned this from your own experience attempting to execute well-conceived plans in previous years. What you need, in order to make the skill of *accountability* commonplace in your life, is the power that comes from the *Personal Leadership Driver passion*. If you are not *accountable*, even the best plans will evaporate in the face of the normal rejection you encounter during any sales year.

**Accountability in
Professional Selling:**

1) A system or process of
measuring performance
relative to established goals,
plans, and strategies. 2) The
reporting of personal
performance in a written
format at established time
intervals, usually weekly. 3)
The work of being held
responsible for both territory
potential and personal sales
potential. 4) The process of
accepting responsibility for
the execution of the sales
plan.

Chances are, if you don't know why you are climbing the mountain, when you come to steep passes, you will look for either an exit strategy or a place to lie down. Learning to *be accountable* is the process of linking all the powerful images about the sources of your own motivation to what you are doing today. If you can't learn to do that effectively, you will constantly be frustrated by seeing the *vision* of your own potential and having a viable plan, yet always seeming to work at a level well below your desired outcomes. Self-discipline is great, but in my experience, when it comes to great achievement, it is generally overrated. You will need something else. If you have done all the work of identifying motivators, now would be a good time to start replaying those images.

The lack of consistent *accountability* is what generally separates good plans from great successes. As a rule, one of the most important reasons for the relatively high obscuration rate of viable plans is the inability of sales professionals to connect future outcomes with present responsibilities. In other words, most of us need constant reminding about why we're doing this. This chapter consists of material to help you become more effective in executing the skill of *accountability* and specific ideas for assessing your *accountability* quotient. The discussion topics in this chapter include:

◆ Accountability Improves Performance – a close-up look at systems or practices in your life to insure levels of professional accountability.

- Passion Drives Accountability – understanding the role of the leadership driver that powers this selling skill.

- Assessing Your Accountability Quotient – a summary of eight ways to assess your present level of accountability in your territory.

- Five Steps to Greater Accountability – a detailed look at five different ways to improve standard accountability practices in your territory.

This chapter will conclude with a brief analysis of how improved *accountability* methods can eradicate the symptoms of Sales Paralysis, followed by some short summary comments about practical implementation of *accountability* in your territory.

Principle A. Accountability Improves Performance

Politicians are *accountable* to the electorate. Great athletes have coaches. Teachers assume that role with their students, and most large corporations have governing boards to provide oversight and *accountability*. Governments in free societies are kept in check by the careful scrutiny of the press.

Political promises rarely go unnoticed. Predictions about upcoming wins are remembered for years by adoring fans. Most of us can remember our high school GPA. Exposure of government excess by investigative reporters appears almost daily in local newspapers. We live in a world of *accountability*. Are you *accountable* for the proper execution of your sales plan?

You may be *accountable* for an annual revenue number, but goals and plans are not the same. Revenue goals generally identify what *others* think your market can produce. A territory sales plan describes what *you* think it can produce. If you are *accountable* only for a revenue number based upon last year's performance, you are negotiating a deal that is less than your best effort. At the end of your career you may have a room filled with plaques celebrating consistent goal achievement, but be filled with the empty realization of unfulfilled potential. It is not enough simply to be *accountable* for others' expectations for you. Outstanding achievement in any endeavor will ultimately be determined by your willingness to be *accountable* for your own expectations.

To *be accountable* for your own expectations is a risk. To *be accountable* for the expectations of others is a way to play it safe in life. The projection of others' expectations on you will almost certainly diminish your capability, because you know in your heart what no one else is capable of knowing. You know your own potential. What others can only glimpse is in full view for you every day. The open acknowledgement of your ability, in the form of a viable plan purposely designed to move you and your territory toward optimum potential, is a daring stroke of personal validation. It allows you to leave the shadows of personal doubt and institutional acceptance and declare your own liberation from mediocrity. It is a bold step toward your potential.

Being accountable is accepting the reality that reaching the greatest summits in life often requires using the footholds others have left for you. It is accepting that the greatest achievements in life are rarely commenced or completed in isolation. More often they are the natural product of seemingly ordinary people, bound together in a common cause and driven to make something extraordinary of their lives. *Accountability* recognizes the role others play in your ascent to higher elevations in your career. It acknowledges the reality that help is required even when most of the energy consumed is your own.

A person who is only *accountable* to himself hides from his own potential. Too many deals are cut and far too many exceptions are made, when you bargain with yourself about the execution of the annual sales plan. Even the best athletes need the vigilance of a trusted coach who knows their ability and requires more than what they might otherwise be willing to give. Professional selling is no different. If you can learn to *be accountable* to someone other than yourself, you are learning what will be required to achieve your greatest potential.

Learning to *be accountable* to others for performance levels that you determine will propel you up the mountain, and in most instances you will find that those lofty peaks of personal performance that you could see only in your mind a few years ago are really mere foothills foretelling the grandeur of more splendid climbs ahead.

To seek help in *being accountable* is not to reveal a lack of self-discipline. Rather, it exhibits a strength which acknowledges that arriving at your greatest potential is a journey that should never be done alone. Who are the people in your life that you can trust to hold you *accountable*?

If you are serious about changing the way you manage your territory to produce a noticeable upward shift in revenue production, measure progress in every key area and then report it. This is a severely under-utilized formula for improving both territory revenue production and overall personal performance.

Principle B. Passion Drives Accountability

While *vision* is quantitative and *character* qualitative, *passion* is fundamentally authoritative in nature. *Passion* drives *accountability* and allows you to say to yourself, your boss, your peers, or anyone else who is interested in your career, for that matter, "This is what I have done." It is not about what you will do or are planning to do, or what you hope to do or might do. A willingness to be consistently *accountable* for your goals and plans is a willingness to say, "Here it is. This is what I have done this week, this month, this year."

This is not merely a matter of reporting activity. To *be accountable* you must have the humility to place side by side your plans and your performance for the time period   in question, and you must accept responsibility for the differences. Taking complete, authoritative control over future outcomes in this way requires *passion* for your work.

Learning to *be accountable* requires changing how you work and how you think. It requires the complete integration of your sales plan into your daily work. Far too often the annual sales plan is set aside a few weeks into the year, and the sales professional lapses into old patterns of behavior that are largely reactive in nature, in which the sales professional assumes a defensive rather than offensive posture. Consistent execution of the sales plan is an offensive strategy to move the territory towards optimum revenue potential.

You may ask, "What about urgent problems that arise with customers and need immediate attention?" Unplanned activities that impact the overall quality of a customer relationship are always high-leverage opportunities. So is taking unexpected chances to develop your business with a new account. You may be reacting to new information, but as long as these activities are high-leverage in nature, they will accelerate your push toward achieving your goal. Unproductive, low-leverage activities eat up valuable time and sap any momentum already established toward realizing your goals for your territory.

My experience suggests that the propensity to lay aside a well-conceived plan in favor of "winging it" – not competitors or downturns – may be the single biggest impediment to realizing sales goals. This is an abdication of *Personal Leadership*. It allows the sales professional to squander time on "safe" but unproductive activities. Too many view operational plans as restrictive. They are designed to be precisely the opposite. A viable plan begins with assessing potential; planning conducted in this context is the ultimate form of sales and marketing liberation.

When sales professionals begin to view *accountability* as one piece of a complex puzzle that will allow them to find the freedom to explore their own potential, it will become less of an aggravation and more of an incentive. Great planning without execution and consistent *accountability* makes no more sense than filing a flight plan, loading the cargo bay, then refusing to perform all the necessary preflight checks prior to take-off. The preflight checks do not delay the flight; they insure its ultimate success. The same is true in professional selling. Learning to *be accountable* for goals and plans is a simple and effective way to ensure that the territory will move on a well-conceived path to higher altitudes of revenue production.

Practice 1. Five Steps to Greater Accountability

Step One: Measure Your Performance

Get comfortable with numbers. They are an invaluable ally in the pursuit of your greatest potential. It you are not willing to measure your performance, you are not willing to get better, and nothing I can say in this chapter will change that. Any sales professional who claims to be "bad with numbers" or "more right-brain driven" is hiding something – or hiding from something, usually the inability to exceed the current level of revenue production. Facing what you are capable of producing can be a frightening proposition. It requires you first to acknowledge the reality that you may be currently working to only fifty or sixty percent of your production capability. It requires you to learn to work and think differently. The thought of change is paralyzing to most people, but, if you can learn to embrace change, you are taking the first step toward discovering your full potential.

If there is magic in learning to *be accountable*, it is in the metrics. If you try to lose those few nagging pounds without standing on a scale regularly to assess your progress, you may receive feedback in the sense of how your clothes fit, but if you want pounds off rather than just a smaller pant size, at some point you need to face the numbers. Befriend the numbers, and you will start to feel the exhilaration that comes with moving in a new direction. Without the precision that numbers provide it will be business as usual in the territory. Unfortunately, it often seems that business as usual is what far too many sales professionals want from their careers.

Personal Leadership is the *Defining Skill* in professional selling because leadership is required to make conscious choices to doing hard but necessary things. Most sales professionals don't need to be taught effective methods for planning, execution,   or *accountability*; they simply need to learn how to implement practices they already know on a daily basis in their professional lives. They need to become more skilled in the discipline of *Personal Leadership*. Leaders take control of their lives and their territories and deploy assets and resources to highly productive activities. Only sales professionals who have learned the skills of *Personal Leadership* experience the satisfaction of working at a level congruent with their talent and ability. The satisfaction that comes from aligning performance with potential trumps even the most important recognition at the annual awards banquet.

Develop a personal tracking system that works for you. It should allow you to account for all key elements of your sales plan that are measurable. Record your performance. Then periodically, perhaps weekly but certainly at least monthly, assess your performance relative to your established benchmark. If you can't do this simple exercise, the nagging feeling of unrealized potential will follow you around like a hacking cough that never seems to go away. This is not complex work, but it does force you to face a few unpleasant things about how you work.

In practicing *accountability* you will weigh every possible aspect of your performance that can be measured against your plans and goals. This will allow you to make the necessary adjustments to insure the complete execution of your sales plan. Trust your plan. Trust your judgment about your market assessment. Trust your ability to move the territory forward in pursuit of sizeable revenue gains. Trust your ability to execute the plan by building the safeguard of *accountability* into your daily regimen. Once you become comfortable that a system of *accountability* is in place, you will also be more comfortable moving the standard of excellence higher during the next sales year.

Here is a simple example of a method of tracking your progress toward achieving annual sales goals by measuring your performance weekly. Whatever method you choose, it should be something that includes both your stated goal and a place to record your actual performance.

Weekly Progress Report

Week of _____

Activity	Goal	M	T	W	T	F	Total
Prospecting	2 hours per day						
Follow-up	1 hour per day						
Hours with Customers	10 hours per week						
New Presentations to Customers	1 per week						
Contract Closing	1 hour per day or 15 contacts						

The activity goals above are taken directly from the sales plan on page 70.

This progress report provides an easy way to transfer activity goals from your sales plan into your weekly work regimen. It is not important that anyone else see this information, but it should be accessible to you daily. I think it is helpful to keep an electronic copy of all your weekly reports and to have a printed copy of your present week with you in your planner. The sooner this simple report becomes a constant ally, the sooner you will develop the needed confidence that the process of moving activity goals into the daily operation of your sales territory can take place with regularity. More importantly, you will come to recognize how daily *accountability*, through making just a few notes on a paper, can change how you think and work in your territory.

Step Two: Find a Partner
Like most people, you probably think you can do this alone. The truth is that most people don't do it alone. Most likely it will not be necessary for you to engage someone else in the activity goals noted in your weekly progress report, however, it will be necessary to seek some help with the overall execution of your annual sales plan. There are undoubtedly a lot of sales plans that look great in January, but by March they are nowhere to be found. Much of this tendency to discard thoughtful planning comes from the fact that the planning was never really that thoughtful. It was done to satisfy an annual assignment, and once the proverbial planning hoop had been jumped through, it was back to business as usual. For most sales professionals the planning imperative is driven by external rather than internal factors.

If you are still reading this book it is likely that something about *Personal Leadership* in professional selling resonates with you. It is also possible that, as you read through the information presented on the six key selling skills of the *Personal Leadership Model*, you found each of these components consistent with what you already knew about selling and personal achievement. If these concepts make sense to you, then you will probably have little or no difficulty in reaching out to enlist the help of someone else to assist in the process of learning to *be accountable* for your goals and plans for the territory. As capable as you are, the sooner you learn to enlist help from others, the sooner your chances for long-term success will rise, perhaps even exponentially.

Most likely the person you need to be connected to your work will be your direct report in the sales organization. If you are an independent representative selling several different products, find a personal coach. I strongly suggest that you consider hiring someone for a few hours a month. This is an activity that will push you further out toward the end of the bar, increasing the leverage of your work. It will be an important investment in your future.

If you have spent any time at a PGA event, you have noticed that the practice area is nearly always filled with tour players and their coaches. Swing coaches at big time golf events are as commonplace as political consultants at town hall meetings. Even though tour players are conditioned to perform at the highest possible level of their sport, the eyes of a trusted coach can make the difference making and missing the cut. If these world class players need the constant attention of a coach to help them improve and to evaluate their swings almost continuously, maybe you and I could benefit from some periodic "swing analysis" by someone who knows our plan for moving our sales territory forward.

We need regular *accountability* with an associate, another set of eyes, for the express purpose of assessing our progress towards goals and plans for the territory that we established independently. It is simply about becoming your best. It is not about a mythical major championship in selling. It is about making major improvements in your game. It is about working in alignment with your own skill and talents. It is about moving your territory forward in a direction where revenue potential (that perhaps only you can see) can start to be realized in the form of improved sales production. It is not simply about spending more time pounding balls on the range. It is about spending time pounding balls in close proximity to someone who knows your swing and can help you make needed progress, someone who knows your goals and will help keep you on the course you set after a careful assessment of your territory.

Here is what I suggest. When you have identified the right person, define the right role for that person in your periodic *accountability* sessions. This is your agenda and your plan. You are reaching out to either a direct report within your organization or to an outside personal coach to help you implement your strategic vision for the territory. Identify specifically what you would like this person to do, the frequency of contacts, and the methodology of your reporting. Give this person a copy of your territory sales plan and explain that his or her role will be to assess the effectiveness and the consistency of your implementation.

You may want to explain that you are not seeking consultation about the overall merits of the strategy, but that you simply need someone to whom you can make periodic progress reports. This is a one-person advisory board with whom you meet monthly, give or take. In most instances this evaluation session can be conducted in fifteen or twenty minutes over the phone.

If you haven't done something like this before, it will seem a bit awkward and uncomfortable. Try it anyway, and two things will happen. First, your performance will improve noticeably in line with your established goals. You will feel in control of your professional life, even empowered by the process. Second, you will find that you have enlisted a person who will become your biggest ally and your most vocal advocate. That new voice alone will accelerate your progress.

I have had remarkable experiences on both sides of this personal coaching relationship. Several years ago I sensed a need to become a more effective leader. I explained my quest to an associate, who agreed to evaluate my progress in relation to goals I had established for myself. I knew the areas of my life that needed improvement, and I identified three or four specific things that I could do to change my approach to organizational leadership. These were nagging problems that kept me from resolving difficult interpersonal challenges. I lacked the skill to communicate my concerns effectively to underperforming members of the sales team. It was becoming clear that, with my voice muted, organizational mediocrity would be my constant companion.

Explaining to my coach what I needed to do gave me a sense of power in making important changes in my life. Periodic supportive reassurance from a trusted confidant made it virtually impossible for me to relapse into old habits. I made more important changes in one area of my professional life in a few months than   I had made in the five previous years combined.

This isn't a magical formula. It is just common sense. Your performance improves when it is reported. It can improve dramatically when you enlist the support of an ally who will hold you *accountable* for things you have committed to do. If you will learn to practice this one specific means of *being accountable*, your plans will improve, your consistency of execution will improve, your satisfaction in selling will improve, and, most importantly, you will improve. Needless to say, when you improve, your sales numbers can only move in one direction.

Step Three: Report Weekly
The weekly planning session is one of those subjects that always receive an approving nod from members of the sales team during training sessions. It is like listening to your dental hygienist expounding the virtue of regular flossing to insure healthy gum tissue. We all get it. The problem isn't that we don't understand the concept; the problem is that we don't practice the principle. Weekly planning sessions are a lot like regular flossing; when we do them consistently we can virtually eliminate decay in our territories.

The term *weekly* might seem to suggest that the planning session could be done anytime during the week. That may be true, if you are simply checking off things on a task list. For this meeting to have meaning, it really needs to be held at the beginning of the week. Think of it as a regular *Monday morning* planning session. The first thing you do at the beginning of the week is take a deep breath, plan your week, and evaluate your progress in implementing your sales plan. Sometimes the evaluation is as important as the planning.

For most of us who spend our lives answering phones calls, returning e-mail, retrieving voice mail messages, and prepping for the next appointment, regularly scheduled planning and evaluating sessions provide order amid the chaos. This is like scheduled CPR, the resuscitation you need to stay on top of a busy sales territory. The tools needed at this meeting are your planner, your sales plan, and your weekly progress report. By the end of the year, your sales plan should have tattered pages, margin notes, water spots, and a crumpled cover. If it is not being used more than your XM radio, something is seriously wrong.

This Monday morning planning session provides the conduit to move the activity goals in your sales plan directly into your weekly activities. It is the way your planning and executing become fully integrated. It is not just about planning your week; it is also purposely designed to facilitate a level of oversight as you implement your sales strategy. It is a way for you to *be accountable* for your plans weekly. It doesn't need to be long. It just needs to be long enough to (1) review and plan the week, (2) review the sales plan and identify areas that need to be implemented in your schedule, and (3) briefly assess your work from last week in relationship to your goals.

Holding your weekly planning and evaluating session is like doing all the requisite stretching exercises prior to a challenging workout. It improves your flexibility in assessing critical strategic components of your sales plan that still need implementation. It enhances your overall dexterity in accomplishing a variety of activities in narrow time windows. It is fundamentally preventative in nature, in that it assists you to identify in advance issues that could significantly impact your revenue during this sales year. Weekly planning sessions ultimately produce healthier sales territories.

Step Four: Continuous Self-Evaluation
The process of *accountability* needs to be ongoing, continuous, and consistent. It will never be enough to periodically refer to your sales plan throughout the year and hope by the time the annual sales meeting arrives that you will be at your number. If you are passionate about being successful in your profession, you must be committed to a process of continuous *accountability*.

The primary purpose of Tactical Work's *accountability* component is to move you closer to your potential as a sales professional, and in turn to push the territory more in line with overall revenue potential. When your annual territory sales plan is designed in the context of a comprehensive market assessment, you have not only identified the revenue potential for the current sales year, but you have also constructed a viable map leading to your intended revenue goal. And while most of the elements of *accountability* we have discussed in this chapter pertain to the execution of your sales plan, we also should discuss specific ways for you to assess your own personal growth and development as a sales professional.

Your territory's potential will be realized as you consistently work your plan. Your ability to work your plan consistently will be greatly influenced by your improvement in key aspects of the selling process and your improved skills as both a leader and a territory manager. In other words, just making more presentations to potential buyers will probably not be enough to realize your product's full market potential. You have to be a more skilled presenter, a better listener, a more thoughtful collaborator, a more disciplined prospector, and a more detailed problem solver. You simply have to improve. Realizing your product's market potential is directly linked to achieving your own potential. In order for you to move closer to your potential, you must also consider specific ways to *be accountable* on a regular basis for the needed progress in your professional life. Here are a few areas that you should assess continuously throughout the year.

Presentations. Too often members of the sales team settle into a comfortable routine of product presentations. Over time they come to lack freshness, and become less current and relevant in a changing market. Good presentations, like good gardens, need to be vigilantly tended, or they can become overgrown with things that destroy their primary purpose. We tend to become complacent about our material; it can become more generic and less specific to the needs of customers. Excellent presenters are perpetual tinkerers. They always seem to have the basic components of their presentation strewn around the office, because they are always rebuilding. They are also constantly in search of new ways to communicate ideas and solve problems more effectively and more succinctly.

It is good to have someone who is familiar with your product periodically listen to you make a presentation, then offer a candid critique. Another person in the room can listen to you present the material, observe all the visual signs from the client, listen to questions, and evaluate your ability to respond to difficult questions. You should also continually assess your presentation's effectiveness on your own. Here are a few self-assessment questions:

◆ When was the last time you made significant changes to your basic presentation?

◆ Is your presentation current with recent product, industry and competitive changes?

- Is your presentation adaptable to the unique needs of a wide range of customers?

- What is the overall quality of questions you receive during and after your presentation?

- What one or two changes could you make to your presentation that would more favorably demonstrate the unique benefits or solutions you are proposing to your customers?

Most of us like to believe that our presentations are clear and relevant to the customer's needs. Unfortunately, many of us are wrong. This is a pivotal point in leading the customer toward a final buying decision. If this element of the selling process is weak, so are your chances of securing an order. If you are serious about improving, you will need to be serious about evaluating and receiving regular feedback on your presentation.

Product knowledge. Few things encourage customers to trust the competency of a sales professional more than that professional's broad knowledge of both the product and the industry. Product training is a building block of virtually every sales training program, but all too often there remains a nagging complaint among customers that sales professionals are deficient in critical technical aspects of the products they represent. When it comes to selling commodity-type products, the technical skill of the sales professional frequently becomes the benchmark for product differentiation. This is one area of professional selling that must never be taken for granted. You sell in a dynamic environment that is constantly changing. Markets change, products evolve, customer attitudes shift, and competitors continue to innovate. Your knowledge of the product and the industry needs to keep pace.

Many industries have certification programs for sales professionals to periodically test their baseline knowledge of the industry in which they work. Some companies offer similar programs for their own products. Whether or not your company or industry has a well-defined continuing education program, you need to be committed to continued learning. Here are a few questions to help you assess your progress:

- Do you spend time each week learning something new about your product, your company or your competitors?

- Are you able to answer ninety percent or more of the technical questions customers ask about your product?

- Are you very familiar with all of the changes to your product that have been made in the last year?

- Are you very familiar with all of the changes your two nearest competitors have made to their products in the last year?

- Are you regularly reading industry periodicals or attending educational conferences to stay current with trends, market forecasts and other important developments in your industry?

- Do you regularly seek assistance from the corporate technical team to review product changes in detail?

- Do you find yourself cramming before important client meetings to avoid being tripped up by technical questions?

- Do your customers routinely call you as a resource for technical questions?

Your technical proficiency with your product is a good barometer of your commitment level as a sales professional. If your command of all the technical aspects of your product and industry is high, it is a good indication that you are programmed to produce excellent work. If your doctor were not current on the latest medical research and practices, you would be looking for a new physician. Your customers have already come to the same conclusion. Your potential as a sales professional will rise and fall with your technical competency.

Problem solving. In many instances your ability to solve problems for the customer will have more impact on the ultimate buying decision than any other single aspect of the selling process. You need to have your head in the game, or it is likely that important opportunities will sail past you and into the welcoming arms of your competitors. The entire process, from the initial customer contact to the execution of the order, most often resembles a gauntlet that is fraught with problems to solve, deadlines to meet, budget constraints to satisfy and performance standards requiring compliance. If you can maintain a high level of energy for problem solving, which at time demands the most exasperating critical thinking and consensus-building among key company associates, you will find that market revenue potential is within reach of your ability.

Problems are opportunities. Look for them. Think about them. Reinvent your approach to selling; become a customer problem solver. The more complex the problem is, the greater is the need for collaborative solutions. Customer problems that require a deeper level of involvement from you should raise your concentration levels and inspire your best creative thinking about potential solutions. Here are a few questions to help you assess your commitment to customer problem-solving:

- Do you enjoy finding solutions to complex problems?

- Do you find that you generally are able to propose multiple solutions to the concerns and problems encountered by your customers?

- Can you readily identify a wide range of solutions your product can provide? Are you technically competent in all of these potential solutions?

- Do your existing customers regularly contact you about problems they are having that might involve your product?

- Do you regularly conduct a thorough need analysis with new clients?

- Is your product presentation solution-based or product-based?

- Are you constantly looking for new and innovative solutions to customer problems?

I like to work with and be around creative problem solvers. It is like cycling with strong riders who create a draft that will pull even the weakest of us along at a faster pace. They have learned from their experience that customer problems represent the "ground zero" of the selling process. Outstanding sales professionals are somewhat like skilled first responders who arrive before everyone else, conduct a critical assessment, and work to stabilize a patient, then actively participate in solving problems in their particular area of expertise. They start with a clear assessment of a problem and from there mobilize all available resources to assist in the relief effort. Effective problem solving ranks near the top of the list of core skills required by every sales professional. This is a basic competency that you should regularly evaluate in your professional life.

Communication skills. As we have previously discussed, selling in its purest form is the process of influencing buying decisions. This doesn't happen by coercion or manipulation. Influence comes from trust, which encourages collaboration about both product selection and final buying decisions. Your ability to communicate clearly and effectively with customers will help you move more quickly towards collaboration. One of the distinguishing characteristics of every outstanding sales professional I have known is the ability to be an effective communicator. They speak clearly about objectives and purposes and articulate solutions in the customer's language. They know that listening is an essential element of communication, and they have learned the basic skills of technical writing.

While we are on the topic of writing, let me make a brief digression, since I believe this is a vital part of communicating with customers. Early in my career, most direct customer communication was in person or over the phone, and periodically supported by written correspondence. In recent years, electronic communication has reshaped the transmission of ideas, opinions, and solutions. The speed of this new communication is as mind-numbing as its expanse.

The world now is at our fingertips. That's the good news. The bad news is that the world is at our fingertips. Digital images often lose the intonation and inflection that communicates urgency, concern, regret or understanding. If you are not careful in selecting your words and constructing sentences and paragraphs, even your best intentions can fall prey to the limitations of a form of communication that is largely one-dimensional. E-mail is a great way for me to stay connected with my kids, but it could never replace spending time with them. Most customers, like most children, need more from you than short greetings and one-line follow-up messages. You need a high level of competency in all forms of communication.

So while the communication resources available to us in the twenty-first century are unparalleled in the history of the world, none of this will compensate for an inability to communicate clearly. More becomes less, if our intent cannot be communicated effectively by whatever medium we choose for speaking with our customers. That was true fifty years ago, and it remains so today.

- Here are a few questions that may help you evaluate how effective you are in all the essential forms of communication:

- What problems have you experienced the past year with your customers, which could have been solved with more effective communication? What are you doing to prevent their reoccurrence?

- Do you make careful notes of all conversations with clients? Do you provide a brief written summary of your notes to your customer, to insure that all relevant items were understood?

- After conducting a need analysis, do you review your assessment with your client to confirm that your understanding of the problem (needs) is consistent with your customer's?

- Are you prompt in responding to every customer inquiry or question?

- Do you address the client's concerns when questions are raised, or do you try to defer them to a later time?

- Do you honor time commitments that were made when you scheduled a client meeting?

◆ Do your presentations contain esoteric language or blatant techno-babble that may confuse customers even as it massages your ego?

Communication in selling is like heavy machinery in manufacturing. If it doesn't work and is not properly maintained, the output will be marginal. Most manufacturing facilities have an ongoing preventive maintenance program to minimize the down time of essential equipment. In your territory you must manage the preventive maintenance and regularly inspect the "equipment" that produces revenue in your territory. This is not a complex task. It simply requires a commitment to periodic *accountability*.

Response times. Your clients' business is important to them. It should be important to you. When they need help solving a problem or collecting relevant data, response time is nearly always a factor. Delays in responding often suggest a lower assigned priority. How quickly you respond to all questions, problems and information requests dramatically affects your image as a sales professional in the minds of your customers. You may be the most technically competent sales professional in your industry, but if your customers can't get you to return a phone call promptly, your bright mind will provide less value than a lighthouse does to a passing motorist. It may be interesting, but it provides very little value to the journey.

I have said previously that outstanding sales professionals work with a sense of urgency. *Personal Leadership* in selling includes the ability to filter out red herrings. It includes having the judgment to assess quickly which problems, phone calls, e-mails and voice mail messages require an immediate and urgent response. Not all phone calls are created equal. Problems vary. Leaders can differentiate among them based on their understanding of the client's unique needs and circumstances. The common characteristic that all customers share is a need to be valued; for this reason, though response times may vary, a slow response to a customer should be a rare exception.

◆ Here are a few questions to help you assess your responses:

◆ Do you return all customer phone calls quickly? Within an hour? The same day?

- Do you put off returning calls to customers, because you still don't have all the information?

- How often do you receive voice mail messages from customers complaining that you are difficult to reach? Do associates in your organization make this same complaint periodically?

- Do you respond to urgent messages urgently?

- Do you acknowledge the receipt of every message from a customer, even when there was no specific request for a reply?

- Do you deliver on all promises of timely bid proposals, technical data or other customer requests?

- Do you have a reliable system in place for when you are away for an extended period of time?

For many customers, response time is a reliable method for assessing the congruency between the sales presentation and sales performance. Where these give different accounts, building trust is difficult, and so is progress toward a final buying decision. A clear assessment of your commitment to responding to customers will help insure that your territory is making healthy progress toward its full potential. It is also a key indicator of your personal effectiveness as a sales professional.

Step Five: Regular Self-Development

It may seem a bit odd that a discussion about self-development would be included in a chapter about *accountability*. Allow me to explain why I chose to locate this material in this section. The philosophy that supports the skill of *accountability* is based on the notion that optimum revenue production is a bi-product of optimum performance levels. Learning to *be accountable* contemplates performance relative to potential. It is *not* simply about the consistent execution of the sales plan, although that is an important part of the work of *accountability*.

This program of self development is about the pursuit of personal potential and differs from the continuous improvement program discussed on page

34 which is designed primarily to address specific deficiencies in how you sell. Without a wellconceived plan in place to consistently improve your ability as a sales professional, you will have about as much chance of reaching your potential in selling as you do of catching flies blindfolded. Self-development is a process that helps you move toward realizing your professional potential. It is the golfing equivalent of spending time on the driving range or putting green.

Self-development is continuous improvement. For most of us, it should move beyond being just an interesting idea and become a more or less formalized program. If your company does not currently have a program to encourage self development, I suggest that you consider two essential components as you design a program that will work for you:

- Health and fitness

- General proficiency

For most of the past twenty years, we have used a program in our organization that is based on these two areas. I find that the more sales professionals invest in themselves, the greater level of commitment they feel to the selling profession. In addition, this simple process of self-improvement allows customers to make buying decisions based upon the comparative skill and competency of the product representative, rather than just a rudimentary evaluation of the product.

Health and fitness. There are endless resources available on this topic. As it relates to establishing an annual self-development program, I just suggest that you outline a specific plan that meets your physical needs and your overall personal fitness goals. What the plan looks like is not as important having a plan and consistently working to achieve your goals. It is hard to argue that improved fitness levels don't impact energy levels, improve concentration, and increase your capacity to shrug off rejection and the disappointment of lost sales.

As you improve your overall fitness, you will experience corresponding gains in all six of the key selling skills in the *Personal Leadership Model*. Regular health and fitness activity is high-leverage work. It is another demonstration of your effectiveness as a leader. It is one of those areas where even a small investment a few times a week can make a significant difference in how you feel. Feeling well improves your chances of selling well.

General proficiency. In addition to establishing an annual personal fitness goal, all members of our sales team are expected to complete one program each month in one of the following four areas:

- Character

- Competency

- Motivation/Desire

- General Elective

As a rule, most of these programs consist of either reading a book on topical material or listening to audio recordings in one format or another. Members of   the sales team complete three programs each year in each of the four categories. They also prepare a short summary of each program and discuss its specific relevance to professional selling.

Examples of programs that could be completed in the area of character include inspirational biographies like:

- *John Adams*, David McCullough

- *Truman*, David McCullough

- *The Founding Fathers: The Politics of Character*, Andrew Trees

- *Benjamin Franklin*, Walter Isaacson

- *No Ordinary Time*, Doris Kearns Goodwin

- *Depths of Glory*, Irving Stone

- *South*, Ernest Shackleton

- *The Speed of Trust*, Stephen M. R. Covey

Competency programs should reflect your specific industry or product type. These can consist of books, seminars, or online learning programs.

Motivation/Desire programs might include reading such books as:

- *The Basics of Success: Keys to Achieving Your Potential*, Tim Connor

- *Building Trust: How to Get It! How to Keep It!*, Hyler Bracey

- *Confidence*, Rosabeth Moss Kanter

- *Thinking for a Change*, John C. Maxwell

- *Think Big: Unleashing Your Potential for Excellence*, Ben Carson

- *Life Matters*, Roger Merrill

- *The Power of Full Engagement*, Loehr & Schwartz

- *The Power of Purpose*, Richard Leider

- *It's Only a Mountain*, Dick Hoyt

- *The 7 Habits of Highly Effective People*, Stephen R. Covey

The final category in the self-development program includes three elective programs. These may be of general interest and may not be directly related to your profession. They could involve a hobby or perhaps a new skill you are trying to learn.

It is the commitment to continuous learning and improvement that makes selfdevelopment essential to your growth as a sales professional.

The program you choose to incorporate in your professional life doesn't have to be this formal. It just has to be enough to push you to invest in your profession regularly. Public seminars on industry topics are widely available through various trade associations; local colleges and universities also offer a wide range of subjects that may be relevant to your profession. I suggest that you write a short plan for selfdevelopment and include a summary of your goals and plans in your annual territory sales plan.

General assessment. If you are internally driven by a need to explore your own potential as a sales professional, the questions that need to be examined in the course of each sales year are, "Am I improving?" and "What can I do this week (or month) to enhance my skills as a sales professional?" These are important considerations that can foster an attitude of continuous self-improvement in your professional life. It is that commitment to improve regularly that will better align your performance with your potential. The closer these two assessments become, the more your territory will grow in a similar fashion. Significant revenue production will track closely with any effort you make to approach your best work as a sales professional.

I know that focusing on one area of your professional life to improve each week or each month seems like a rather benign concept. It starts out that way, but over time the accumulated weight of those small changes will fundamentally alter nearly every aspect of your professional life. It is like the constant dripping of the faucet; if it continues long enough there will be enough water to float a large boat. Even a modest obsession with improving your selling skills will produce noticeable changes in how you work and the revenue you produce. However, even small droplet-sized changes are unlikely to take place unless you hold yourself *accountable* from week to week. Here are a few questions for you to consider periodically:

- What are the two or three most important changes I have made in the past month to improve my skill and competency as a sales professional?

- What are the three most important areas in my professional life that need to be improved? What can I be doing this week or this month to work on those needed changes?

- What is the single most important reason that I am not achieving my potential as a sales professional?

- How can I obtain the needed feedback about how I sell to insure that I am making improvement in important aspects of my territory?

- How do I know that I am making needed improvements?

I find it interesting that the top sales professionals I have worked with are nearly always the ones who are fixated on improvement. In some years, the person who receives the top sales award also qualifies as the most improved member of the sales team. What many on the sales team don't seem to understand is that selling more is not about luck or the geography of the territory. It is not about being more intelligent or more naturally outgoing or more naturally anything. Great sales territories don't just fall into place overnight. They are developed by hardworking people who excel in Personal Leadership. These are people of vision, character and passion. They are people just like you.

Practice 2: Assessing Your Accountability Quotient

This section will give you an opportunity to complete a short self-assessment exercise about key elements of your attitude towards *accountability*. More specific information about standard practices will follow in the next section, "Five Keys to Greater Accountability." Like most work in selling, having the right mindset is often the best predictor of the overall quality of the execution.

It is possible that *accountability* is the least understood, least practiced and most underutilized component of the *Personal Leadership Model*. There are solid gains to be had in your performance if you will spend some time in this area. This is not difficult or unpleasant work. Most often it can be done in your home before you leave for work on Monday morning. For most of us getting thirty minutes of stimulating cardio exercise isn't that difficult either, but we allow expensive aerobic equipment in our homes to grow old in peace. It is time to make some noise and disturb the silence. You can get your heart rate up in a hurry by starting the week with some critical thinking about the most important things to get done in the days ahead.

Most of us need a little push to get started, if we have developed habits that don't include consistent *accountability*. For many *accountability* suggests external control, compliance, rigidity and conformity, and seems to crush the spontaneity to which many have grown accustomed in professional selling. Spontaneity is overrated, and fears about control in a territory led by consistent *accountability* are without merit. Great territories are not built by winging it. Neither are great lives. The truth is that the greater your *accountability*, the more control you will have over your progress toward your greatest potential. Once you are on that path, any fears about the constriction of your time or the absence of spontaneity will quickly evaporate.

The following paragraphs summarize eight ways to evaluate your overall commitment to *accountability*. As you read each one, assess your progress toward *being accountable* for implementing all elements of your sales plan in your territory.

Don't procrastinate the hard stuff. There is a reason that I have listed procrastination first. This problem alone is probably responsible for more casualties in the form of poorly executed sales plans than any other aspect of human performance. There isn't an easy formula for overcoming it, other than simply making a conscious choice never to procrastinate difficult tasks. If you can learn this one skill, much of your work in learning to be *accountable* will be accomplished, and you will experience improved relationships with customers and company associates.

Move the hard stuff for any given day to the top of the list. Let's face it, implementing your sales plan and working towards your potential isn't easy. But it is within your capability. If you are struggling to spend the needed time doing prospecting work, schedule the number of hours and the specific days on the weekly progress report and make a commitment to complete the work before you leave the office. Not only will the tasks get completed more consistently, but you will also experience noticeable improvements in the results. Most importantly, you will feel yourself moving in a new direction, and soon you will experience noticeable gains in your territory. Learning not to procrastinate requires self-discipline. So does achieving your potential. This is a skill that will serve you well in your career and distinguish you from most other members of the sales team.

While avoiding procrastination may be hard at first, I think you will find considerable satisfaction in clobbering a few hard tasks during the early morning hours. You will also find that much of the rest of day will seem like coasting downhill. I have yet to find an entrenched procrastinator who consistently works at full potential. Don't kid yourself into thinking you will be the one exception.

Identify some rewards. Some of the most highly motivated sales professionals I have worked with program into their work day some personal incentives for completing challenging tasks. Selling can be difficult and exasperating. Rejection of your product feels personal, and in some ways it is. I am not aware of another profession that is constantly subjected to rejection more than selling. The accumulated weight of reoccurring *no*'s can sap your enthusiasm and dull your responsiveness. If you have been selling very long, you know what that feels like. You can become like a fullback who has had his bell rung one too many times, who now shies away from hard contact.

In order to avoid the sluggishness that can come from working through difficult problems or challenges, you need to work constantly to "move the chains" by accelerating your work pace nearer to optimum levels. If you start working in a way that allows you to avoid hard contact, there will be few, if any, first downs in your immediate future. Set some daily intermediate goals and factor in a few personal incentives to move you through the rough patches. It could be something as simple as a few minutes at a nearby putting green, a slow walk through the park, a milkshake, or even some quiet time to read another chapter of a book you want to finish. It doesn't need to cost anything or consume much time. You know the buttons to push to keep your head down and your feet moving, trying to gain valuable yardage. A cheering crowd does this for a fullback. What works for you?

Write it down. This doesn't mean you need to keep a diary of the work completed during the day. For the most part, the notes you record in your planner and in the weekly progress report constitute a reasonable summary of the week's activities. I suggest that, in your monthly meeting with your direct report or personal coach, you prepare a one-page summary of your progress in the past month. This short summary should specifically address the key strategic initiatives of your annual sales plan. If you do this for the entire year, you will have a twelve-page, rather detailed account of your progress when the year is over.

Writing will almost require you to think critically about your territory and your progress toward important goals. That alone is empowering. Writing is also a very effective tool in insuring a high level of *accountability* in your performance. You will find that, as you prepare a one-page summary of your progress, along with some thoughts about key areas of focus for the next month you will see two things happen. You will develop a greater sense of commitment to the complete execution of your sales plan. This is a key component of *accountability*. And you will have new insight about subtle changes or course corrections that need to be made to better position your territory to take advantage of changing market conditions. It is nice to think about your territory and possible changes. It is better to write about it and construct a logical case based upon solid reasoning.

Visualize accountability. I discussed this topic in a previous chapter, but some of that material bears repeating, because of the relative importance of this concept for your ability to be fully engaged in the critical work of *accountability*. The planning component of Tactical Work is on paper. Execution is measured by a host of different metrics.

To a degree the process of learning to *be accountable* is invisible. Perhaps this is what makes it so elusive for most sales professionals. It needs to take on a distinct, recognizable form. Until it does so, it will remain the one aspect of the *Personal Leadership Model* that is never fully implemented. Realizing the full potential for your territory depends upon consistent *accountability*.

Think about becoming completely *accountable* for the potential that you have determined exists in your territory. The more you believe in the power of *accountability*, the more likely you will be to include this work in your daily and weekly routine, to the point that it takes on a distinct, recognizable form. It must be visible to you.

Accountability will be seen in how you integrate your sales plan into the daily work of your territory. The more you visualize the transfer of the sales plan into your activities today, the more you are assuming *accountability* not just for a revenue number, but for territory potential. Visualization is controlled thinking about your desire for specific outcomes. When you have learned to visualize the complete execution of your sales plan, *accountability* is no longer invisible.

Do something important daily. One good way to measure your progress toward becoming fully *accountable* for your territory's potential is to do at least one thing everyday that specifically relates to your sales plan. For example, one of your key strategic initiatives might be to make fifty presentations to pre-qualified customers who are not currently buying your product. You don't need to make one presentation a day to meet that goal, but you will need to do some phone work to schedule the appointments. A simple task like this may only take a few minutes to complete, but it creates a continual connection with your sales plan. It is this regular connection to your plan that fosters a high level of *accountability*.

Judgments about the relative importance of a particular task are a matter of *Personal Leadership*. The more consistent you become in making good judgments about utilizing your time, the more you are growing as a leader. The *Defining Skill* in professional selling is *Personal Leadership;* nowhere is this more apparent than in the continual alignment of your weekly schedule with critical objectives of your sales plan. There are many ways to assess how you allocate your time. Most of them have been discussed already in various places in this book. Staying connected to your plan by making daily progress in completing even just one essential task will always be an important and effective use of your time.

Avoid distractions. Distractions destroy momentum, delay attention to important projects, and disrupt otherwise productive days. Distractions come in a host of different shapes and sizes and are delivered in ways that can be difficult to ignore. Most often, the challenge is not to dismiss the overt time-wasters, but to sort out the subtle ones that can suck away time faster than a computer virus can shut down your hard drive. They look benign enough and may even come wrapped as opportunity. Far too often, by the time you dig to the bottom of the box, the most productive hours of the day have evaporated.

Effective leaders filter distractions. They quickly sift through the fancy packaging and assess whether the contents are important or will sap needed minutes out of an already overscheduled day. Effective leaders are inoculated from consuming precious time on unproductive activities. It is not that they encounter fewer potential distractions; it is simply that they have the ability to distinguish a good use of time from a better one. Choosing against bad allocations of time is easy. It is in the choices between good and best where most sales professionals stumble.

Stay positive. Negative thinking and speaking can suffocate any sales territory. Consuming and regurgitating negative material changes thinking patterns and paralyzes a person's ability to visualize creative solutions to complex problems. Negativity destroys energy levels and seriously impairs collaboration. The more you complain about the economy, competitors, corporate pricing policies, compensation plans, territory boundaries, customers, product delivery schedules, gas prices, and the results of the last election, the more you succumb to a sense of victimization that will rob you of your ability to influence outcomes.

Sales professionals who are consumed by negative thinking rarely hold themselves *accountable*. They reserve *accountability* for people and things out of their immediate control. They are free *falling* when they could be free-*wheeling*. They are consumed with doubt, when just a morsel of hope would liberate them. I have never worked with a successful sales professional who was immersed in fear and doubt. Staying positive when the winds of doubt swirl is a conscious choice effective leaders make. Leaders know that, even amid howling winds, opportunities blow by unexpectedly.

Embrace the numbers. We have all been taught that numbers don't lie. What we often forget is that the truth they tell can lead us to uncover our weaknesses as a sales professional. You may find that what some people in your life won't tell you, a simple comparative analysis will.

You don't need to be a math whiz to get numbers to start talking to you. You need a simple willingness to embrace the numbers as an effective and reliable ally in your ongoing effort to be *accountable* in your sales territory.

There is an almost linear relationship between bid totals and contract revenue for most products. It is not difficult to understand, in order to sell more you will likely have to bid more. This doesn't simply mean the gratuitous tendering of bids to unqualified prospects. It means legitimate bid offerings to solid prospects that are ready to make buying decisions. This is only one example. A host of other numerical voices offer ways for you to improve in various aspects of your professional life. Prospecting hours, new customer contacts, weekly hours with clients, cost of sales ratios, gross margin percentages, and new product presentations are just a few of the numbers that can give you critical feedback in your territory without even involving another person. The more you embrace the numbers, the more effective you will be in becoming completely *accountable* for the revenue potential in your territory.

Accountability Quotient	
Score 1 - 10 (1 = Strongly Disagree 10 = Strongly Agree)	
	YOUR SCORE
1. I do not procrastinate doing difficult tasks.	
2. I take time to plan short term rewards.	
3. I prepare a written summary of my performance at least monthly.	
4. I visualize my efforts to be consistently accountable.	
5. I work to complete a minimum of one important task daily.	
6. I concentrate on avoid time activities that waste time and drain energy.	
7. I work to stay positive.	
8. I enjoy using numbers to assess and report my progress towards important goals.	
9. I am passionate about the execution of my sales plan.	
10. I evaluate my performance in all areas of selling regularly.	
TOTAL POINTS	

Accountability and the Eight Symptoms of Sales Paralysis

The skill of learning to *be accountable* impacts six of the Eight Symptoms of Sales Paralysis. And while the impact on these symptoms is split equally between "low" and "medium," I believe that assessment alone fails to provide an accurate summary of the overall contribution of *accountability* on the success of any sales territory.

Symptom	Impact	Comments
The Passion is gone	LOW	Solid reporting methods can revive the *Passion*.
Inattentive listening	LOW	Regular accountability keeps your head in the game.
Winging it	MEDIUM	It's hard to "wing it" if you have to make an accounting.
Lack of a sense of urgency	MEDIUM	Reporting progress regular elevates a sense of urgency.
Feelings of frustration	LOW	Accountability helps you maintain perspective.
Blaming others	MEDIUM	This skill forces you to look inward.

Passionate people who are driven to execute the sales plan suffer from very few of the symptoms of Sales Paralysis. Where there is no viable mechanism in place to insure *accountability*, the onslaught of paralysis starts to raise its ugly head. What results most often is a territory that is in disrepair and a sales professional who is reacting to events daily rather than executing a systematic plan developed from long-term critical thinking and analysis. The work of *accountability* is a way to move your hands closer and closer to the end of the bar.

Be Accountable: The Practical Implementation of Passion

In Strategic Work passion becomes the driving force in sustaining the level of motivation necessary to achieve personal potential. In Tactical Work *passion* pushes the sales professional toward clearly identified objectives. Implementing a regular system of *accountability* increases the prominence of tasks and their objectives in the minds of sales professionals.

In Strategic Work, the absence of any one of the three skills virtually nullifies the entire process. The same is true of Tactical Work. These distinct skills, bundled together, have the potential to produce extraordinary outcomes. Planning might be compared to creating architectural drawings. Execution is the actual construction of the building. *Accountability* is the periodic assessment and acceptance of the work by local regulatory authorities and the owner's representative. All three different skills are critical to the project's successful completion.

The jade lions that adorn one of the bookshelves in our home are a constant reminder of how the choices we make can have costly consequences, but you don't need jade lions. You have a monthly sales report. *Account-ability* is the skill that insures your performance is consistent with your plans. Don't assume that good plans will be enough. At some point the "credit card statement" for your territory will arrive, and if you are not working daily to be consistently *accountable*, an elevated heart rate and cold sweaty hands may be the least of the consequences that result.

The Relationship of Principles and Practices in Developing the Skill *("Learned Power")* **to Be Accountable**

Principle A. Accountability improves performance.

    Supporting Practices:

        1. Regularly assess your "accountability quotient"

        2. Practice the "Five Steps" to improve personal accountability

Principle B. Passion drives accountability.

    Supporting Practices:

        1. Regularly assess your "accountability quotient"

        2. Practice the "Five Steps" to improve personal accountability

---

Epilogue

CHAPTER 9

An Infusion of Leadership Produces Forward Motion

THIS BOOK is written to help you improve your ability as a sales professional to move your territory closer to its overall potential. It is leadership that allows potential and performance to merge. When every aspect of your sales life is immersed in leadership, the prospect of embracing your professional potential is   as close as your next sales presentation. *Personal Leadership* is what makes it possible to keep moving forward, even when the nagging symptoms of Sales Paralysis cast a shadow on your work.

When you work to become a leader, the mark of *Personal Leadership* begins to appear in all aspects of the selling process. As you learn to exert a sense of *vision* you will manifest this leadership trait in assessing potential and in the development of a viable territory sales plan. The same can be said of the other two *Personal Leadership Drivers*. The more you develop and implement these *Personal Leadership* traits, the more effective your selling skills will be in pushing the territory to new levels of revenue production. For this reason, *Personal Leadership* is the *Defining Skill* in professional selling.

Hopefully, the more we have talked about *Personal Leadership* in selling, the easier it has been for you to recognize how improving your leadership skills will correspondingly impact revenue growth in your territory.

When I was young, my grandfather would periodically ask me and my brothers to pull weeds on his farm. At the time I was only eight or nine years old. He would give us some instructions to start the day and send us off to separate the weeds from the wheat, corn, or whatever crop he was growing. My older brothers were constantly badgering me about uprooting grandpa's crop, because, at least for me, the weeds were difficult to distinguish from the young corn sprouts.

Leaders easily recognize the difference between things that make the territory flourish and things that don't. Much of that recognition is learned. If *Personal Leadership* is the *Defining Skill* in professional selling, then it is imperative that you learn what leadership looks like in every possible form, so that you don't mistakenly pull up the valuable sprouts that could become a bumper crop at the end of the year.

The *Personal Leadership Model* introduced in this book is designed to infuse the practice of *Personal Leadership* into the selling process. For that to happen in your territory, it will be critical for you to know precisely what *Personal Leadership* in selling looks like. Let's look at a few more of the many faces of *Personal Leadership*, to help you recognize the opportunities and qualities that need to be cultivated, not uprooted, to meet your highest expectations for revenue growth.

Effective leaders, like effective farmers, tend to:

- Start early

- Fertilize and plant

- Irrigate regularly

- Spray as needed

Start early. Like farmers, leaders understand the value of work. To start early is to work hard; productive territories, like productive farms, thrive on hard work. Hard work alone will not insure success, but not working hard will almost always prevent it.

Personal Leadership is about working smart, which should never be misconstrued as an alternative to working hard. Great territories and great farms are built by tireless, intelligently directed hands.

For a leader, starting early is not only about maximizing the work hours of every day; it is also about planning well in advance for desired outcomes. Leaders seldom work in twelve-month cycles; their vision of the territory spans several years, while their plan generally applies to one season. Sales professionals who start early also know that often the most productive hours in the day come when energy levels are high. Navigating through tough tasks frequently requires the best thinking of fresh minds, working in the early morning hours of the day.

We have a member of a sales team who has a daily ritual that he calls "Dialing for Dollars." This exercise involves following up on projects where clients have received proposals. He does it with the same consistency as a farmer milking the cows. He no longer asks whether or not the work needs to be done; he simply has established a pattern of starting everyday with this highly productive task. It works well and, believe me, his sales totals are worth mooing about.

Fertilize and plant. Leaders know from experience and careful analytical work where the fertile spots of the territory are and where the soil needs nourishment. They tend the parcels of ground that have been productive, while simultaneously working on the barren patches that could produce desirable yields in the future. They study the soil and understand when to apply treatments that will improve productivity, and they also recognize when it's time to plant the seeds of ideas that will yield future revenue in a coming season.

Over ten years ago a member of our sales team determined that a possible selling opportunity might exist with a Fortune 100 company. The process that followed was complex, tedious, and time-consuming. It required multiple layers of review and analysis within the company. Months passed, and, before we knew it, years came and went, and despite a lot of attention the account was still little more than   a potentially fertile piece of ground, generating no appreciable yield.

Fortunately for us, this member of the sales team was the type of farmer who knew a good spot of ground when he saw it. Within a few years more, after some vigilant fertilizing and careful planting, the account produced an abundant harvest of revenue for nearly ten years. It became the single largest source of revenue in our business.

Leaders recognize opportunities. They have learned when to use available resources to turn barren soil into cash crops.

Irrigate regularly. Leaders know that identifying customer needs and presenting viable solutions is like providing water to a sun-baked field of corn. Sales territories are in constant need of watering. Customers wilt in a dearth of fresh ideas and finetuned responses to pressing challenges. Leaders know that sales territories, like farms, will decay without constant irrigation, where new ideas flow like fresh spring water into the minds of anxious prospects.

There was a point early in my career when it seemed that, as a company, we should have had a spectacular farm. A new line extension held a lot of promise, but we were getting little or no traction in the market. It seemed that we had all the right equipment: a solid product, a motivated sales team, the required approvals and a surging market. We had everything we needed except sustained revenue growth. In other words the fields were all planted; we just could not get anything significant to grow.

This new product was really a new venture. It resembled the old line of products, but the new features reclassified it into an entirely new industry. Consequently, we needed to explore a whole new set of realities with our existing customers. I remember a conversation with a long-time consultant in this new industry, who explained in five minutes what we had been trying to figure out for five years. Simply put, he gave us a lesson in the virtues of irrigation.

What seems simple now was, at the time, enormously complex. It changed my thinking about the product line and reshaped our message to our customers, enabling us to speak with new clarity about solutions. When solutions began to arrive, the floodgates were opened, and our customers could start drinking in ideas that resolved pressing concerns. Ideas are the wellspring that both feeds customers and builds thriving territories.

Spray as needed. For leaders in selling, spraying is a preemptive measure designed to eradicate infestations of bugs that can prove fatal to the territory. Most commonly, these pests are found in the selling habits of the sales professionals.

Eight of these common ailments – known here as the Eight Symptoms of Sales Paralysis – were outlined in Chapter One. The chapters that followed demonstrated how the skills found in the *Personal Leadership Model* are the keys to exterminating these pesky bugs

Sales Paralysis is not the only condition that may require the territory to be sprayed. Sales professionals invested in *Personal Leadership* watch carefully for any signs of decay that require remedial action to insure the health of the territory. They also realize that, as on the farm, over-spraying may damage the crops more than the bugs do.

Leaders in selling are vigilant about the quality of their relationships with clients. A decline in trust, a shift in buying preferences, and a hesitation to collaborate are a few of the indicators that warrant greater involvement by the sales professional to preserve a relationship with a valued client. Slow response to the first signs of annoying bugs could render even the most ardent attempt at spraying ineffectual later. Leaders respond with urgency to the first hint of problems that might impact a relationship with a client.

A few years ago a member of our sales team learned that a large customer had essentially established a moratorium on any future product purchases from our company. There had been little or no direct customer contact with this account for months. In fact, when the member of our sales team called to schedule a meeting with the client, it was with a person he had never met. The customer was justifiably upset. The issues were resolvable; the question that remained was whether or not the relationship could be saved by some last-minute spraying that should have been done months earlier.

We had mismanaged the relationship and jeopardized future business by ignoring signs of decay. We were arrogant and presumptuous, when we should have been attentive and proactive. In the end, we solved the problems and saved the account, preserving a strong and loyal customer to this day. But it would have been better to avoid the problems in the first place.

Sales professionals who are skilled in *Personal Leadership* don't just look for signs of decay; they take preemptive measures to insure that client relationships remain at the highest possible levels of trust. Leaders know that on their farm the most important harvest is the trust of valued customers.

Whatever product you are selling, the one constant that will have the greatest impact on your long-term success will be how successfully you in incorporate *Personal Leadership* into the management of your territory. If you can infuse it into your work, you can predict successful outcomes and maximize your product's revenue in your market.

Careers in selling are demanding, but they can be the most rewarding of any experience in business. Selling uniquely provides you with an opportunity to explore the upper limits of your professional potential and compensates you accordingly. If you are serious about maximizing your potential, it will require some changes in how you think and how you work. It will require a new model for selling.

My guess is that since you have completed this book you are a highly capable sales professional who is committed to improving your performance and increasing revenue production. You are precisely the type of person who will find a new sense of power from implementing the skills presented in this book. Achieving your potential in selling is closer than you think.

www.ingramcontent.com/pod-product-compliance
Lightning Source LLC
Chambersburg PA
CBHW070629290526
45790CB00001B/57